Advances in Well-Being

Advances in Well-Being

Toward a Better World

Richard J. Estes and M. Joseph Sirgy

ROWMAN &
LITTLEFIELD
INTERNATIONAL

London • New York

Published by Rowman & Littlefield International Ltd.
Unit A, Whitacre Mews, 26–34 Stannary Street, London SE11 4AB
www.rowmaninternational.com

Rowman & Littlefield International Ltd. is an affiliate of Rowman & Littlefield
4501 Forbes Boulevard, Suite 200, Lanham, Maryland 20706, USA
With additional offices in Boulder, New York, Toronto (Canada), and Plymouth (UK)
www.rowman.com

British Library Cataloguing in Publication Data
A catalogue record for this book is available from the British Library

ISBN: HB 978-1-7866-0346-3
         PB 978-1-7866-0347-0

Library of Congress Cataloging-in-Publication Data Is Available
ISBN 978-1-78660-346-3 (cloth : alk. paper)
ISBN 978-1-78660-348-7 (electronic)

∞™ The paper used in this publication meets the minimum requirements of American
National Standard for Information Sciences—Permanence of Paper for Printed Library
Materials, ANSI/NISO Z39.48–1992.

Printed in the United States of America

This book is dedicated to Harry and Kay Halloran and to Joseph "Tony" Carr—three remarkable visionaries who appreciate the rich contributions made by quality-of-life and well-being scholars in helping to improve the world within which we live. Without their investment of resources and time, and their dedication to the promotion of the science of well-being, this book would never have been possible. Together with the Halloran Team, the authors are committed to "fostering the science and application of well-being research" in "bringing about the world we all want."

Contents

PART V **251**

Foreword

It has been a passion of mine, as a businessman, to understand that which has been vitally important for human progress. Few forces rival the energy and creativity of the human spirit to achieve betterment, and I for one truly believe that most people possess this desire to improve their human condition and the prospects of their children. Indeed, this "life force" permeates a vast range of human activity, including our philosophies, our religions, our traditions, and nearly all modes of expression including music and the arts. Moreover, many of us in the business world are driven by the same pursuit of prosperity, coupled with the will to do something good for community and society.

The vision of the Halloran Philanthropies, as set out in 2007, has been to focus on and support social innovation and leadership in various areas including livelihood, health, and education. Yet, for us to do this well, it became clear that we needed a far more substantive understanding of the *history* of well-being. Where did our human race begin on the grand canvas of human development, and how far have we come?

Our thinking needed to be informed by the fundamental ingredients that have served the achievement of human well-being, namely, the key facets of health, education, and livelihood that serve as the cornerstones for enabling well-being outcomes for the greatest number. This is particularly salient in an era where our thoughts, feelings, and perceptions are largely shaped by media that fail to champion a rigorous analytical lens based on fact and empirics. Together with our esteemed editors, Professors Richard Estes and Joseph Sirgy, we undertook an extremely rigorous research exercise over a period of three years to aggregate the high-quality inputs of quality-of-life experts from all corners of the world. This work culminated in the volume entitled *The Pursuit of Human Well-Being: The Untold Global History*, published by

Springer (Estes & Sirgy, 2017) earlier this year. With Human Development Index (HDI) indicators as a starting point (United Nations Development Programme, 2016), we explored the extensive data that underpin the rich fabric of human experience, uncovering at the same time a complex tapestry that integrates Eastern, Near Eastern, and Western philosophical conceptions of what it means for humans to "live well."

We live in an era in which world average per capita income levels have improved by nearly 140 percent since 1990. The world's developing countries have remained the major drivers of global growth, accounting for about 60 percent of the increases in world gross product between 2016 and 2018. The rate of extreme poverty has been cut in half just since 2000 and is expected to be cut in half again by 2030 in response to the ambitious poverty alleviation priorities embodied in the United Nations Sustainable Development Goals initiative. Two billion people lived in extreme poverty in 1981; by 2013, this number declined by more than one billion. Most babies born in 1900 did not live past age fifty, yet life expectancy rose to 71.5 years in 2014, an increase of almost twenty years—just since 1960. Everything about the face of humanity on the planet has changed and evolved, mostly for the better. Yet we do not really "hear" about these tremendous advances nearly as much as we lament the instances of decline, tragedy, or conflict that are outlier events. The confirmation that well-being is improving in all regions of the world is nothing short of a revelation for me that unites all of us by a common force for good and a desire to tread confidently forward on the path of human progress toward the world we all want.

Harry Halloran
Halloran Philanthropies
West Conshohocken, Pennsylvania

REFERENCES

Estes, R.J., & Sirgy, M.J. (2017). *The pursuit of human well-being: The untold global history*. Dordrecht, NL: Springer.
United Nations Development Programme. (2016). *Human development report, 2016: Human development for everyone*. New York: United Nations Development Programme.

Preface

INTRODUCTION

When reflecting on the state of the world's nations and diverse peoples, many readers may visualize images of environmental failures, rapid rates of population growth, recurrent political calamities, as well as a mixture of war, diversity-related social conflict, and even the involuntary movements of large numbers of migrants across national and even international borders. Many of us also visualize the persistence of extreme poverty in a world with plentiful resources, including the poor who live in our own nations and communities. These significant challenges to human well-being are likely to persist despite our collective efforts to rid them from our planet (Brown, 2015; Cameron & Neal, 2002). Once these challenges are resolved, no doubt new challenges will surface that are experienced as equally compelling and, in the worst cases, initially thought to be beyond our reach to solve. But with carefully orchestrated efforts on the part of all the relevant public–private stakeholders, they, too, likely will be solved.

Among the many successes that have accrued to humanity since the end of World War II is the realization that a major element in solving the serious problems that confront us is the need to reframe our *perception* of the causes of these threats to personal well-being. This internal reframing process requires that we open our minds to new ways of thinking[1] and acting on a wide range of recurring collective problems. Thus, the solution to advancing human well-being first *requires* that we reframe what previously were thought to be impossible problems to solve to situations that, in time, and with a lot of effort, will result in more positive outcomes. Nearly all of us have learned this lesson as we have sought to solve the challenges that have confronted us in our own lives. As emphasized throughout this book, the adoption of a more positivist approach to life and living also contributes to the discovery of new methods for solving complex societal problems that require the active participation of large numbers of people.

This book presents a positive approach to understanding past and contemporary history and assumes that organized activities undertaken with others can help solve even the most complex challenges. One example of our collective success in resolving global challenges has been the magnitude of the life-promoting advances in the care of infants, children, and pregnant women that have been achieved since 1960. These groups, which historically have been highly vulnerable to premature death, are now surviving in larger numbers and at higher rates than at any other time in history. Significant progress in these areas continues to occur as increasingly larger numbers of infants and children survive the perils of birth and early childhood and as larger numbers of vulnerable women deliver their babies safely and under more sterile conditions. Significant gains in the health sector are also reflected in the worldwide success in extending the average years of life expectancy from forty-seven years in 1900 to more than seventy-eight years in 2015, a net gain of 66 percent over the span of a single century.

The underlying drivers that contributed to these dramatic successes in life extension and other sectors of human development are the principal subjects of this book. As we shall see, these critical life-enriching accomplishments cut across all areas of human activity and across all levels of social and political organization at both the local and global levels. The emergence of a more positivist perspective in all sectors of human well-being has resulted in advances in standards of living and quality of life never experienced in history (Estes & Sirgy, 2017).

We shall elaborate further on these principles throughout the Preface and in the chapters that follow. First, though, let us identify some of the transformational breakthroughs that made possible the realization of the remarkably high levels of well-being that now exist for large numbers of people in many regions of the world. None of these achievements would have been possible without the innovations that occurred in the late nineteenth and throughout the twentieth centuries to the present. Nor would they have occurred without the adoption of a positivist attitude on the part of the innovators who were most directly responsible for these phenomenal advances in human well-being.

TOWARD A MORE POSITIVE PERSPECTIVE OF HUMAN WELL-BEING

The critical breakthroughs that we have inherited from the innovations achieved during the first half of the nineteenth century, for example, offer considerable support for a more positivist view of humanity's remarkable advances in well-being. Consider, for example, the dramatic progress that occurred in the biological and technical sciences during this period as well as the equally extraordinary achievements during the same period that took place in communications, transportation, economic production, management styles, entertainment, leisure time activity, food production and preservation, and so on, that continued to impact the well-being of societies long after World War I ended in 1918. These advances improved the living standards and quality of life for people everywhere, including those living in the polar regions and in remote rural communities. Today, all of humanity is benefiting from the achievements made during the nineteenth and early twentieth centuries that made possible the even greater technological and other achievements during the middle- to late twentieth century. The human synergy that resulted from these earlier advances in quality of life has contributed to even more rapid advances in human well-being in our own lifetime.

SOCIAL AND TECHNOLOGICAL PROGRESS ASSOCIATED WITH THE INDUSTRIAL REVOLUTION AND WORLD WAR II

Consider, for example, the remarkable advances that preceded and followed the Industrial Revolution that began in Europe in the 1850s, namely, the use of coal and other fossil fuels, especially oil, to generate the energy needed to produce electricity and steel; the development of the internal-combustion engine; and the formation of assembly lines in the manufacturing industries that predominated in major urban centers. Other transformational changes occurred in response to the introduction of telephones and telegraphic systems and the laying of steam- and coal-powered railroads across much of Europe and North America and in selected regions in Central and East Asia and on the Indian subcontinent. Effective and efficient approaches to mass education, especially to advance adult literacy, were introduced during the late nineteenth century, as were highly successful programs of urban sanitation and the establishment of preventive public health services in virtually all regions of the world (e.g., vaccinations, the establishment of neighborhood health centers, remarkable programs of pre- and postnatal health care, and major public- and private-sector investments in research and development).

Consider, too, the important advances that occurred in the social sciences and the humanities that laid the foundation for much of contemporary thought and practice in the theoretical and applied social sciences, namely, the conceptualization and widespread utilization of the concept of a "middle class," the emergence of empirically based *psychology* (e.g., Wilhelm Wundt's physiological conception of the mind), the emergence of empirically based *sociology* (e.g., Auguste Comte's approach to understanding social problems using statistical data and scientific positivism), and the emergence of empirically based *history* (e.g., Leopold von Ranke's rejection of history based on tradition and, instead, placing an emphasis on the use of documentary evidence to support findings and generalizations). Darwin's theory of natural selection, Einstein's theory of relativity, and Sigmund Freud's unraveling of the unconscious mind also emerged during these decades, as did the formation of the sixty-member League of Nations (1920–1946), the predecessor organization to the United Nations (1945). These extraordinary advances in human well-being provided us with entirely new windows into our understanding of the heretofore unseen worlds that make up the human mind and the larger universe of which we are but a part. They also provided the foundation for the equally impactful advances in human well-being in all sectors of development that were to follow.

On the technological front, major innovations and inventions emerged in the decades that followed or preceded World War II (figure P.1): the development of flight (1903); the introduction and widespread adoption of consumer banking (1904); the introduction of recorded music to mass markets (1906); air conditioning introduced in homes and many office workplaces (1906); the invention of the first efficient light bulb (1910); the opening of the forty-eight-mile Panama Canal that gave ships access to both the Atlantic and Pacific oceans (1914); the beginning of the women's liberation movement (1920); the development of insulin, which saved hundreds of thousands of lives each year and provided critical insights into the functioning of the endocrine system (1921); the introduction of frozen foods (1924); the invention of liquid fuel rockets (1926); the introduction of television, which became an immediate commercial success (1926); Charles Lindbergh's flight across the Atlantic Ocean, which opened the eyes of people everywhere to what might be possible for the future (1927); the introduction of antibiotics and penicillin, which saved countless lives (1928); the introduction of paperback books, which brought affordable literature and pulp fiction to mass markets, including to many previously illiterate adults (1935); the emergence of unions and workers' rights movements throughout the industrialized world that, in time, brought better incomes and working conditions to factory and office workers (1935); the invention of the photocopy machine, which was widely adopted by commercial enterprises (1938); and the introduction of plasma and blood typing that made possible successful transfusions and related health innovations (1939). These are just some of the transformational changes that took place in society during the immediate post–Industrial Revolution period and the early twentieth century.

These highly practical social, political, and economic achievements were not restricted to one population or to one region of world; rather,

Figure P.1. Nineteenth-century cotton gin, used around 1940. *Source*: (Photo from the US Department of Agriculture; at https://c1.staticflickr.com/7/6109/6302864824_9c3a 0f6a1e_b.jpg; public domain)

they influenced the quality of life and well-being of people everywhere, including those living in the most remote regions of the planet—including deeply impoverished peoples living in the slowest developing countries of sub-Saharan Africa, Asia, and Latin America. They contributed to a level of cross-national interaction that spread swiftly throughout the world and helped to unite its diverse populations. They also laid the foundation for the even more spectacular advances in human well-being that preceded and followed World War II (1938–1945).

ADVANCES IN HUMAN WELL-BEING ASSOCIATED WITH THE PERIOD SURROUNDING WORLD WAR II

Even more technologically sophisticated innovations were introduced either before, during, or after World War II. These advances in human well-being occurred worldwide and resulted in higher living standards and a better quality of life for people everywhere. Among others, they included the invention of the electron microscope (figure P.2), permitting us to see worlds within ourselves that were never previously imagined or visualized (1940); the introduction of the world's first, but expensive, office and laboratory computers (1946); the founding of the United Nations (1945); the development

Preface

of democracy and other participatory forms of governance that spread rapidly among post–World War II nations (1945); the introduction of publicly financed primary- and secondary-level education for the masses virtually everywhere (1947); the process of racially integrating commercial sports, which began in the United States (1947); the introduction of the transistor by

Figure P.2.   Electron microscope (Siemens 1-A Electron Microscope). *Source*: **(Photo by Stahlkocher; at https://upload.wikimedia.org/wikipedia/commons/6/6e/Elektronenmikroskop.jpg; GNU Free Documentation License)**

Bell Laboratories, which laid the groundwork for the development of silicon chips—the microprocessors on which much of our contemporary computer-based civilization depends (1947); the introduction of the credit card, forever changing the nature of credit-based economies (1950); the introduction by Bayer Laboratories of the aspirin tablet (1951); the introduction of first-generation psychotherapeutic drugs for the treatment of patients with severe mental illnesses (1952); the discovery of DNA and biotechnology in response to Watson and Crick's isolation of the helical structure of DNA (1953); the introduction of vaccines against polio, small pox, and other infectious diseases in the years that followed, resulting in the saving of tens of millions of lives every year (1954); the introduction of fiber optics (1955); the use by modern hospitals of external defibrillators and other high-tech electronics that soon spread to work and cultural venues where large numbers of people congregate (1956); the introduction of the alkaline battery that powers hundreds of millions of small electronic appliances (1959); the launching of the European unification campaign amid considerable controversy over challenges to national autonomy (1960); the development and widespread availability of the birth control pill, thereby giving women for the first time control over their reproductive cycles (1960); the launching of communication satellites into space (1962); the publication of Rachel Carson's best seller, *Silent Spring*, which inspired the global environmental movement (1962); the performance of the first heart transplant by Christian Barnard in South Africa (1967); the launch of space exploration with the first landing on the moon (1969); the identification of HIV, a cause of death for hundreds of thousands of people annually in rich and poor countries alike, and the beginning of the quest for effective treatments (1983); and the fall of the Berlin Wall (1989) and later of the politically oppressive Soviet Union (1991).

OUR WORLD TODAY

Our world today continues to build on the advances in well-being that took place during the twentieth and the early part of the twenty-first centuries. Contemporary advances in the biological, engineering, medical, mathematical, and related sciences are equally as impressive as those that occurred during earlier decades. So, too, are the advances that continue to be made in the social sciences, humanities, performing arts, architecture, and music. Many of these contemporary changes have been made possible through the creation of high-speed "supercomputers" (figure P.3), more efficient air travel that moves people from continent to continent in the space of a few hours, the further miniaturization of personal electronic devices that are now essential to our way of life, new discoveries in metallurgy (including the extraction of the rare earth elements used in the production of electronics), and the reasonably steady supplies of energy from a wider range of politically secure sources—nuclear, solar, wind, solid waste—to generate gas and electricity. Today, we are on the brink of being able to transcend time and space through interplanetary travel planned to be launched in the near term. And who, just a decade ago, could have imagined that he or she could hold the sum of all human knowledge in a small handheld electronic device connected to huge banks of supercomputers? Yesterday's science fiction is now part of our contemporary reality, which, no doubt, will be reshaped dramatically in the years and decades ahead.

Advances in the medical sciences—especially in the neurosciences, organ transplants, and life extension—have been especially impressive. These achievements were built on the legacy of Christian Barnard, the South African physician who performed the first human-to-human heart transplant in 1967, and the incredibly ingenious international team of medical and biological scientists responsible for cloning the first mammal, a Finn-Dorset lamb

Figure P.3. One unit of a super computer. *Source*: (Photo by Raul654; taken at Supercomputing 2006; at https://upload.wikimedia.org/wikipedia/commons/a/a7/Blue GeneL_cabinet.jpg; Creative Commons Attribution-Share Alike 3.0 Unported license)

named "Dolly" (1997). Other recent medical achievements include automated gene sequencing, restoring body-part functioning through robotics, the reconstruction of lost limbs using computer-driven prostheses, gene-based cancer therapy, and the development of highly effective antiviral agents.

The inclusion of racial, ethnic, religious, sexual, and other minorities into the mainstream of most societies has been an extraordinary accomplishment and made possible the availability of talents that otherwise would have gone unnoticed or undervalued. The election of Nelson Mandela as South Africa's first black president (1994–1999) marked the end of the incredibly cruel system of apartheid and restored responsibility for the governance of nations from oppressive minority racial groups to members of a country's majority population. Gender parity is now a reality in most economically advanced societies and is steadily increasing in economically less-advanced countries. Women today are joining their male counterparts as heads of nations, members of parliaments, internationally recognized scientists, professors, and as skilled workers, as was the case for an eighteen-year-old Princess Elizabeth, now Queen, as a truck mechanic fixing Red Cross trucks during the latter years of World War II. Women today excel not only as mechanics and plumbers but also as specialists in all areas of the arts, humanities, and sciences. Indeed, most of the undergraduates attending universities in Europe and the United States today are women. The underlying dynamics of these breakthroughs in the social sciences had their genesis in the liberation and equality movements that began in the 1920s and slowly took hold.

Extreme poverty has been cut in half since the beginning of the twenty-first century. The preponderance of improvements in income security through paid employment has been concentrated in China, India, and other countries of South and Southeast Asia. Significant advances in the alleviation of poverty have occurred among the developing nations of sub-Saharan Africa and in many subregions of the Caribbean and Latin America. These significant gains in the economic status of previously poor people have occurred in response to the near-laser-like focus of the *Millennium Development Goals* campaign and, now, the even more ambitious goals associated with the just launched *Sustainable Development Goals* campaign. International businesses and private philanthropies have been and are contributing to these successes as well, a role that both have carried over centuries of international exploration and development. Working in close partnership with a generous nongovernmental development assistance community, businesses, governments, and nongovernmental organizations have brought about levels of economic and social progress within just a few decades never thought achievable (World Bank, 2015). The elimination of extreme poverty for so many of the world's poor has stimulated economic growth as well as the capacity of workers to consume the products of their labor (the principle used by Henry Ford in the nineteenth century to keep the price of the cars he produced at a level his workers could afford).

Simultaneously with these achievements, more self-sustaining family and community systems have come into being (e.g., racially blended and same-sex families and economically sustainable single-parent families). Much of this advancement in human well-being was achieved through the relocation of high-paying jobs from urban centers to suburban and rural communities, including to the "corporate parks" found throughout both economically developing and developed countries.

Peace throughout much of the world has made possible high levels of economic growth and a sense of security largely unknown to earlier generations. The number of deaths from militarized conflicts has reached historically low levels, as have the number of men and women disabled in such conflicts. Peace is rapidly becoming the "new normal" and, despite the tragedies associated with impersonal violence and terrorism, is expected to become more widespread in the years ahead (Halloran, 2016; Pinker, 2012). Along with increasing peace has come increasingly more democratic and participatory forms of governance and increased freedom of the press, freedom of assembly, the European Union, and the nearly complete resumption of independence by former colonies of European nations in Africa and Asia (Freedom House, 2017a, b).

Obviously, certain qualifications exist when making such bold statements, but the empirical evidence generated by leading social scientists provides ample evidence in support of these statements. Several of these sources already have been identified, but others include the *Stockholm International Peace Research Institute* (2016), the Berlin-based think tank *Transparency International* (2014, 2016), and the Washington-based think tank *The Fund for Peace* (2017). Other writers, of course, express contrarian views concerning this conclusion, especially concerning the sharp decline in rates of interpersonal and international violence reported by the Harvard psychologist and linguist Steven Pinker (Gray, 2015). Even so, the pattern of a more peaceful world has been firmly established and is expected to continue as problems of global terrorism and the tragic events occurring within many of the nations of Middle East and West Asia subside.

THE STRUCTURE OF THIS BOOK

The book is divided into six chapters, two substantive appendices, and original artwork. We also have a Foreword written by our benefactor, Harry Halloran, chairman of the Board of Directors of Halloran Philanthropies. Each section of the book contributes to the story of the positive changes that have occurred in human well-being since the beginning of the twentieth century.

Chapter 1 introduces the major themes discussed throughout the book to provide a framework within which the data-rich chapters that follow can be better understood. Chapter 2 focuses on the philosophical foundations of human well-being. It includes a full discussion of the Aristotelian perspective on well-being and of the intellectual enhancements to this perspective in Western civilization during the 2,300 years since Aristotle's death. The chapter also discusses the equally rich East Asian and Islamic traditions in terms of the pathways one should consider if one wants to attain the highest possible levels of personal and collective well-being. Chapter 3 focuses on one of the three most critical pillars of human well-being—health. The extraordinary gains that have been attained in increasing the average years of life expectancy parallel the equally significant gains that have been achieved in reducing rates of infant, child, and maternal deaths. The chapter also identifies the achievements that have been made worldwide in public health, especially in the areas of improved living conditions and safer work places. Attention is also given to successes in extending preventive health services to people living in remote polar and rural communities. Chapter 4 discusses the critical role that economics contributes to advancing human well-being everywhere in the world. The chapter focuses on wealth and poverty but addresses more central worldwide changes that have taken place in per capita and household income and consumption patterns since the end of World War II. The chapter also focuses on the important economic partnerships formed between rich and poor countries, including the use of foreign remittances, official development assistance, and foreign direct investments to hasten the pace of economic growth in poor countries. Chapter 5 reports the important advances that have been made in providing basic and advanced education to the largest possible number of people worldwide. The chapter also discusses major investments that are being made in research and development and in the extension of the Internet and consumer devices (e.g., computers and iPhones) needed to access the Internet by the largest possible number of people. Chapter 6 provides a comprehensive overview of the book's previous chapters and identifies the underlying drivers that inform each of the sectors as well as the important overlap that exists between and among the various drivers of advances in human well-being for the seventy-year period since the end of World War II. The chapter also speaks to the positive future that can be achieved with all of us working together to advance shared values, technologies, and other goals that have already been achieved—many during our lifetimes.

Richard J. Estes
M. Joseph Sirgy
September 2017

REFERENCES

Brown, A. (2015). *World history: Ancient history, United States history, European, Native American, Russian, Chinese, Asian, Indian and Australian history, wars including World War 1 and 2*. Amazon.com: CreateSpace Independent Publishing Platform.

Cameron, R., & Neal, L. (2002). *A concise economic history of the world: From Paleolithic times to the present* (4th ed). Oxford and New York: Oxford University Press.

Cognitive Reframing. (2017, March 1). In Wikipedia, the free encyclopedia. Retrieved June 15, 2017, from https://en.wikipedia.org/w/index.php?title=Cognitive_ reframing&oldid=767985669

Estes, R. J., & Sirgy, M. J. (Eds). (2017). *The pursuit of human well-being: The untold global history*. Dordrecht, NL: Springer.

Freedom House. (2017a). *Freedom in the world 2017: Populists and autocrats: The dual threat to global democracy*. New York: Freedom House.

Freedom House. (2017b). *Freedom of the press 2017: Press freedom's dark horizon*. New York: Freedom House.

Fund for Peace (FFP). (2017). The Fragile States Index, 2017: Factionalization and group grievance fuel rise in instability. Washington, DC: FFP. Retrieved June 1, 2017, from http://fundforpeace.org/fsi/category/analysis/fsi17/.

Gray, J. (2015, March 12). *Steven Pinker is wrong about violence and war*. London: The Guardian. Retrieved June 8, 2017, from https://www.theguardian.com/books/2015/mar/13/john-gray-steven-pinker-wrong-violence-war-declining.

Halloran, N. (2016). The fallen of World War II. [Video on YouTube]. Retrieved June 10, 2017, from https://www.youtube.com/watch?v=DwKPFT-RioU

Pinker, S. (2012). *The better angels of our nature: Why violence has declined*. New York: Viking.

Stockholm International Peace Research Institute (SIPRI). (2016). *SIPRI yearbook 2016* Armaments, disarmament, and international security. Stockholm: SIPRI.

Transparency International. (2014). *Exporting corruption: Progress report 2014: Assessing enforcement of the OECD Convention on Combating Foreign Bribery*. Berlin: Transparency International.

Transparency International. (2016). *Corruption perceptions index 2016*. Berlin: Transparency International.

World Bank. (2015). *A global count of the extreme poor in 2012 data issues, methodology and initial results*. Policy Research Working Paper #7432. October 2015. Washington, DC: World Bank. Retrieved February 12, 2017, from http://documents.worldbank.org/curated/en/360021468187787070/pdf/WPS7432.pdf.

Acknowledgments

This book is a companion volume to our previously published book, *The Pursuit of Human Well-Being: The Untold Global History* (2017). The *Pursuit of Human Well-Being* is an edited book (edited by the authors of this book, Richard Estes and Joe Sirgy) involving many contributions from well-being scholars from around the globe. The current book was written by the editors of the previous book. The aim of the current book is to translate and extend the information presented in the previous book in a unified and more readable format so as to make it more reader friendly to an educated lay audience. The edited book is more suitable for academicians, scholars, and researchers interested in the study of the quality of life and human well-being. We owe our gratitude to all the authors, consultants, advisory board members, support staff, and reviewers of the previous book.

Most importantly, we express our sincere gratitude to our sponsor, the Halloran Philanthropies, the Halloran Philanthropies team, and our previous publisher, Springer International Publishing. Both books (the edited book and this authored book) were envisioned by *Harry Halloran*, a generous philanthropist who has dedicated his life to the enhancement of human well-being across the globe. Halloran Philanthropies has a magnanimous record of supporting many projects designed to enhance well-being in different walks of life. Harry Halloran has provided not only the financial resources but also the vision and inspiration. *Joseph Anthony (Tony) Carr*, president of Halloran Philanthropies, was also an inspiration to us. He has been highly instrumental in translating Harry's vision into concrete guidelines that shaped the entire project. *Audrey Selian*, the program officer at the foundation, has done an extraordinary job in further translating much of Harry's and Tony's vision and guidelines into an operational plan for both books. She worked closely with us to make the entire four-year project highly productive.

Our gratitude also extends to our support staff. *Pamela Fried* played two roles in this project—copyeditor of both books and technical production manager. She has done a great job managing these roles. *David Walker* also played two roles—that of graphic designer and that of webmaster. He created all the graphics and has done a wonderful job. He also excelled at developing the Web site for the project (click the *History of Well-Being* tab on the MIQOLS' Web site at www.miqols.org). *Pamela A. Jackson* of Radford University provided the administrative talent and oversaw the finances of the entire project.

We also are grateful to our remarkable team of editors, reviewers, and production staff at Rowman & Littlefield International in London. The team provided us rich feedback for all aspects of this book. We especially appreciate the initial administrative work carried out by *Anna Reeve* and *Michael Watson* in acquiring the book for Rowman & Littlefield. *Dhara Snowden* and *Rebecca Anastasi* saw the book through to completion and added many useful suggestions for its improvement, including recommendations made to Rowman & Littlefield by its independent external reviewers. Dhara and Rebecca also worked closely with the art and production departments, as well as with the authors, in preparing the book's cover and the several states of proofs in the most favorable manner possible. We are especially grateful to them for their flexibility with the requests made of them by the authors.

We would also like to recognize the contribution of our benefactor, *Harry Halloran*, for writing the Foreword, and of *Lylia Carr* of Fresno, California, for providing the original artwork used to separate the parts of the book. The artwork adds considerable richness to the book and makes use of the Maya calendar numbers appropriate for dividing each section of the book. Thank you again, Lylia, for giving us permission to incorporate your vivid and civilization-connecting artwork into the book.

This project was administered through the Management Institute for Quality-of-Life Studies (MIQOLS; www.miqols.org). MIQOLS is a think tank devoted to the generation of knowledge related to the science of human well-being and the dissemination and utilization of such knowledge by societal institutions worldwide. The institute is in Dublin, Virginia, and maintains a data-rich Web site that includes further information about this book.

Much of the data used in this book came from international bodies such as the United Nations Development Programme, the World Bank, and the International Monetary Fund. We are much indebted to these institutions for collecting data on human well-being at regular intervals.

Finally, we would like to recognize the support of our academic institutions (University of Pennsylvania and Virginia Tech) and, of course, that of our spouses (*Gail Buchanan Estes*, wife of Richard Estes, and *Pamela Jackson*, wife of M. Joseph Sirgy). We could not have undertaken the writing of this book without their support and encouragement. Thank you! Thank you! Thank you!

NOTE

1 "Cognitive reframing" refers to a psychological technique that consists of identifying and then disputing irrational or maladaptive thoughts. Reframing is a way of viewing and experiencing events, ideas, concepts, and emotions to find more positive alternatives. In the context of cognitive therapy, cognitive reframing is referred to as cognitive restructuring. Cognitive reframing, on the other hand, refers to the process as it occurs either voluntarily or automatically in all settings (Cognitive Reframing, 2017).

Part I

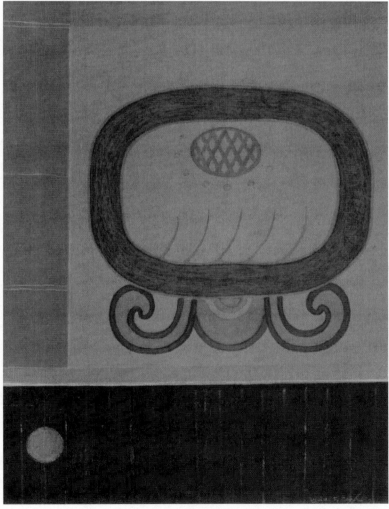

Imix'—First day of the Maya calendar. Mixed media on paper—22″ × 30″. © 2015. Lylia Forero Carr. Used with permission.

Chapter 1

Advances in Human Well-Being

Humankind has arrived at a dramatically different level of well-being in 2017 than that which existed fifty years ago or that which characterized people worldwide at the outset of the twentieth century. The advances we have the privilege to witness today reflect changes in the quality of life of people everywhere, and the forward momentum we would like to focus on continues with the promise of even more significant advances in the years ahead. While distinct drivers for the progress we discern are difficult to isolate in terms of causality, the rich tapestry of multistakeholder and multisector collaboration that has made this dramatic story possible stems from what we believe to be a near-organic, DNA-level imperative in human beings to "make life better for oneself and others." In health and life expectancy alone, people in North America and Europe are living thirty-one years longer on average (as of 2015) than in 1900, a net increase in the average number of years of life expectancy from forty-seven to somewhat more than seventy-eight years in the span of a single century. An increase of this magnitude is extraordinary and reflects social progress across a broad range of social, political, and economic sectors.

Most importantly, our children appear to be surviving at higher numbers the often harsh and precarious experiences of birth and early childhood encountered by earlier generations of children. Rates of infant and child mortality, which have posed major threats to child survival worldwide, are now at historically low levels—down from an average of sixty deaths per 1,000 live born in economically advanced societies in 1990 to an average of well below five or six infant deaths per 1,000 live born infants in these same societies by 2015. Figure 1.1, which covers the 100-year period from 1950 to 2050, confirms that the same pattern of child survival is occurring in all regions of the world including those that comprise the nonindustrialized nations of Africa, Asia, the Caribbean, and Latin America (United Nations, 2009). As

3

with the dramatic increases in average years of life expectancy, the high level of child survival that characterizes the world today is unparalleled in human history or in our contemporary sense of well-being. These gains have had a secondary effect that, increasingly, allows families to voluntarily reduce the number of children or to space pregnancies consistent with their level of economic resources, especially in situations where they have sufficient numbers of male children, who are expected to support their parents in old age (van Soest and Saha, 2012). Fertility rates also are expected to drop even more once income security for the aged and other vulnerable populations is put in place. In either case, parents need no longer "expect" that large numbers of their offspring will die before reaching the first year of life or during the years that follow. Rather, more and more families can add to their numbers as they judge appropriate without fearing that some of their children will die before reaching adulthood (figure 1.1).

Similarly, mothers are more likely to survive childbirth. Rates of maternal mortality have declined dramatically almost everywhere in the world as increasing numbers of pregnant women gain access to quality prenatal care, improved diets and nutritional supplements, and safer, more sterile deliveries in health centers staffed by skilled health care professionals. These include mostly midwives, but in economically advanced societies include physicians and physician assistants with access to at least midlevel diagnostic equipment. The number of maternal deaths associated with hemorrhage, infection, sepsis, genital trauma, and unsafe abortions has declined dramatically everywhere in the world by an average of at least 13 percent (World Health Organization, 2017). Enabling safe pregnancies and deliveries for women

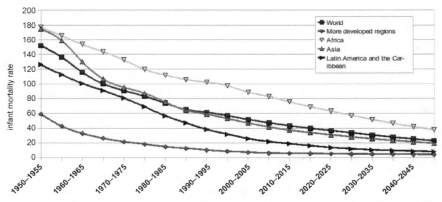

Figure 1.1.   Infant mortality rate by region, 1950–2050. *Source*: (Graph by Rcragun; source UN World Population Prospects, 2008. https://commons.wikimedia.org/wiki/ File:Infant_Mortality_Rate_by_Region_1950-2050.png; Creative Commons Attribution 3.0 Unported license)

living in remote rural communities remains one of the greatest challenges facing humanity, but the knowledge and the resources needed to solve this challenge are gradually becoming available.

THE DEMOGRAPHIC CHALLENGE

More people in the early part of the twenty-first century are being born and living longer than ever before in human history. This simple demographic reality has changed the face of our communities for many decades into the future and, in doing so, has reshaped the set of responsibilities for promoting the well-being of their growing number of citizens by both the state and private sectors. Indeed, two remarkably similar trends across societies dominated, namely, a *continuing* high rate of child fertility in combination with *high rates* of population aging. At some point in the near term, child fertility patterns in developing countries are expected to decline as the percentage of their populations sixty years of age and older increases (Population Reference Bureau, 2016). This means that today and in the years ahead, fewer babies will be born, and people will continue to live longer. Most developing countries must thus inevitably struggle with a wide range of policy issues related to rapidly increasing numbers of age-dependent persons relative to numbers of working-age individuals (persons aged fifteen to sixty-four years) who generate most of the wealth needed to build the society and to support their families and the larger community. Chronic joblessness of young people, including university graduates, and uncertain income streams for the elderly are among the most frequent demographic challenges that developing countries face as they seek to increase their competitiveness in global markets while maintaining social stability at home (Estes & Tiliouine, 2016). The solutions needed to solve this challenge are not simple and will require active participation by all segments of society working together toward a shared set of solutions.

Figure 1.2 identifies the years of average life expectancy for males and females for the world's ten most populous countries. The data are for midyear 2016. Added together, the combined population of these countries equals about 58 percent of the world's total population. Of interest is that only one of these countries, the United States, is classified as an economically advanced society; the remaining nine are classified by the World Bank as either "low-income" or "developing" countries (World Bank, 2017). All ten of these countries, though, engage in robust trade with one another, and this trade has added new resources to the economies of all of these nations for use in supporting a wide spectrum of advances in well-being.

Using bubbles to represent the comparative population size of each country, figure 1.2 also shows the years of average life expectancy for males

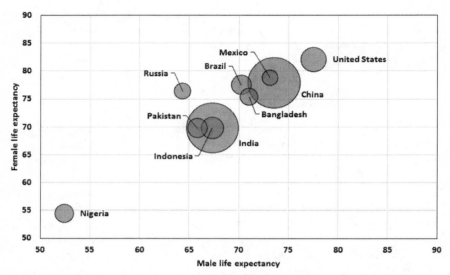

Figure 1.2.   The world's ten most populous countries in 2016 by gender distribution. *Source*: (Data from United Nations Population Division, 2016; illustration by David Walker)

and females residing in each of the countries. The intention in using bubbles in the figure is to graphically summarize three variables: (1) to represent the different population size of each country, (2) to report average years of life expectancy by gender, and (3) to reflect gender-based disparities in average years of life expectancy. The use of this type of data visualization makes it easier for the reader to readily discern complex patterns that are not so clearly visible when examining columns of numbers alone. (The authors are indebted to the late Swedish medical statistician Hans Rosling for promoting the use of such approaches for presenting complex data patterns more simply.)

The population and gender data reported in figure 1.2 are for mid-2016. The data confirm the relationships that exist in population size when disaggregated, using gender as a control factor. The figure also confirms that highly populated countries, though advancing at different rates, are moving in the same direction in extending the lives of their residents and are doing so quickly. This is an especially important finding since these very large nations must work not only toward advancing the longevity of hundreds of millions of people but also toward establishing the means required to provide for at least the basic needs and wants of their rapidly increasing numbers. The demands placed on the governments of these nations are especially intense for improved health care, better education, and more secure employment. These are not easy well-being outcomes, even for affluent nations to accomplish. At the same time, the challenge for highly populated developing countries is to achieve the same outcomes as more economically advanced countries but to do so with fewer material resources. And, yet, the majority of the world's most populous nations have achieved this outcome, including all four of the population "super giants" shown in the figure, that is, China, India, the United States, and Indonesia.

Figure 1.2 also confirms the existence of increased parity in average years of life expectancy among the ten most populous countries. Women, as is the case worldwide, in each of the ten countries live longer than men by an average of four to five years, often longer, but both men and women are living substantially longer on average than did earlier generations. This pattern is expected to continue over the near term as rich and poor countries achieve average years of life expectancy that are increasingly comparable to one another. These changes will occur most dramatically in countries with accelerated rates of economic growth, improved health conditions, and greater availability of at least basic education. The steady introduction of reasonably secure "social safety" nets also will add to this advancement in well-being among developing countries, as will decline in average family size and, viewed globally, the size of the total world population (International Social Security Association, 2017; United Nations Population Division, 2016).

The very significant positive gains just reported are confirmed by the strikingly upward direction in which population longevity is increasing in nine of the ten countries. This is the case even for Nigeria, the major outlier shown in the figure, which continues to struggle with a legacy of poverty, high levels of diversity-related social conflict, classism, and political instability—all despite the great oil wealth of the country. Even so, today, men and women are living longer in Nigeria than during earlier decades despite their lagging economic and political positions.

Today, people living everywhere in the world are enjoying longer, healthier, and better-educated lives than at any time in human history. In combination with emerging and the already secure social safety nets that exist in most economically advanced countries, the quality of life of hundreds of millions of people already has been improved. In the decades just ahead, even more gains in population longevity and fertility control are expected. When that threshold is reached, the world is expected to experience a stabilization of population growth rates and an overall, in time, reduction in the overall size of the world's total population (United Nations Population Division, 2016).

Looking ahead, figure 1.3 shows the expected rate of population increase for the world by developmental stage. Included with each stage are the expected patterns associated with births, deaths, and rates of natural increase and decrease that result from patterns of births and deaths. The dynamics of child fertility and population aging are reported in the bottom boxes of the figure. The chart presents a picture of the general pattern of economic change

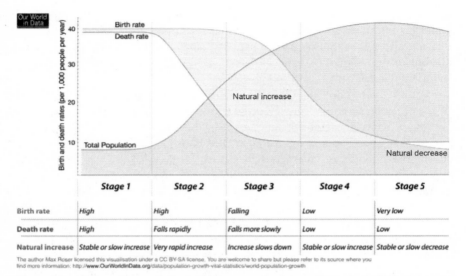

Figure 1.3. **Expected rate of population increase for the world by stage of development, birth rate, death rate, and rates of natural increase and decrease.** *Source*: (Roser, M., & Ortiz-Ospina, E., 2017; Creative Commons Attribution-ShareAlike 4.0 International License)

that most countries undergo as they move from stage 1 to stage 5 of population growth.

These generally "expected" patterns are useful in comparing the population trends occurring within and between various groups of nations. In applying this framework, we can easily see variations that may prevent countries from moving from one development stage to another.

The differences that exist in population distribution patterns are apparent in charts such as that portrayed in figure 1.4, which summarizes the important age and gender distributions that take place in countries. Figure 1.4 illustrates what is referred to as a "population pyramid," which groups national populations by gender and age. The information summarized in the figure is for Mexico in 2015. The ideal pattern, of course, is to have many economically active persons (ages fifteen to sixty-four) who generate the resources needed to provide for age-dependent family members and to support the overall development of the community

Mexico's population pyramid reflects the imbalance that exists between the numbers of noneconomically productive children, youth, and older persons vis-à-vis the numbers of persons in the economically active age group. In Mexico, the percentage is much lower than that of most postindustrial societies because of the large number of children in most Mexican families. The growing number of older persons, though still small, also makes large

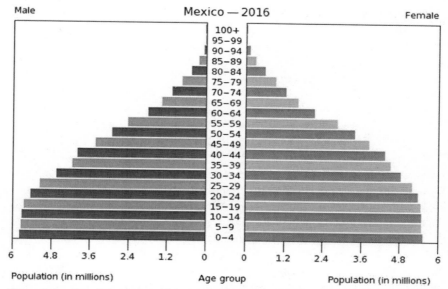

Figure 1.4. **Population pyramid for Mexico by age and gender, 2016.** *Source:* (Central Intelligence Agency, 2017; public domain)

demands on the financial resources of the family and of the country. Taken as a percentage of Mexico's total population, the volume of demand for support placed on Mexican families by their children and their elders is large. At the same time, the proportion of economically active age groups in Mexico is steadily shrinking, which imposes yet another set of policy demands on a midlevel developing country.

What does this all mean? The economic burden placed on Mexico's economically active workforce is high as it struggles to meet the needs of so many children and a steadily increasing population of elderly persons. The demographic challenges for Mexico represented by these trends are substantial and have major well-being implications not only for Mexico but also for the world. Moreover, increased gender inequality, a lingering problem in Mexico, in combination with moderate to high rates of economic growth, has caused families to voluntarily reduce their birth rate and invest more in their elders (Ghose, 2013). Despite the complexity of these trends and the range of drivers that support them, there is little determinism or fatalism that may be applied to these dynamics. These decisions are made by families themselves, and they, as with nearly all families, hold in their own hands the power to enhance their overall quality of life, standard of living, and well-being.

Private decision making and public policies formulated by policy makers in support of families play a vitally important role in enhancing the quality of life in society across the board. Evidence-based decisions of this kind provide the foundations upon which individuals, families, and societies achieve their collective progress. This is one of the many results of adopting a *positivist* approach to understanding and acting on the challenges that confront all sectors of personal and communal life.

DECLINING RATES OF INFECTIOUS AND COMMUNICABLE DISEASES

Perhaps most exciting and least appreciated in terms of making headlines has been the impact of modern medicine on the preponderance of infectious and communicable diseases such as diphtheria, pertussis, tetanus, polio, cholera, malaria, and tuberculosis. Each has declined to its historically lowest levels in response to aggressive health outreach services to large numbers of urban and rural dwellers. Vaccinations against crippling childhood diseases— diphtheria, pertussis, tetanus, and polio—now reach nearly 80 percent of the world's infants and children. If we think about this, this level of achievement in human progress is nothing short of a modern miracle. These diseases are entirely preventable, especially in their early stages, and the cost of vaccines has dropped to historically low levels. The recently launched United Nations Sustainable Development Goals initiative has been designed to reach the remaining 20 percent of unvaccinated, difficult-to-reach children. Every expectation exists for believing that this goal will be achieved by no later than 2025. Progress in treating drug-resistant tuberculosis likely will proceed more slowly, given the complexities of both the disease and the health delivery systems needed to treat the disease at its earliest stage.

The global sanitation movement, which is inextricably tied to the spread of communicable diseases, has fully taken hold. From the World Toilet Organization (http://worldtoilet.org/) down to the most dogged social enterprise working on the ground, teaching people about the dangers of open defecation, progress has been achieved to move the needle. Local communities around the world have developed highly effective approaches for processing liquid and solid wastes that previously littered their streets and even their homes.

The world's most environmentally aggressive communities formulate carefully thought through plans for disposing of solid and liquid wastes with an emphasis on waste reduction, waste reuse, and waste recycling. Less emphasis is placed on waste disposal and waste recovery given the expense of these approaches and their often-negative impact on the poor into whose communities these wastes are often dumped. Rather, the most effective and, on balance, least expensive approach to waste management has been to carefully "mine" the wastes to extract anything of value and, then, to use the remaining solid wastes for use as fuel in the production of low-cost energy delivered to communities with little or no previous access to the electric "grid" (Waste-to-energy, 2017).

Thanks to these rapidly spreading approaches for the effective and efficient management of waste, a larger share of the world's population need no longer depend on a single light bulb (or candle) to light their homes after dark. Instead, even low-income urban dwellers can have multiple outlets for receiving and using electrical services. This innovation, along with the significant advances that have occurred in the health, education, and economic sectors, has added measurably to the quality of life and well-being of many poor and low-income communities. The remaining challenge, of course, is to bring low-cost energy to the many hundreds of millions of rural dwellers who do not yet possess the ability to convert waste into low-cost energy. But this challenge is expected to be met in the decade just ahead.

EDUCATION AND WELL-BEING

Housing and neighborhood living conditions also have improved significantly since 1950. Clean water is a new reality for the rich and the poor, one of the primary drivers of improved health conditions worldwide. The availability of clean piped water in developing countries has significantly improved the social situation of women and girls, who previously spent most of their time carrying heavy buckets of unsafe water from distant streams to their homes. At the same time, illiteracy is rapidly becoming a problem of the past, given that increasing numbers of children and adults have access to at least literacy education (figure 1.5). The reduction of drudgery for the fulfillment of basic needs has created more space for other activities, not least of which include learning and the application of other basic productive skills in even the most deprived areas.

The global literacy rate for all men is 90 percent, and the rate for all women is 82.7 percent. The rate varies throughout the world, with developed nations having a rate of 99.2 percent (2013); Oceania, 71.3 percent; South and West Asia, 70.2 percent (2015); and sub-Saharan Africa, 64.0 percent (List of countries by literacy rate, 2017).

Never in human history have we seen the major fundamental improvements in day-to-day living conditions and quality of life that have occurred during the decades following the end of World War II. Today, women and men and their school-age children can carry out such routine tasks as reading newspapers, doing homework assignments, writing to others, and reading and interpreting treatments prescribed by health service providers and pharmacies. Until now, the number of children who died because they or

Figure 1.5. Two women reading on a verandah at Ingham, Queensland, Australia, ca. 1894–1903. *Source*: (Photo by Harriet Brims around 1903; State Library of
Queensland; GL-59 Harriett Brims Photographs. At https://upload.wikimedia.org/wiki
pedia/commons/c/c9/StateLibQld_1_132733_Two_women_reading_on_a_verandah_
at_Ingham%2C_ca._1894-1903.jpg; public domain)

their illiterate parents were unable to read or understand labels on bottles of
medicines prescribed by health care providers was very high (Northwestern
University, 2007).

None of the preceding advances in human well-being would have been
possible without the gains made in basic health, education, social welfare,
engineering, and technology. Nor would they have been possible without
the significant advances in community literacy levels, access to primary and
secondary school education, and access to postsecondary education (colleges,
universities, qualified evening schools, and continuing education programs
designed to reach populations to which basic and advanced education were
previously inaccessible). Major advances in vocational and technical training
programs also have contributed to our century-long advances in health and
education that serve as the cornerstone for improved quality of life everywhere in the world.

All the preceding efforts at advancing human well-being were supported
by central and local governments and by an extraordinarily large number of

generous private philanthropies. They also have been built on the foundation of economic growth and the foresight of informed business leaders and their enterprises that contributed to significant increases in per capita and household income levels—another of the critical drivers of advances in well-being (Gopal & Tikhvinsky, 2008).

Significant gains in social progress since 1900, but especially since 1950, have been made in bringing historically disadvantaged population groups into the mainstream of society. These gains have been especially significant for women and girls who, increasingly, are achieving equity with men and boys. Most of the world's women are now able to vote and can participate fully as members of representative parliaments and congresses nearly everywhere in the world. Women and other members of historically disadvantaged population groups (e.g., child and youth, the elderly, sexual minorities, racial and ethnic minorities, migrants) also are receiving increasing levels of legal protection against occupational discrimination with the result that many are employed in the same types of positions as men, although the incomes of most women have not yet achieved full parity with those paid to men performing the same jobs. That situation, too, is changing rapidly as the so-called glass ceiling has more and more cracks. The contemporary achievements of women and other previously disenfranchised population groups in the sciences, business, education, health care, the performing arts, and competitive sports are especially noteworthy and have resulted in an entirely new cognitive "reframing" of their role in rich contribution to male-dominated societies (UN Women, 2015).

It is truly notable that poverty rates throughout the world have declined dramatically. The rate of extreme poverty has been cut in half since 2000 and is expected to be cut in half again by 2030 in response to the ambitious poverty alleviation priorities embodied in the United Nations Sustainable Development Goals initiative with its thousands of local, national, and international private and public partners. Average income levels of previously poor families have increased appreciably since 2000, and these averages are expected to continue to increase as the poor acquire new job skills and pursue training opportunities that previously were not available to them. These gains in poverty reduction have affected the rural poor most dramatically, especially in the poorest nations of East (China) and South Asia (India, Bangladesh, Pakistan), where hundreds of millions of the extreme poor have been lifted out of poverty. Every expectation exists for believing that this significant advance in human well-being will continue over at least the near term, during which time hundreds of millions of additional previously poor people will gain secure employment and stable incomes that exceed national and global poverty thresholds (World Bank, 2017).

THE DRIVERS OF SOCIAL PROGRESS, TECHNOLOGICAL INNOVATION, AND WELL-BEING

In addition to the dramatic social advances in human well-being just identified, major advances have been made in improving worldwide access to science and technology. These advances in the collective scientific, technological, and engineering accomplishments are responsible for the impressive achievements that have been made since 1960 across all sectors of society. Many of these transformational innovations and inventions were described in the Preface, but the following warrant a restatement, namely, completion of the sequencing of the human genome, gene-based treatment of cancers and other life threatening diseases, phenomenal advances in the neurological sciences, and heretofore unimagined advances in the miniaturization of electronic devices along with the use of these devices for unparalleled ease of interpersonal communication and access to the sum total of all human knowledge, using these devices to connect to supercomputers housed elsewhere ("the Cloud"). Technological advances in the medical sciences (including medical imaging such as computed tomography and magnetic resonance imaging, bioengineering approaches to aiding physically disabled persons, minimally invasive surgical techniques, and more effective medications for treating persons with serious mental illnesses) have emerged at a pace never previously experienced. These movements, too, will continue in the future, as will the broad-based political and economic innovations occurring in other sectors of social development.

ORGANIZATION OF THE BOOK

The book is divided into six chapters, each of which is intended to provide a different snapshot of the well-being of people individually and collectively over the approximately 120-year period from 1900 to 2016. Special emphasis is given to the remarkable advances in well-being that have taken place worldwide since the end of World War II in 1945. The rich interrelationships that exist between the various sectors that contribute to advances in well-being are illustrated in figure 1.6, which identifies many of the major sectors and the interactions between them that result in well-being. This basic framework is discussed throughout the book and helps to simplify many of the complex relationships that exist between health, economics, education, and other sectors of human activity that contribute to the improvements in quality of life that we seek.

The chapters are data rich in their philosophical and empirical presentations and confirm the validity of the major findings reported in each chapter.

Figure 1.6. Selected overlapping dimensions of well-being. *Source*: (Illustration by David Walker, based on the writings of Hardy Stevenson and Associates Ltd)

Illustrations and other visual presentations have been used to present often complex tables of numbers in a more easily understood graphical format. This chapter provides an overview of the central concepts that are considered throughout the book and that are discussed more fully in the Preface. Chapter 2 offers a description of the major philosophical and religious traditions that have guided different segments of humanity in their pursuit of well-being. Each of the socio-philosophical-religious perspectives presented in the chapter reflects the well-being pursuits of literally hundreds of millions of people worldwide. An even fuller discussion of these perspectives is summarized in *The Pursuit of Human Well-Being,* the authors' companion volume to this book (Estes & Sirgy, 2017).

   The remaining chapters of the book are basically intuitive in their content and placement. The dimensions of human well-being are many and varied. Figure 1.6, as already noted, shows the most common dimensions— physical well-being, social well-being, environmental well-being, economic well-being, and psychological well-being. The book focuses on three major dimensions of human well-being that comprise the United Nations' Human Development Index, namely, the health (chapter 3), economic (chapter 4), and educational (chapter 5) dimensions of human well-being. Health well-being is reflective of what is commonly construed as "physical well-being," and educational well-being is traditionally viewed as a major element of social well-being. These critical components of human well-being offer both direct and indirect measures of well-being (United Nations Development Programme, 2016). For our purposes, we have chosen to focus on each of these dimensions to describe more fully the positive changes and, in some cases, the obstacles to those changes that have contributed most significantly to advancements in human well-being over the past century. The last chapter, chapter 6, summarizes the major shifts that have occurred over the past century in advancing human well-being. Sections of chapter 6 also suggest additional major advancements in the health, education, and economic sectors that we anticipate in the decades following 2017.

The book also contains two appendices for readers with special interests: (a) Human Development Index (see page 237) scores for selected groups of nations compiled since the initiation of the Human Development Index in 1980 to the present and (b) a selection of scholarly and popular readings (see p. 241). Many of the latter readings are available electronically and can be accessed directly, often without cost, using a wide variety of handheld electronic devices.

The authors welcome readers to embark on the remarkable journey that is just ahead. We feel confident that the lessons learned from the journey will prove to be truly wondrous in their variety and importance.

REFERENCES

Central Intelligence Agency. (2017). *World factbook*. [Public domain]. Retrieved June 15, 2017, from https://www.cia.gov/library/publications/the-world-factbook/geos/mx.html.

Estes, R. J., & Sirgy, M. J. (Eds.). (2017). *The pursuit of human well-being: The untold global history*. Dordrecht, NL: Springer.

Estes, R. J., & Tiliouine, H. (Eds.). (2016). *The state of social progress of Islamic societies: Social, political, economic, and ideological challenges*. Dordrecht, NL: Springer.

Ghose, T. (2013, April 29). The secret to curbing population growth. *Live Science*. Retrieved June 11, 2017, from https://www.livescience.com/29131-economics-drives-birth-rate-declines.html.

Gopal, S., & Tikhvinsky, S. L. (Eds.). (2008). *History of humanity: The twentieth century* (vol. VII). Paris: UNESCO.

International Social Security Association. (2017). *Social security programs through-out the world*. Geneva: ISSA.

List of countries by literacy rate. (2017, June 13). In Wikipedia, the free encyclo-pedia. Retrieved June 14, 2017, from https://en.wikipedia.org/w/index.php?title=List_of_countries_by_literacy_rate&oldid=785506073.

Northwestern University. (2007, July 26). Low literacy equals early death sentence. *ScienceDaily*. Retrieved June 13, 2017, from https://www.sciencedaily.com/releases/2007/07/070723160224.htm.

Population Reference Bureau. (2016). 2016 World population data sheet: With a spe-cial focus on human needs and sustainable resources. Retrieved March 30, 2017, from http://www.prb.org/pdf16/prb-wpds2016-web-2016.pdf.

Roser, M., & Ortiz-Ospina, E. (2017). World population growth. [Online Resource]. Retrieved June 15, 2017, from https://ourworldindata.org/world-population-growth/

UN Women. (2015). *Progress of the world's women, 2015–2016: Transform-ing Economies, Realizing Rights*. New York: UN Women. Retrieved June 14, 2017, from http://www.unwomen.org/en/digital-library/publications/2015/4/progress-of-the-worlds-women-2015.

United Nations, Department of Economic and Social Affairs, Population Division (2009). World population prospects: The 2008 revision, highlights, working paper No. ESA/P/WP.210 Retrieved June 14, 2017, from http://www.un.org/esa/population/publications/wpp2008/wpp2008_highlights.pdf.

United Nations Development Programme. (2016). *Human development report, 2016: Human development for everyone*. New York: United Nations Development Pro-gramme. Retrieved June 14, 2017, from http://hdr.undp.org/en/2016-report.

United Nations Population Division. (2016). *2015 Revision of world population pros-pects*. Volume I. New York: UNPOP-DESA. Retrieved June 13, 2017, from https://esa.un.org/unpd/wpp/publications/files/key_findings_wpp_2015.pdf/.

Van Soest, A., & Saha, U. (2012). Birth spacing, child survival and fertility deci-sions: Analysis of causal mechanisms. Center Discussion Paper Series No. 2012–018. Retrieved June 13, 2017, from https://papers.ssrn.com/sol3/papers.cfm?abstract_id=2009852.

Waste-to-energy. (2017, May 25). In Wikipedia, the free encyclopedia. Retrieved June 14, 2017, from https://en.wikipedia.org/w/index.php?title=Waste-to-energy&oldid=782153311.

World Bank. (2017). Countries. Washington, DC: World Bank. Retrieved June 10, 2017, from http://www.worldbank.org/en/country.

World Health Organization. (2017). *Ten years of transformation: Making WHO fit for purpose in the 21st century*. Geneva: WHO.

Part II

Ik'—Second day of the Maya calendar. **Mixed media on paper—22″ × 30″.** © 2015 Lylia Forero Carr. Used with permission.

Chapter 2

The Concept of Well-Being

Philosophical Wisdom from the Ages

THE PHILOSOPHICAL FOUNDATIONS OF
HUMAN WELL-BEING

The pursuit of *well-being* has been one of the most enduring quests of human civilization. The search for well-being permeates our philosophies, religions and religious traditions, rituals and rites of passage, music, visual arts, and, of course, the performing arts in all their varieties. It is reasonable to suggest that all human beings have sought at least some measure of well-being and others have regarded its pursuit as a central life interest. Before we go further, let us first pin down the concept of well-being. Scholars conducting research on well-being have referred to this concept by different names: happiness, quality of life, well-being, subjective well-being, life satisfaction, hedonic well-being, emotional well-being, psychological well-being, quality of living, eudaemonia, and social indicators, among others. This is not to say that these terms are perfect synonyms. They are overlapping concepts in that they have something to do with the overarching concept of well-being (figure 2.1).

What is the highest of all the goods achievable in action? . . . .
   most people . . . call it happiness, . . .
   But they disagree about what happiness is.

—(Aristotle, 1934)

In this chapter, we discuss the concept of well-being primarily from a philosophical point of view, though we do provide some empirical data to support selected findings. Overall, we try to shed light on how philosophers over the centuries have treated this concept from a Western perspective, an East Asian perspective, a South Asian perspective, and an Islamic perspective. The statistical data-rich chapters follow this one.

21

Figure 2.1.   Aristotle. *Source*: (Photo by Jastrow, 2006; statue, National Museum of Rome, Palazzo Altemps, Ludovisi Collection; at https://commons.wikimedia.org/wiki/ File:Aristotle_Altemps_Inv8575.jpg#file; public domain)

WESTERN PHILOSOPHY AND THE CONCEPTION OF WELL-BEING

Alex C. Michalos, a renowned well-being scholar from the University of Northern British Columbia, and Dan Weijers, a philosopher and the founding coeditor of the *International Journal of Wellbeing*, wrote a chapter "Western Historical Traditions of Well-Being" in *The Pursuit of Human Well-Being* (Michalos & Weijers, 2017). They presented a selection of major notions of well-being from the known history of the Western world. They discussed ancient views of well-being, focusing on aristocratic values in ancient Greece—the notion of the good life, harmony as the key to well-being, and the experience of pleasure. They also discussed religious conceptions of the

Figure 2.2.   Alex C. Michalos. *Source*: (Personal photo; used with permission)

good life, as expressed through the Middle Ages and beyond. They also discussed other secular conceptions of well-being (figure 2.2).

Michalos and Weijers made the case that much of the historical writings of the Archaic Age (c. 750–c. 480 BCE) reflected well-being in the prescriptive sense—what is the best life for an individual and what the individual should do to become the best person he or she can be. What is strength of character? People should be honest, courageous, just, generous, compassionate, hospitable, and so forth. Virtue and character capture much of the philosophical discourse about well-being during that time.

> *Happiness depends on ourselves.*
> —(Aristotle, n.d.)

Moving forward in time, harmony emerged as the focal point of the well-being discourse (in the period 550–250 BCE). Harmony became central to the concept of well-being but in different forms. Philosophers at that time emphasized harmony as reflected in nine different attributes of the good life:

1. *The soul's harmony with itself* (i.e., striving to bring increased harmony to the soul to improve the individual's chances for trading up rather than down in the next life—trading up means to come back as a higher form of being);

2. *Harmony among one's species, nature in general, and ideal law* (i.e., the good life is living in a community and willingly following the community's customs and conventional laws in a manner consistent with the divine law);

3. *Harmony as blending daimones with a supreme being* (i.e., *daimones* are considered as exalted entities having special status—higher than that of souls but lesser than that of gods; e.g., love is viewed as a cosmic force bringing together elements such as earth, air, fire, and water to produce a world in which the *daimones* are blended with a supreme being);

4. *Harmonious balance among an individual's internal atoms and the external atoms of his or her environment* (i.e., good health is achieved by achieving harmony between the atoms in one's body and the atoms in the environment);

5. *Harmonious balance among the individual's physical constitution, humors, diets, exercises, geography, seasonal climates, heavenly bodies, and government*;

6. *Harmonious combination of well-ordered souls in well-ordered cities* (i.e., well-being is achieved when rational souls are reconciled with ideal cities);

7. *Ascetic harmony with nature* (i.e., the best life is that lived by, or in harmony with, our animal nature);

8. *Harmonious mixture of an active life with goods of the soul, goods of the body, and external goods* (i.e., a good life requires a good mind and body—internal goods—as well as external goods such as noble birth, friends, wealth, and honor); and

9. *Harmony with nature through virtue* (i.e., the good life involves living in harmony with nature through virtuous action).

> *Holding fast to these things, you will know the worlds of gods and mortals which permeates and governs everything.*
> *And you will know, as is right, nature similar in all respects, so that you will neither entertain unreasonable hopes nor be neglectful of anything.*
> —(Strohmeier & Westbrook, 2003)

Western philosophers from 550 to 250 BCE wrote much about *pleasure* as well-being. Many of the writings during this era reflected four views of well-being as pleasure:

1. *A life of personal pleasure regardless of its impact on others* (i.e., an individual experiencing the good life is an individual who regards the pursuit of pleasure as the end for humans);

2. *A life of measured pleasures exceeding pains* (i.e., a person experiencing well-being is a person who makes careful observations, thinks rationally

about what causes distress and joy, and makes decisions and acts to maximize pleasure and minimize pain; as such, the good life is a life lived with measured pleasures greater than measured pains);

3. *A life filled with experiences of transient pleasures* (i.e., we derive knowledge from transient experiences; as such, well-being or ill-being must be subjective and based on concrete pleasures based on transient experiences); and
4. *Pleasure in the form of peace of mind and a healthy body* (i.e., the chief goal of human beings is tranquility and good health).

> *It is impossible to live a pleasant life without living wisely and well and justly agreeing neither to harm nor be harmed), and it is impossible to live wisely and well and justly without living a pleasant life.*
>
> —(O'Keefe, 2005, p. 134)

Moving forward in history, the rise of Christianity during the time of the Roman Empire created a shift in the Western conception of well-being. Instead of the ancient Greek view of well-being as controlled primarily by the individual through purposeful action, the Christian view of well-being was fatalistic. Human well-being exists only on earth; spiritual well-being is attained only in Heaven in the afterlife. Also, human well-being cannot be influenced directly by individual, purposeful action. If there is such a thing as human well-being, it is a gift from God. People who follow the religious path toward God could enjoy a semblance of well-being on Earth, followed by true well-being in Heaven. True happiness can only be experienced in Heaven after we die. Life on Earth is Real Hell. A life lived religiously could lead to Real Paradise in Heaven. In other words, imperfect happiness can be attained while living, but true happiness can be attained only in Heaven. As such, earthly happiness (or imperfect happiness) constituted a life of many satisfying experiences and a few dissatisfying ones. To achieve earthly happiness, we need wisdom, and God gives us wisdom to allow us to achieve this semblance of earthly happiness, paving the way to heavenly happiness. This religious view of well-being persisted for hundreds of years.

> *St. Augustine assumes in his main discussions of morality that the starting point for such reflections is how to live a happy life, and explains why the love of God and neighbor that Christ commands in all four gospels is the true path to happiness.*
>
> *St. Thomas Aquinas follows Aristotle in beginning his most famous discussion of morality with a treatise on happiness, and concludes with Augustine that God alone can fulfill the restlessness and longing that marks all human persons.*
>
> —(William III, 2008, pp. 25–26)

Imperfect happiness, the earthly happiness, was emphasized during the Enlightenment; the intellectual and scientific movement of eighteenth-century

Europe was characterized by a rational approach to religious issues. It was common during this period to view well-being in terms of happiness—both personal and public happiness. This view of well-being during the Enlightenment can be characterized as follows (figure 2.3):

1. Well-being is essentially earthly happiness;
2. Earthly happiness is viewed as a preponderance of pleasure over pain;
3. Personal happiness is more of a tranquil state, more reflective on avoiding pain than on experiencing pleasure;
4. Personal happiness can be achieved by being generous and moral, not greedy and immoral;
5. Public happiness is essentially utilitarian in character. That is, ethical decisions can be made by selecting courses of action that can maximize pleasure and minimize pain for the greatest number of people; and
6. Personal and public happiness can conflict in that decisions geared to maximize personal happiness can conflict with public happiness and vice versa.

The creed which accepts as the foundation of morals, Utility, or the Greatest-Happiness Principle, holds that actions are right in proportion as they tend to promote happiness, wrong as they tend to produce the reverse of happiness.

Figure 2.3.   John Stuart Mill. *Source*: (Photo by London Stereoscopic Company, ca. 1870; Hulton Archive; public domain; at https://commons.wikimedia.org/wiki/File:John_Stuart_Mill_by_London_Stereoscopic_Company,_c1870.jpg#file)

By happiness is intended pleasure, and the absence of pain; by unhappiness, pain, and the privation of pleasure.

—(Mill, 1879, chapter 2)

Following the Enlightenment period, the philosophical discourse shifted toward loftier goals, a departure from teleological ethics and utilitarianism. The philosophy of well-being shifted to focus on values—community, meaningful work, and God. This shift in the philosophy of well-being was a pushback to the greed manifested in those economies that embraced capitalism. It was a pushback to the perception that people had become obsessed with making money and that wealth and acquisition of material possessions became the mantra of living—the ultimate purpose of life. Philosophers of well-being decried that there is more to life than happiness as utilitarians have defined it. There is more to human well-being than happiness in the hedonic sense. Well-being requires a heavy dose of meaning and authenticity. If so, public happiness should not be the goal of society and public policy. Moral, social, and religious goals are more appropriate. Following is a quote from Michalos and Weijers (2017) related to meaning and authenticity (figure 2.4):

. . . the contemporary idea of governments measuring happiness and using happiness research to guide policy is likely unpopular among the older generations partly because their longer view of history has taught them that being forced

Figure 2.4.   Daniel Weijers. *Source:* **(Personal photo; used with permission)**

to be free is a much better guarantor of their well-being than any roughshod attempt to force them to be happy. State force has been abused so many times in the past (and even still now) that many people prefer that their governments provide them with the tools they need to pursue their own view of well-being in their own way, a way that is meaningful to them. For this reason, useful proxy measures of well-being might be thought to be measures of health, education, civil and political liberties, and wealth, because these are the basic enablers of the freedom to pursue well-being in all of its forms.

—(Michalos & Weijers, 2017, p. 54)

EAST ASIAN PHILOSOPHY AND THE CONCEPTION OF WELL-BEING

Shawn Arthur and Victor H. Mair wrote a chapter on this topic in *The Pursuit of Human Well-Being: The Untold Global History* (2017). Shawn Arthur (figure 2.5) is an assistant professor of Chinese religions at Wake Forest University and is a specialist in all East Asian religions. Professor Mair (figure 2.6) is an American sinologist and professor of Chinese studies at the University of Pennsylvania. The focus of their chapter is the conception of well-being as embedded in the history and culture of China (including Tibet and Taiwan), Japan, and Korea (North and South). These three geopolitical regions also

Figure 2.5.   Shawn Arthur. *Source*: **(Personal photo; used with permission)**

share the religions of Confucianism, Buddhism, and Daoism, which provide the foundation for sociopolitical thought and ultimately the conception of well-being. The authors discuss the East Asian conception of well-being in terms of five dimensions—prosperity and wealth, love of virtue, good health and peace of mind, longevity, and fulfilling destiny and following the will of Heaven.

With respect to *prosperity and wealth* as a major element of human well-being, Arthur and Mair argue that people from East Asia have traditionally glorified the extended family that is closely knit with plenty of material resources: having lots of children, especially male descendants; living in a major housing compound; and sharing a single surname. A common tradition in China is to pay homage to the God of Wealth and celebrate good tidings of financial success by hanging colorful paintings of groups of male children playing amid gold and silver ingots, which symbolize wealth and prosperity. Displaying images of the God of Wealth in religious temples, people's homes, and retail stores is also a common tradition (figure 2.7).

With respect to *love of virtue* as a key dimension of well-being, the Confucian tradition focuses on upholding four major groups of virtues:

1. Family responsibilities and obedience;
2. Commitment to and acceptance of group norms, solidarity, and harmony;
3. Commitment to hard work and education; and
4. The cultivation of a proper disposition including austerity, humility, self-control, and frugality.

Upholding these values in everyday life should lead to happiness and well-being of self, family, community, and society at large. The central tenet of Confucianism reflects virtue ethics. The virtues valued by Daoism and Buddhism include equality, consideration, respect of diversity, contentment, noncompetitiveness, humility, patience, quietude, and simplicity. Well-being, then, involves the virtues of taking care of one's health, living harmoniously with others and nature, and living a life with integrity.

Just as treasures are uncovered from the earth, so virtue appears from good deeds, and wisdom appears from a pure and peaceful mind.

To walk safely through the maze of human life, one needs the light of wisdom and the guidance of virtue.

—(Buddha, n.d.)

With respect to *good health and peace of mind* as an important component of human well-being, Arthur and Mair (2017) (figures 2.5 and 2.7) have argued that the classical Chinese medical tradition is predicated on the notion

Figure 2.6.   Victor Mair. *Source*: (Personal photo; used with permission)

that well-being reflects balanced, strong, smooth-flowing *qi* along the body's energy pathways. The ancient Chinese believed that the universe and the human body was heavily influenced by *qi*, material energy (wood, fire, earth, metal, and water) that provides the body with energy of movement and is the basis for the ability to function. Harmonious and balanced *qi* flow leads to health and well-being, whereas blockage of *qi* flow leads to illness. As such, the Chinese medical tradition calls for cures such as acupuncture, herbal remedies, massage, and lifestyle changes designed to calm the spirit, regulate diet, engage in proper exercise and breathing, moderate emotions, and avoid excesses of drinking, eating, and sexual activities. Peace of mind, based on Chinese tradition, means contentment, serenity, stillness, and quietude. It is about achieving harmony with oneself and the cosmos. It is about achieving balance between the *yin* and *yang*. The *yang* involves emotions manifested because of excesses that people experience in life in the form of greed, war, and corruption, and the emotions manifested from these experiences such as anger, hatred, worry, fear, sadness, and euphoria. The *yin* is the countervailing force that brings a person back to a state of harmony with him- or herself and nature—regaining balance through maintaining calm, quietude, relaxed breathing, and tranquility.

> As "to heal" means "to make whole," [all the methods of the larger Chinese health care system] *serve to transform human beings from simple discrete entities separate from the outside world into active participants in the triad of*

Figure 2.7.   The God of Wealth. A contemporary God of Wealth shrine on Mount Tai in Eastern China. *Source*: **(Credit: Shawn Arthur, China 2013; used with permission)**

heaven, earth, and humanity. Chinese health methods not only cure and vitalize people's bodies and minds, but aim to join them harmoniously with the larger cosmos. Health accordingly does not just mean the absence of illness or symptoms, but is an integrated balance of physical well-being, personal happiness, good fortune, and harmony.

—(Kohn, 2005, p. 3)

With respect to *longevity* as a primary dimension of human well-being, Chinese tradition has long focused on being prosperous and "living a long life." The most ancient desires and aspirations of the Chinese people are the prolonged life and a natural death. Chinese society offers prayers for longevity, even immortality. Throughout history, Chinese people strove to find ways to prolong life—health rituals, herbs and medicine, mineral elixirs, visualization and breathing practices, ascetic dietary regimens, astrology, sexual practices, and physical exercise.

We now turn to the final dimension of human well-being, *fulfilling destiny and the will of Heaven.* One of the most important moral tenets in Confucianism is the relationship between oneself and one's family. Chinese folklore reminds people that they are merely a continuation of their ancestors. This view is typically manifested in folk sayings such as "the inheritance of the family line," "raising sons for one's old age," "having three generations living together under one roof," "happiness for the elderly is from their children pleasing them by living with them," and "harmony in the family is the basis for success in any undertaking." As such, part of fulfilling one's destiny includes being filial to one's ancestors, having filial children, maintaining the health and wealth of the family, and protecting the family from life's hazards. Part of fulfilling destiny and the will of Heaven is to ensure safety—safety for the self, the family, the community, and the country. Maintaining safety is a cherished custom in Chinese society. It is about safety from infectious diseases, safety from epidemics, safety from wars and foreign invasions, and safety from natural disasters.

SOUTH ASIAN PHILOSOPHY AND THE CONCEPTION OF WELL-BEING

Isabelle Clark-Decés and Frederick M. Smith wrote a chapter on the conception of well-being from a South Asian perspective in *The Pursuit of Human Well-Being: The Untold Global History* (Clark-Decés & Smith, 2017). Isabelle Clark-Decés is a professor with the Department of Anthropology at Princeton University, and Frederick M. Smith is Professor of Sanskrit and classical Indian religions with the departments of religious studies and Asian and Slavic languages and literature at the University of Iowa. Much of the following discussion comes from their chapter.

Professors Clark-Decés and Smith (figures 2.8 and 2.9) have argued that well-being in South Asia is viewed in terms of health, prosperity, longevity, community, and harmony with others and nature. Although South Asia comprises a large geographical area that includes India, Pakistan, Bangladesh, Nepal, Bhutan, Sri Lanka, and Afghanistan, much of the discussion here focuses on Indian culture and history as these relate to the conception of well-being. Thus, the conception of well-being in this region of the world has been mostly influenced by Indian religious doctrine (primarily Buddhist, Hindu, and, later, Islam). Based on their research, Professors Clark-Decés and Smith demonstrate that the concept of well-being has been captured in classical Sanskrit to reflect several states:

1. *Sukha* (i.e., satisfaction, happiness, ease, agreeability);
2. *Hita* (i.e., sound beneficial, or healthy state mostly a result of gift-giving or religious practice);
3. *Kusala* (i.e., suitability, competence, and cleverness);
4. *Aucitya* (i.e., appropriateness);

Figure 2.8.   Isabelle Clark-Decés. *Source*: (Personal photo; used with permission)

Figure 2.9.   Frederick W. Smith. *Source*: **(Personal photo).**

5. *Svasti* (i.e., auspiciousness);
6. *Svasthya* (i.e., "established in oneself");
7. *Islam* (i.e., intactness, peace, safety, and security).

The Buddhist tradition in South Asia emphasizes *nirvana* and the ultimate state of psychological well-being. People who achieve *nirvana* realize that the world and all its parameters are in a constant state of flux; we live in a temporary and transient state; there is no permanence. Everything (idea, thought, object, or life condition) is dependent on prior conditions that reach back indefinitely and infinitely. Life is essentially all about suffering and the alleviation of suffering. Hence, well-being, by definition, is a state characterized by lack of suffering. To achieve *nirvana* the Buddhist tradition mandates an "Eightfold Path" (i.e., the right view, the right intention, the right speech, the right action, the right livelihood, the right effort, the right mindfulness, and the right concentration) (figure 2.10).

> *There is a safe place in view of all, but difficult of approach, where there is no old age nor death, no pain nor disease. It is what is called nirvana, or freedom from pain, or perfection, which is in view of all; it is the safe, happy, and quiet place which the great sages reach. That is the eternal place, in view of all, but difficult of approach. Those sages who reach it are free from sorrows, they have put an end to the stream of existence.*
>
> —(Kanna, 2011, p. 26)

Eventually, the influence of Buddhism in South Asia diminished and was replaced by Hinduism and Islam. The image of well-being from a Hindu

Figure 2.10. Garuda from India. *Source*: (Photo courtesy of Hyougushi/Hideyuki KAMON from National Museum in *Delhi, India*; https://commons.wikimedia.org/wiki/File:Garuda_by_Hyougushi_in_Delhi.jpg; Creative Commons Attribution-Share Alike 2.0 Generic license)

tradition depicts themes of love, beauty, humor, health, and friendship. This image of well-being was pursued through a caste system. The caste system categorizes people into four hierarchical classes that reflect occupational divisions: priest, warrior, merchant, and laborer. The caste system was bolstered as a social system to maximize societal well-being. Religiously, well-being, at least among the priests, warriors, and merchants, was construed in terms of reward and punishment in the afterlife. Those who lived a good, productive life and stuck to social customs (*dharma*) would be rewarded in the afterlife by being reincarnated in exalted states.

> *Thus, one's ideal state of well-being was viewed as dependent on a naturalized order: A warrior must be a warrior, a merchant a merchant, a priest a priest, a laborer a laborer. This naturalized and sanctified order was certainly a reflection of the dominant social order in northern India at the time. But the notion of collective well-being revealed here undoubtedly helped perpetuate power structures inherent in this social order, which in turn reinforced notions of well-being as dependent on the purity of caste.*
> —(Clark-Decés & Smith, 2017, p. 90)

Based on the Hindu religion, four stages of life have direct implications for well-being:

1. *Studentship*: This stage involves the first twelve years of life during which the young man studies philosophy, literature, science, and language. Well-being is experienced to the extent that the student adheres to role expectations related to education and socialization.
2. *Householder*: This stage of life involves marriage and raising a family. Well-being in this stage is reflected in the way the person adheres to societal expectations related to family roles.
3. *Retiree*: This stage is defined by the empty nest, in which children are out of the house and parents retire to a forest dwelling to pray and contemplate. Hence, well-being is experienced to the extent that the retirees assume the retiree role.
4. *World renouncers*: This stage of life reflects the fact of the retiring couple renouncing their worldly goods to seek *nirvana* in preparing for their death and reincarnation.

> *Nothing is higher than Dharma.*
>> *The weak overcomes the stronger by Dharma, as over a king.*
>> *Truly that Dharma is the Truth (Satya).*
>> *Therefore, when a man speaks the Truth, they say, "He speaks the Dharma";*
>> *and if he speaks Dharma, they say,*
>> *"He speaks the Truth!" For both are one."*
>> —*Brihadaranyaka Upanishad, 1.4.xiv* (Horsch, 2004, pp. 423–48)

Islam in South Asia took hold in the mid- and late second millenniums. In that context, Islam was viewed as a path to well-being through adherence to the *Qur'an* and Islamic law (*Sharia*). Within Islam in this world region, other religions took hold that influenced people's conception of well-being. One notable religion was Sufism. Well-being guided by Sufism was viewed in terms of states of ecstasy and rapture through sacred music and living one's life guided by the saints of Sufism. We discuss the influence of Islam on the conception of well-being in some detail in the next section.

The last few centuries of the second millennium witnessed a further shift in the conception of well-being in South Asia. A major reason for this shift was the primary health care centers run by Christian missionaries. These centers provided medical services and served as models for Hindu and other religious and secular health care providers to follow suit. The diffusion of these medical organizations resulted in the popularization of well-being based on health and medicine.

ISLAMIC PHILOSOPHY AND THE CONCEPTION OF WELL-BEING

Mohsen Joshanloo wrote a chapter on the conception of well-being from an Islamic perspective in *The Pursuit of Human Well-Being: The Untold Global History* (Joshanloo, 2017). Joshanloo is an assistant professor of psychology at Keimyung University in South Korea. He has published several articles on well-being in non-Western cultures; therefore, we view him as an expert on the topic of the interface between Islam and well-being. Much of the discussion in this section is based on Joshanloo's chapter (figure 2.11).

Islam is a comprehensive ideology that has significant implications for the concept of well-being as practiced by many of the Muslim people and Muslim countries around the world. There are 1.6 billion Muslims; they comprise 23 percent of the world's population. Islam is widespread among forty-nine countries that have Muslim majorities. Muslims are concentrated in South Asia, Southeast Asia, West Asia, and North Africa. Furthermore, many countries have significant minority segments that claim to be of the Muslim faith—successor states in Central Asia of the former Soviet Union, China, Europe, and the Americas. The guidelines to human well-being are spelled out in the *Qur'an,* which is considered by Muslims to be the literal word of *Allah* (God) as revealed to the prophet Muhammad through the angel Gabriel (figure 2.12).

In the *Qur'an,* well-being is permanent bliss experienced in the afterlife (i.e., Heaven). It can be achieved only through submission to the will of *Allah.* To achieve this state of well-being, the individual must have absolute faith in *Allah* (as the one and only God) and follow the teachings of the *Qur'an* in conducting his or her daily affairs. *Allah* has the power to reward and punish people's deeds not only in the afterlife but also in this world. *Allah* is to be revered and feared because *Allah* can reward people by many worldly blessings and punish with great vehemence by inflicting pain and suffering in many forms. To submit to *Allah* and ultimately attain well-being in this world (at least partly) and the next, people must follow Islamic law and the moral code (the *Sharia*).

Figure 2.11. Mohsen Joshanloo. *Source*: (Personal photo, used with permission)

Figure 2.12. The *Qur'an*. *Source*: (Photo courtesy of Nahidh Salman. Downloaded from http://www.rgbstock.com/photo/nQz76Lu/Quran2)

The *Qur'an* states that human beings have two natures: one angelic, one demonic. The angelic side (or good side): Human beings are created with an inclination for good (*fitra*). The *fitra* is a motivational force to submit to the will of *Allah* and follow the *Sharia*. Thus, people are inherently good because they are intrinsically motivated to help their fellow man, to be compassionate, generous, loving, hospitable, protective, and just. The demonic side (the dark side): Human beings are equally motivated to do evil—to commit murder, to be cruel to their fellow man, to be selfish, to rob and disobey, to ignore and act mindlessly, and so on. This is the satanic element of human nature. As such, human beings are in a constant state of internal conflict between good and evil. People win this battle in favor of the good when they mobilize their will and inner strength to do good and prevent sinful conduct and evil. This facet is the essence of what Muslims call the *jihad*—the inner struggle to resist temptations of the carnal self and to act in accordance with the will of *Allah*. Thus, the *jihad* is to embrace the *Sharia* and follow its many prescriptions. As such, well-being is not construed as subjective states of experience (e.g., life satisfaction, positive/negative affect, hedonic well-being, or happiness) but a lifelong devotion to worship and serve *Allah*, which means following the *Sharia*. The achievement of well-being is not an outcome state but a never-ending work in progress (i.e., a process) with the outcome being intense, permanent spiritual pleasure in the hereafter. The greatest pleasure experienced in the hereafter is proximity to *Allah* in Heaven. To reiterate, well-being in this world is nothing more than being on track to achieve well-being in the hereafter.

> *Know that the key to happiness is to follow the Sunna and to imitate the Messenger of God in all his coming and going, his movements and rest, in his way of eating, his attitude, his sleep and his talk. Al-Ghazali*

—(Ruthven, 2012)

Happiness, according to Islamic law, is intellectual. It is the recognition of oneness with *Allah*; it is to be close to *Allah*, to realize that one is following the path to salvation. Bodily desires may conflict with intellectual happiness. Hence, bodily desires should be suppressed through virtuous activity and piety, which entail subjugating bodily desires to ascetic practice as spelled out in the *Sharia*. Happiness cannot be obtained by strictly focusing on one's self. The focus should be on the community or society at large. It should be noted that the term *jihad* has a very different meaning to militant Muslims. Militant Muslims have a passionate anti-Western sentiment. They use terror and violence in their fight against Westerners and other Muslims allied with a Western way of life. Martyrdom in Islam, according to the militants, is a way to attain genuine well-being experienced in the afterlife. Hence, the *jihad* is not necessarily an inner struggle between inner angelic and demonic forces but an external struggle between the Western way of life (i.e., demonic) and the Islamic way of life (i.e., angelic).

CONCLUSIONS

From this discourse on the philosophy of well-being, we see that the concept of well-being is indeed elusive and multifaceted. Philosophers throughout the millennia and from the vast corners of the earth have produced conceptions of well-being that are dramatically different.

Western philosophers from the ancient Greeks conceptualized well-being in terms of strength of character and virtues. Roman philosophers referred to well-being in terms of harmony—inner harmony, social harmony, harmony with nature and the cosmos, and so on. Philosophers who followed focused on pleasure and utilitarian concepts of the greater good. Christian philosophers focused on spiritual well-being, the type of well-being that can be attained only through salvation in the afterlife. The latter is perfect happiness, but a less-perfect form of happiness can be attained by living a Christian life as revealed in the Bible. The focus then shifted to values—community, meaningful work, and God.

East Asian philosophers have long viewed the concept of well-being in terms of prosperity and wealth, love of virtue, good health and peace of mind, longevity, and fulfilling destiny and following the will of Heaven. South Asian philosophers focused on *nirvana*, the ultimate state of psychological well-being. *Nirvana* allows the person to prepare for reincarnation into a higher being. To achieve nirvana, one needs to follow the eightfold path that reflects the caste system. Maintaining the caste system by doing what one is destined for (priest, warrior, merchant, and laborer) allows people to achieve a social order that produces the highest form of collective happiness—preparing people for reincarnation in the form of higher beings.

Islamic philosophers, like Christian philosophers, have long viewed the concept of well-being as submitting to the will of *Allah,* worshipping God, and following a path leading to salvation and Heaven in the afterlife. The path to the afterlife is achieved by following the rules and mandates spelled out in the *Qur'an* (the *Sharia, or* Islamic law).

The concept of well-being, when treated comprehensively, comprises three key dimensions: economic well-being, health well-being, and educational well-being. These three dimensions of well-being reflect the popular measure of human well-being developed by the United Nations Development Programme. It has a long, rich history of social indicator and quality-of-life studies. We use these three dimensions to document advances in human well-being during the past fifty or more years. We believe that these three dimensions are consistent with the varied concepts of well-being construed by philosophers from every corner of the globe and throughout the history of human civilization. Although one's perception of well-being may differ depending on one's philosophy (e.g., *nirvana*, salvation, perfect happiness, oneness with God, harmony with the cosmos), the common denominator is the requisite state that should be achieved to attain the final state. Most philosophers agree that to achieve personal and collective well-being, societies must be organized to deliver the means to enhance economic well-being, health well-being, and educational well-being. These three states of well-being should provide people with the "right path" to come closer to God or gods, the ultimate state of well-being.

REFERENCES

Aristotle. (1934). *Nicomachean ethics*. (H. Rackham, Trans.), Loeb Classical Library. Cambridge, MA: Harvard University Press.

Aristotle. (n.d.). Aristotle: Quotes. Retrieved June 16, 2017, https://www.goodreads.com/author/quotes/2192.Aristotle.

Arthur, S., & Mair, V. H. (2017). East Asian historical traditions of well-being. In R. Estes & M. J. Sirgy (Eds.), *The pursuit of human well-being: The untold global history*. Dordrecht, NL: Springer.

Buddha. (n.d.). Brainy Quote. [Web site]. Retrieved June 16, 2017, from https://www.brainyquote.com/quotes/authors/b/buddha.html.

Clark-Decés, I., & Smith, F. M. (2017). Well-being in India: A historical and anthropological report. In R. Estes & M. J. Sirgy (Eds.), *The pursuit of human well-being: The untold global history*. Dordrecht, NL: Springer.

Horsch, P. (2004). From creation myth to world law: The early history of Dharma. *Journal of Indian Philosophy, 32*, 423–48.

Joshanloo, M. (2017). Islamic conceptions of well-being. In R. Estes & M. J. Sirgy (Eds.), *The pursuit of human well-being: The untold global history*. Dordrecht, NL: Springer.

Kanna, Y. (2011). *Nirvana: Absolute freedom*. Mumbai: Kamath Publishing.

Kohn, L. (2005). *Health and long life: The Chinese way*. Cambridge, MA: Three Pines Press.

Michalos, A. C., & Weijers, D. (2017). Western historical traditions of well-being. In R. Estes & M. J. Sirgy (Eds.), *The pursuit of human well-being: The untold global history*. Dordrecht, NL: Springer.

Mill, John Stuart. (1879). *Utilitarianism*. Reprinted from *Fraser's Magazine*, 7th edition. [Project Gutenberg]. London: Longmans, Green and Co. [Project Gutenberg]. Retrieved June 16, 2017, from http://www.gutenberg.org/files/11224/11224-h/11224-h.htm.

O'Keefe, T. (2005). *Epicurus on freedom*. Cambridge, MA: Cambridge University Press.

Ruthven, M. (2012). *Islam: A very short introduction* (p. 54). Oxford: Oxford University Press.

Strohmeier, J., & Westbrook, P. (2003). *Divine harmony: The life and teachings of Pythagoras*. Berkeley, CA: Berkeley Hills Books.

William III, C. (2008). *Introducing moral theology: True happiness and the virtues*. Ada, MI: Brazos Press.

Chapter 3

Health

The Cornerstone of Well-Being

It is health that is real wealth, not pieces of gold and silver.

—Gandhi, M. (n.d.)

The 1948 *Constitution* of the World Health Organization (WHO) defined health in the broadest terms possible and defined it as a basic human right to which people everywhere should have access: *Health is a state of complete physical, mental and social well-being and not merely the absence of disease or infirmity* (World Health Organization, 1948).

The WHO went on to specify the core values that informed its definition of health and, more broadly, of health well-being. These values were judged to be so important that they, too, were included in the opening paragraphs of the WHO *Constitution*. We have included these core values in box 3.1.

BOX 3.1   Core Values Underlying the WHO Definition of Health and Health Well-Being

- The enjoyment of the highest attainable standard of health is one of the fundamental rights of every human being without distinction of race, religion, political belief, economic or social condition.
- The health of all peoples is fundamental to the attainment of peace and security and is dependent upon the fullest cooperation of individuals and States.
- The achievement of any State in the promotion and protection of health is of value to all.

- Unequal development in different countries in the promotion of health and control of disease, especially communicable disease, is a common danger.
- Healthy development of the child is of basic importance; the ability to live harmoniously in a changing total environment is essential to such development.
- The extension to all peoples of the benefits of medical, psychological and related knowledge is essential to the fullest attainment of health. Informed opinion and active co-operation on the part of the public are of the utmost importance in the improvement of the health of the people.
- Governments have a responsibility for the health of their peoples which can be fulfilled only by the provision of adequate health and social measures.

(World Health Organization, 1948)

The WHO definition of health and health well-being is far-reaching and includes mental and behavioral health as well as lifelong rehabilitation services as essential components of comprehensive health care services. The definition also defines health as a basic human right and specifies the role of governments, nongovernmental organizations, and people themselves as the primary actors in promoting advances in health status. The WHO's inclusion of historically disadvantaged population groups in its list of core values also is noteworthy.

The WHO definition of health parallels that of the more general understanding of well-being discussed in this book. The definition is at the center of public and private efforts designed to reduce disease and disability and to promote health well-being. Not surprisingly, the definition figures prominently in the goals that inform *The Right to Health* (Office of the United Nations High Commissioner for Human Rights, 2008), another seminal document related to health for all passed by the governing body of the United Nations Office of the High Commissioner for Human Rights. Further, the combined goals of these documents are associated with at least half of the seventeen *Sustainable Development Goals* on which the 193-member states of the United Nations agreed in 2015 (United Nations Development Programme, 2015). They also provide the framework adopted by many of the world's major international nongovernmental development assistance organizations in promoting health and in reducing worldwide rates of early death and disability (Doctors without Borders, 2017; Save the Children, 2017; World Vision International, 2017). Many local development councils and organizations also have adopted these goals as the central focus of their health promotion activities (Hague Academy of Local Governance, 2016; Tortajada, Joshi, & Biswas, 2013).

FOCUS ON HEALTH

This chapter identifies the significant developments that have taken place in advancing the health well-being of people everywhere, including the important global initiatives undertaken by the United Nations in collaboration with businesses and business leaders and with the head of major philanthropic foundations and social services organizations that are committed to advancing the well-being of people everywhere. These collaborative efforts and funding partnerships have resulted in major social, health, educational, and employment well-being never previously encountered. These collaborative efforts between the public and private sectors have brought about a level of advance in human well-being never previously experienced as have the well-coordinated global action plans that resulted from the Millennium Campaign (United Nations, 2015) and the recently launched Sustainable Development Goals (SDG) campaign (United Nations, 2016). Though housed within the structure of the United Nations and its many and varied technical agencies, these campaigns are expected to result in even higher levels of human progress than those we collectively experienced over the seven decades since the end of World War II. A high level of success also is assured given that many actors from the private sector are contributing their time and effort to ensuring the success of the campaigns, that is, by introducing a wide range of economic programs, ensuring adult access to at least a grammar school–level education, and ensuring a steady flow of low-cost vaccines and other essential biological materials to people in all walks of life.

Of interest is the *Health for All* agenda of the World Health Organization and the recently implemented SDG initiative of the United Nations (2015–2030) mentioned in the previous paragraph. *Health for All* is a programming goal of the World Health Organization that has been popularized since the 1970s. It envisions securing the health and well-being of people around the world but with emphasis on the health promotion needs of people residing in developing countries. It is the basis for the World Health Organization's primary health care strategy to promote health, human dignity, and enhanced quality of life (Health for All, 2017). Throughout the chapter, we also refer to the United Nations Millennium Campaign (2005–2015) that provided the foundation for dramatic progress in advancing the health status of people everywhere during the next fifteen-year period, 1995–2020 (World Health Organization, 2017b).

The chapter draws on a broad set of data to illustrate the various discussions contained in each of the sections. These empirical data are presented for major world regions and, for the most part, for the world. Nation-specific data are reported only when needed to illustrate major comparisons. The centrality of health activity within nations makes clear that many governments and peoples regard access to quality health care services as a basic human right, even if such access brings with it high fiscal costs. The data reported in the chapter were obtained from public and private international data gathering and reporting sources as well as from our recently published book *The Pursuit of Human Well-Being: The Untold Global History* (Estes & Sirgy, 2017). Where necessary, statistical estimates are used for selected groups of countries for indicators for which reliable empirical data are not currently available, a pattern that characterizes the data-reporting capacity of the world's poorest nations.

ALTERNATIVE VIEWS

Quality health care does not necessarily convey the same meaning all over the world. At least three major approaches to or understanding of health care exist in most societies: (a) Western medicine, (b) Eastern medicine, and (c) alternative medicine. All three approaches share many elements of health care, but they are also characterized by distinctive differences.

Western Medicine

Western medicine reflects a bio-psycho-social approach to health care.[1] This approach is illustrated in figure 3.1, which reflects both the complexities and richness of the varied actors that contribute to shaping the macro environment of the Western approach to health services. The model was formulated by Sr. Kathleen Popko, executive vice president, Strategy and Ministry Development, Catholic Health East, Newtown Square, Pennsylvania. Though focused primarily on the delivery of comprehensive health services to older adults living in the community, the model also offers unique insights into the structure and functioning of health care across many specialty practices serving highly diverse population groups (Popko, 2008). Further, the model illustrates the complex environment within which health care exists and identifies the varied inputs, throughputs, and outcomes associated with health, health care, and health services in Western societies—the systems-based model that we have used throughout the book. We have also emphasized the importance of evidence-based practice and decision making as key aspects of Western health care. These functions, too, are presented in the assessment, monitoring, evaluation, and dissemination functions suggested by the model.

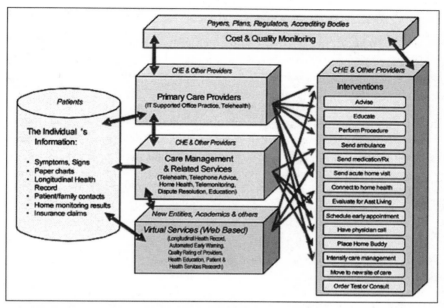

Figure 3.1. The Continuum of Quality Services, developed by Sr. Kathleen Popko. CHE is an acronym for "Catholic Health East—a healing ministry in a variety of settings across the continuum of care." The model is used to describe the multilayered approach to improving comprehensive health services for the aged. *Source*: (Figure from Popko, 2008; permission granted from Health Progress, January–February 2008. Copyright © 2008 by the Catholic Health Association of the United States)

Western Primary Health Care

Primary health care is principally preventive in nature. Its goal is to eliminate the environmental causes that contribute to poor health, for example, lack of access to clean, safe water; inadequate, heavily congested housing; inadequate methods of sanitation and solid waste disposal; high levels of illiteracy; and failure to ensure the quality and safety of foods, drugs, and other consumable products. Effective primary health care resolves each of these problems and engages in the early detection of infectious and contagious diseases (World Health Organization, 2017a; World Toilet Organization, 2017). Vaccinations and other immunizations are major aspects of primary health care, given its emphasis on the prevention of disease and illness. Thus, preventive community health services are at the center of primary health care and overlap directly with mass education campaigns, all of which add significantly to growth at all levels of economic productivity.

Western Secondary Health Care

Secondary health care in Western medicine, by far the largest segment of health care provision, involves the treatment of sick, injured, and temporarily disabled people. This level of health care utilizes a wide spectrum of drugs, antibiotics, radiation, and surgical procedures that are designed to restore people to their level of functioning prior to the occurrence of the illness or injury. This aspect of health care is very expensive to administer and accounts for 10 percent to 20 percent of the gross domestic product (GDP) of most nations (World Bank, 2017). The cost to individuals, as a percentage of their income, is often high. In the United States, secondary health care is responsible for the largest share of personal bankruptcies filed in the country's courts (Himmelstein, Thorne, Warren, & Woolhandler, 2009).

Western Tertiary Care

Tertiary health care in Western medicine is devoted to the care of people with long-term illnesses and permanent disabilities. The goal of this level of care is to help patients and their families function at the highest possible level because a return to full levels of health is rarely possible. Persons with serious spinal cord injuries, the sick aged, those who are losing or have lost their cognitive faculties, severely injured war veterans, and long-term stroke patients are among the largest population groups served through tertiary care. The costs associated with tertiary care are high in all countries given that these patients and their families fall into long-term, usually permanent, categories of care in which all aspects of their needs are expected to be met through various segments of the health system, for example, continuity of care, accessible housing, nutritional services, nursing home and assisted-living care, and, when chosen, end-of-life care.

Eastern Medicine

Eastern approaches to health are ancient and are built on traditional approaches of Chinese medicine that emphasize the importance of the soul and the spiritual aspects of being as the source and cure for the ailments that afflict people. Eastern approaches to health care revolve around harnessing the body's own forces in promoting healing, that is, the qi or chi that flows through major body channels called "meridians" (National Center for Complementary and Integrative Health, 2017a). The qi may be modified or brought back to its previous pattern of internal energy flow using specially designed needles (acupuncture), inverted bottles (moxibustion), bone alignment, massage, and specially prepared herbal remedies designed to treat the specific illness or injury that blocks the flow of healing energy through the body. Usually a combination of these highly person-specific methods is used (Alternative Medicine, 2017; Traditional Chinese Medicine, 2017).

Surgery was once used in the practice of Eastern medicine but, today, given the high risk of infection, it rarely occurs. (Of historical interest, surgical procedures were initially attempted by Chinese, Arab, and early European practitioners of health [including barbers] but were abandoned as the practice of medicine became professionalized. The earliest comprehensive schools of medicine in the East were established in medieval Arab cities including Baghdad and Cairo [Fact of Arabs, 2017; Whitlock, 2010].) Today, body manipulations and medicinal herbs represent the primary approaches used to treat Eastern patients. The overarching goal of these methods, as in Western medicine, is to restore the body to its natural state of regenerative health.

Alternative Medicine

Alternative medicine, often referred to as complementary medicine, includes the use of acupuncture, moxibustion, bone alignment, and massage as staple components of treatment. Such approaches are practiced widely, including in major university medical centers. Herbal treatments, the use of vitamin and mineral supplements, and dietary supervision are components of alternative medicine. Complementary approaches to health care also use a broad range of social approaches in caring for patients with long-term, degenerative illnesses for which no cures currently are available, for example, Alzheimer disease, profound congenital birth defects, permanent disabilities (Alternative Medicine, 2017).

The main goal of alternative medicine is to incorporate the most effective practices in both Eastern and Western medicine into an integrated, holistic system of health care (National Center for Complementary and Integrative Health, 2017b). Alternative medicine has become widely popular in most Western societies and is often practiced under the supervision of a Western-trained health professional.

In societies where alternative medicine is practiced, however, a high level of unease exists with the ambitious claims made by its practitioners. A forceful summary of the criticisms of alternative medicine appears in Wikipedia (Alternative Medicine, 2017):

> Alternative medicine is criticized for being based on misleading statements, quackery, pseudoscience, antiscience, fraud, or poor scientific methodology. Promoting alternative medicine has been called dangerous and unethical. Testing alternative medicine that has no scientific basis has been called a waste of scarce research resources. Critics state "there is really no such thing as alternative medicine, just medicine that works and medicine that doesn't", and

the problem with the idea of "alternative" treatments in this sense is that the "underlying logic is magical, childish or downright absurd". It has been strongly suggested that the very idea of any alternative treatment that works is paradoxical, as any treatment proven to work is "medicine".

Despite these caveats concerning alternative medicine and its practice, its adoption in Western societies continues to attract considerable interest and popularity.

EFFECTIVENESS AND EFFICIENCY OF HEALTH AND HEALTH SERVICES

Measuring the *effectiveness* (the extent to which the intended goals or outcomes have been achieved) and *efficiency* (receiving the highest benefit per unit of cost incurred) of health service systems is one of the most complex and difficult areas of research activity to undertake. The size, complexity, and various administrative and financial arrangements that make up the health sector contribute to the difficulties encountered in carrying out these assessments (Shah, 2011; World Health Organization, 2013b). The task is made even more complex because the health sector may account for as much as 10 percent to 20 percent or more of a country's total GDP and represents a large share of a country's skilled and unskilled workforce (Fuchs, 2013; World Health Organization, 2016d). In many nations, health services are provided through a mixture of public and private systems and are financed through a variety of private insurance schemes, governmental services, and substantial out-of-pocket expenditures made by patients and their families in the form of deductibles and "copayments" (World Health Organization, 2016d). In addition, totally different financing approaches are used to provide health services for the poor. These, too, involve a combination of private and public health care services in combination with out-of-pocket expenditures, many of which are outside the reach of many patients (Bill and Melinda Gates Foundation, 2017). Religiously inspired charity care is also a large component of the health sector in deeply impoverished communities in both developed and developing countries. Countries with a combination of public and private approaches to health care often have centrally administered but programmatically decentralized systems of health care for injured war heroes and retired military personnel and their families (United States Department of Veterans Affairs, 2017).

Many approaches have been developed to undertake the complex task of assessing the efficiency and effectiveness of health care systems. These approaches can be divided into at least five categories: (1) the quality of the services provided, (2) patient satisfaction with the care received, (3) the health outcomes achieved, (4) the efficiency with which the services are provided, and (5) the cost-effectiveness of patient care and of the overall health care systems through which the patients are served. All five levels of assessment are difficult to carry out. Therefore, multiple approaches are generally used with each of the five levels (Cogan & Hubbard, 2011).

To cover each of the five levels for assessing the health care system is beyond the scope of this chapter. Instead, we have chosen to focus on four of the most sensitive indicators of health care worldwide: global advances in extending the average years of life expectancy and advances in reducing infant, child, and maternal death rates.

Living Longer

Worldwide progress in advancing the years of average life expectancy is among the goals of the Millennium Development Goals (MDG) campaign and the Sustainable Development Strategy (SDS) (box 3.2). This measure of global social success is reflected in figure 3.2, which shows the years of average life expectancy for each of the world's regions. The figure also shows the progress in extending years of average life expectancy for three discrete time intervals, that is, 1970 to 1975, 1995 to 2000, and 2000 to 2013. Thus, we have a highly dynamic set of data covering forty-three years.

Years of average life expectancy is considered the paramount measure of the success of a health system. Increasing the average life expectancy requires both quality health services and uniting the health and education sectors in a variety of health initiatives. Long life enables people to add to their family size and to increase the breadth and depth of their extended kinship networks. Many are living long enough to enjoy the birth not only of children and grandchildren but also of great-grandchildren. Indeed, families of three or more generations are now becoming commonplace in most societies.

The ability to realize these significant advances in health figures prominently in the assessments made by people in judging their own quality of life and life satisfaction. They also are important in assessing the overall health status of people individually and globally from a demographic perspective. Increasing from a world average of just 48 years in 1950, world average years of life expectancy exceeded 69.1 years for men and 73.8 years for women in 2015 (United Nations Population Division, 2015). This change represents a major achievement on the part of the world community in advancing overall life expectancy.

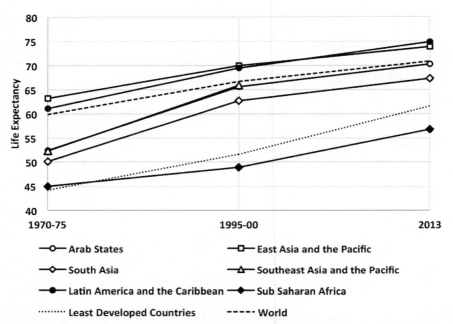

Figure 3.2.   Average years of life expectancy by major world region. *Source:* (Figure 20.7.
Life expectancy, 1970–2013, from *The Pursuit of Human Well-Being: The Untold Global
History*, 2017, p. 702, Estes, R. J., & Sirgy, M. J. [Eds.], ©Springer International Publishing
Switzerland 2017, with permission of Springer)

BOX 3.2   Life Expectancy Increased by Five Years Since 2000, But Health Inequalities Exist

19 May 2016 | GENEVA—Dramatic gains in life expectancy have been
made globally since 2000, but major inequalities persist within and
among countries, according to this year's "World Health Statistics:
Monitoring Health for the SDGs".

Life expectancy increased by five years between 2000 and 2015, the
fastest increase since the 1960s. Those gains reverse declines during
the 1990s, when life expectancy fell in Africa because of the AIDS
epidemic and in Eastern Europe following the collapse of the Soviet
Union. The increase was greatest in the African Region of WHO
where life expectancy increased by 9.4 years to 60 years, driven mainly
by improvements in child survival, progress in malaria control and
expanded access to antiretroviral for treatment of HIV.

(World Health Organization, 2016b)

The country with the highest current life expectancy rates is Japan, with an average number of 86.8 years of life expectancy for both sexes; the country with the least favorable average years of life expectancy is Sierra Leone, where men currently live on average 49.3 years and women 50.8 years. Years of average life expectancy will likely continue to increase in these countries, even in Sierra Leone, which has been besieged by decades of civil unrest, war, and extremely low levels of development. By 2050, years of average life expectancy in economically advanced countries will likely increase to about 100 and by the end of the century to 120 years. Average years of life expectancy are expected to continue to increase in developing countries as well and, most likely, at a pace even faster than that which occurs in economically advanced societies, given the high years of life expectancy they already experience. This trend reflects a remarkable change in worldwide development and is clearly related to social progress associated with national and regional development strategies. Significant advances in preventive health care, as well as the introduction of new health technologies, are also expected to contribute to these advances (Lee, 2013).

The years of average life expectancy are expected to remain at the historically consistent level of 20 percent more years on average for women than for men, even as men live longer and healthier lives. Similarly, life expectancy is highest for people living in economically advanced countries but is increasing rapidly for people living in less economically developed countries. Advances in years of average life expectancy for the latter group of nations will occur for both men and women, given the more peaceful and prosperous conditions that currently characterize these nations. Increasingly larger numbers of infants and children are surviving to adulthood as well, and, even among adults, the numbers of people aged sixty-five years and older also are increasing as a percentage of the total population of countries (United Nations Population Division, 2015).

Regional Variations in Years of Average Life Expectancy

Regional years of average life expectancy are reported in figure 3.2 for three time periods—1970 to 1975, 1995 to 2000, and 2000 to 2013. These data permit us to observe changes that have taken place in years of average life expectancy over nearly half a century. Further, the figure shows data for six of the world's geopolitical regions for the time periods indicated as well as for nations organized by development level and data for the world. All the trends reflected in this figure show steady, impressive gains in average years of life expectancy for all nine of the clusters reported on.

The most striking feature about the figure is the significant rise in average years of life expectancy that all countries, regions, and the world have experienced. Average years of life expectancy increased for all the regions and groups reported in the figure. This overall pattern of improvement in the health sector is especially impressive since the trend lines for each region reflect average years of life expectancy for men and women and for persons at various points on the income spectrum. Life expectancy growth rates are especially impressive for East Asia and the Pacific and Latin America and the Caribbean. The nations of sub-Saharan Africa continue to lag other world regions on this dimension of human development, but the lag is not as great as that which existed between these nations and other nations of the world during the early 1930s and 1960s. All nations are increasing the average years of life expectancy for their populations. This pattern is expected to continue well into the future. In time, the expectation exists that the average years of life expectancy for sub-Saharan African nations will approximate those reported for other regions, although the age trends occurring in East Asia will likely prove difficult for any group of nations to surpass for the foreseeable future.

Almost certainly, the impressive regional gains reflected in figure 3.2 are the result of heavy investments made by economically advanced countries in improving the general health status, including years of average life expectancy, of people living in less-developed countries (Organization for Economic Cooperation and Development, 2016; United Nations Development Programme, 2017). But aging trends in economically advanced countries also are expected to continue to increase at a steady pace until about ninety years on average and perhaps higher, given the socially advantaged level of living that characterizes these countries (Kochhar, 2014).

The population aging prospects discussed previously will also have a significant impact on the economic and educational sectors of societies. The most immediate impact will be on the economic sector, which will need to create innovative approaches to support increasing numbers of noneconomically active members of society, that is, children and youth, older adults, and persons with disabilities. Fiscal needs associated with the continuing education and other lifelong learning experiences for older adults and preschool experiences for young children are expected to be prominent in the budgets of virtually all societies. Funds to support these activities will need to be generated primarily from public sources, but nongovernmental and business leaders are expected to play a major role in supporting these activities as well. These activities will place economic demands on governments that did not exist when population aging was increasing at a much slower pace.

Age Pyramids

Population "pyramids" are constructed to show the distribution of a nation's total population by age group and gender. These pyramids also lend themselves to time-series analysis and provide a simple visual way of understanding complex national demographic changes that take place over time. Thus, population pyramids are prepared each year to monitor changes in population size and composition and to determine how public policies to either promote or slow the rate of population change. Sparsely populated countries such as Norway, Finland, and others with small populations, for example, have developed public policies that promote population growth, as do most of the nations of Western Europe, which are experiencing negative population growth. Densely populated nations such as China and India, however, develop policies that are intended to slow the rate of increase of population growth with the goal of eventually reducing the size of their populations. Most of these policies are expensive and difficult to implement and can have many surprising outcomes such as a preponderance of males over females in societies that prefer the birth of male children (Eager, 2004; Kasun, 1999).

Age Pyramids for a Developed and a Developing Country

Figures 3.3 and 3.4 show population pyramids from 2015 for an economically advanced (Japan) and an economically developing country (Sierra Leone). The pyramids illustrate the changing patterns of national average years of life expectancy by gender and enable strategic and goal-oriented planning in response to these trends. The purposes of the pyramid are twofold: (1) to describe the general characteristics of the populations of the two nations and (2) to point out the dramatic age and gender differences that exist between the two nations (United Nations Population Division, 2009). The resulting population pyramids for the two nations could not be more different from one another, given the high concentrations of young people in developing countries and the high concentrations of persons sixty years of age and older in economically advanced countries.

The differences that exist in each of the population pyramids have a profound impact on the nature of health care that is needed in the two countries. Economically advanced countries such as Japan, for example, must invest more of their health care dollars in providing for the complex, long-term health needs of their aging populations. These costs are extraordinarily high, especially in situations where the elderly have not set aside private resources in support of their care as they age. Health services at a high level are needed in developing countries such as Sierra Leone to care for the complex preventive care typically needed by children, youth, and older young people. The demands for sophisticated health care for all age groups for both types of nations are universally high and increase as populations age.

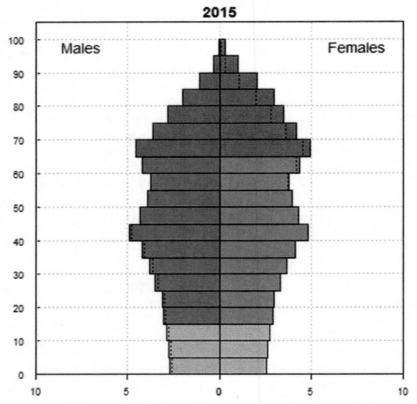

Figure 3.3. Population pyramid for Japan, 2015. *Source*: (United Nations, Department of Economic and Social Affairs, Population Division, 2015)

Aging in Japan

Japan is the world's tenth most populous country (127 million people) as of March 2017 and contains the world's highest concentration of older adults (persons sixty-five years of age and older) and has a comparatively smaller, and diminishing, population of young people under the age of eighteen years (figure 3.3). Further, Japan's age dependency ratio of working-age population (fifteen to sixty-four years) compared with the percentage of older adults, children, and youth was 43.3 percent in 2015. In effect, the percentage of economically active persons in Japan needed to support the country's expansive domestic social systems is less than half of the country's total. This pattern places enormous pressures on the country's slowly increasing

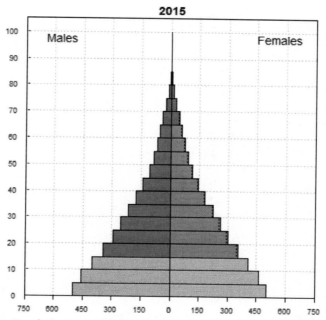

Figure 3.4. Population pyramid for Sierra Leone, 2015. *Source*: **(United Nations, Department of Economic and Social Affairs, Population Division, 2015)**

financial resources with the result that a large percentage of older adults depend primarily on private savings and family care to support themselves following retirement. Fortunately, the country's per capita income level of approximately $26,111, an amount that exceeds the average of other Organization for Economic Cooperation and Development countries, appears to be sufficient to maintain the financial well-being of Japanese children and older adults as reflected by the nation's still low, but increasing, poverty rates for these groups (World Bank, 2017).

Japan's population pyramid for 2015 (figure 3.3) reflects the disproportionate number of children and youth and older adults as a percentage of the total population. This distortion has been increasing for several decades and is expected to increase even more until at least 2025, when the percentage of working-age adults is expected to exceed that of the age-dependent groups. Clearly, Japan's extensive network of social support and respect for older adults have contributed to the country's higher-than-average years of life expectancy. These factors, in combination with the demographic trends just described, support the enhanced years of average life expectancy.

Aging in Sierra Leone

Population size and aging patterns for Sierra Leone differ significantly from those reported for Japan. The size of the population of Sierra Leone in 2015 numbered somewhat more than 6.5 million people, a large percentage of whom (60 percent) lived in poverty. The country's literacy rate is about 41 percent, and 70 percent of its working-age young people are either unemployed or underemployed on a recurrent basis (World Bank, 2017). The country also has a long and current history of political turmoil, a reality that has resulted in the premature deaths of large numbers of Sierra Leone's citizens. Comparatively few of the country's citizens have survived to old age, and the country's high investments in the military sector subvert resources for the health, education, and other social sectors that are needed to provide adequately for the social advancement of the country, individually and collectively.

Years of average life expectancy for Sierra Leone are among the lowest worldwide, whereas its rates of infant, child, and maternal mortality are among the world's highest. Significant advances have been made in these demographic trends, but these advances have proven slow and difficult to achieve, given the high level of social chaos that exists in the country. Inadequate transportation systems, shortages of critical health personnel and facilities, and persistent life-threatening communicable diseases compound health-promoting goals associated with extending average years of life expectancy. A low per capita income level of $500, in combination with the country's comparatively weak social, health, and education systems, compounds Sierra Leone's efforts to improve its health systems in a way that extends years of average life expectancy (World Bank, 2017). Slow to moderate rates of economic growth that average 3 percent also reduce the country's capacity to finance new health and life extension initiatives that are critical to improving the health status of nations.

Sierra Leone's population pyramid for 2015 is shown in figure 3.4. The numbers of children and youth under the age of eighteen are high, a phenomenon that is typical of the demographic challenges confronting most socially least developing countries. However, Sierra Leone's share of the population over the age of sixty-four is low, another characteristic that is shared with other socially least development countries (United Nations Development Programme, 2015). The net result of these trends is that the country's age dependency ratio in 2015 was 81.9 children and elderly per 100 working-age persons (fifteen to sixty-four years)—only one working-age adult for each age-dependent person. This number alone suggests the magnitude of the social and health challenges that confront Sierra Leone's government. Fortunately, Sierra Leone is on the list of countries designated to receive substantive levels of international development assistance as part of the fifteen-year SDG strategy. Sierra Leone is also a designated recipient of substantial programs of bilateral development assistance from some economically advanced countries as well as aid from private nongovernmental organizations (Kargbo, 2012). These international efforts are expected to contribute significantly to the overall health and years of life expectancy of Sierra Leone's large numbers of impoverished persons (International Fund for Agricultural Development, 2012).

GLOBAL SUCCESSES IN PROMOTING CHILD AND MATERNAL SURVIVAL

A variety of approaches can be used to illustrate the dramatic advances that have been made in health care since 1990. In this section, we focus on two of the most critical issues that have eluded the health sector in most developing and socially least developing nations, that is, improving the rates of child survival and significantly reducing the number of women who die during childbirth. Both factors are critical measures of the quality of locally available health services as well as of the ability of people to access them. Further, lower rates of infant, child, and maternal mortality have proven to be acutely elusive to health service providers; unfortunately, this fact accounts for the large numbers of infants, children, and women who die in developing countries each year. These measures of health outcomes are also used as basic indicators in virtually all indexes of social progress, quality of life, and human development, including the Human Development Index of the United Nations Development Programme (2017) and the *Index of Social Progress* (Estes, 2017), among others.

BOX 3.3   Geneva/New York/Washington

Child mortality rates have plummeted to less than half of what they were in 1990, according to a new report released today. Under-five deaths have dropped from 12.7 million per year in 1990 to 5.9 million in 2015. This is the first year the figure has gone below the six million marks.

(World Health Organization, 2015a)

Child Survival in an Age of Uncertainty

Reducing the number of infant and child deaths has been a major challenge confronting all the world's nations (box 3.3). Indeed, so important are
changes in these areas that rates of infant and child mortality often are used as
proxy measures for indicating accessibility to health care as well as gauging
the overall quality of those systems. These indicators appear on nearly every
major index of development and figure prominently in the strategic health
initiatives of nearly all nations.

Infant and child deaths are also directly associated with maternal mortality, given the enormous demands that are made on the bodies of mothers,
for example, excessive bleeding, infection, and the absence of prenatal care,
especially mothers living under difficult economic circumstances. Severe
shortages of skilled health care personnel also contribute to the high rates
of infant, child, and maternal deaths. Consequently, pregnancy and delivery
still constitute major threats to the lives of young women. Poverty, living in
squalor, and the absence of an adequate support network all compound the
problem of women who live in impoverished rural communities.

Recent estimates reported in *Levels and Trends in Child Mortality: Report
2015* (United Nations Inter-agency Group for Child Mortality Estimation,
2015) indicate that substantial gains have been made in infant and child
survival since the launch of the MDG campaign in 2002. Still, the threats
to child survival remain serious and require significantly increased international development assistance and other efforts to reduce them. For example,
approximately 16,000 children under the age of five still die every day. The
53 percent drop in under-five deaths occurs within the first month of life,
most on the day of or within a few days after birth. Further, the worldwide
gains that have been made in reducing the incidence of child deaths were not
enough to fully achieve the MDG of reducing early child deaths by two-thirds
between 1990 and 2015 (World Health Organization, 2015b). As individual
nations and as a world community, we have a long way to go in achieving
our child survival targets. Fortunately, new programmatic strategies and progressively higher levels of investment in child health remain central to the
recently launched SDS.

Forty-five percent of all child deaths occur within the first twenty-eight
days of life. One million babies die each year on the first day of life, and two
million die within the first week of life (World Health Organization, 2016a).
The causes of these deaths are primarily prematurity, pneumonia, complications that occur during delivery, diarrhea, sepsis, and malaria. The unavailability of clean water also is a major threat to infant survival.

Infant and child death rates are highest among the developing nations of
sub-Saharan Africa and Southern Asia; five of ten child deaths occur in the

nations of sub-Saharan Africa and three in ten occur among the low-income nations of Southern Asia (World Health Organization, 2016a). Child survival also is a major problem for financially poor mothers and their children living in many economically advanced countries. The challenges are especially severe among population groups living in rural and remote communities. Estimates of the rate of rural child deaths range from two to three times that of children born to families who reside in urban settings, even for families who live in poorer sections of these urban settings (World Health Organization, 2015d).

Dr. Flavia Bustreo, assistant director general at the WHO, in *The Global Strategy for Women's, Children's and Adolescents' Health* (World Health Organization, 2016a), noted that most of the means needed to halt the epidemic of infant and child deaths in low-income developing countries already are within reach—early skin-to-skin contact, exclusive breastfeeding, and extra care provided by skilled health personnel. These actions are believed to offer children the best chance for a healthy start in life. Yet many countries continue to struggle with meeting even these most basic goals.

Infant Deaths by Major World Regions

Infant mortality rates reached a high of 150 births for every 1,000 live born children in 1990. Most of these infants died immediately following birth or during the first day of life, but more than 90 percent perished within the first week of life. Tragically, infant mortality rates at these levels characterized virtually all the world's regions and are directly related to the poor conditions under which these children were born. The absence of clean drinking water and inadequate food contributed to these high rates of infant deaths (figure 3.5). Complications during delivery and inadequately trained midwives added to the high incidence of infant deaths virtually everywhere. Sadly, the infant deaths were rarely reported to official governmental agencies, given the arduous travel that frequently must be undertaken to reach regional government statistical agencies. Thus, until recent years, official infant and child deaths were significantly underreported, and therefore, the data shown in figures 3.5 and 3.6 must be considered the best estimates of the actual infant and child deaths that took place.

Few people can imagine the sense of anguish experienced by the families of infants who die during childbirth or, in the case of young children, before these boys and girls reach five years of age. The grief experienced by these families is profound and almost always forms a major part of the life narrative reported by mothers to friends and others who express interest in learning about their personal histories (Weiss, 2017). The progress in reducing the incidence of infant and child deaths reported in figures 3.5 and 3.6

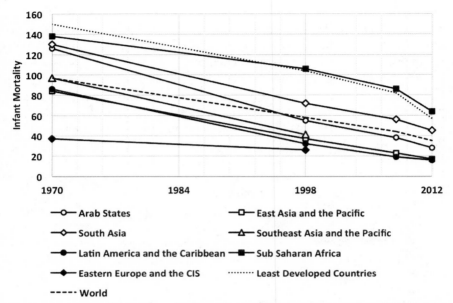

Figure 3.5.   Rates of infant mortality by major world region. *Source*: (Figure 20.8. Infant mortality, from *The Pursuit of Human Well-Being: The Untold Global History*, 2017, p. 703, Estes, R. J., & Sirgy, M. J. [Eds.], ©Springer International Publishing Switzerland 2017, with permission of Springer

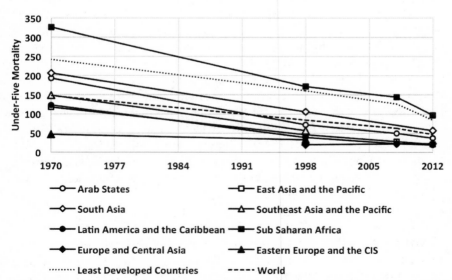

Figure 3.6.   Child mortality rates by major world region. *Source*: (Figure 20.9. Child mortality, from *The Pursuit of Human Well-Being: The Untold Global History*, 2017, p. 703, Estes, R. J., & Sirgy, M. J. [Eds.], ©Springer International Publishing Switzerland 2017, with permission of Springer

significantly reduces the tragedies experienced by these families. The sharp declines in such deaths from 1970 to 2013 that have resulted from major governmental, intergovernmental, and nongovernmental development initiatives implemented over this period (World Health Organization, 2015b) are impressive.

Significant Improvements in Infant and Child Survival Rates

Despite the often dramatic challenges to the increasing infant and child survival rates shown in figures 3.5 and 3.6, the WHO report *Global Strategy for Women's, Children's and Adolescent's Health* (World Health Organization, 2016a) describes the substantial advances that have been made in improving infant and child health since the launch of the MDG campaign in 2002. Among the most impressive advances were (a) roughly one-third of the world's countries (sixty-two) have met the MDG campaign target to reduce under-five mortality rates by two-thirds, whereas another seventy-four countries reduced child death rates by at least half; (b) the world has experienced considerable progress in reducing infant and under-five child mortality rates since 1990; and (c) ten of the twelve lowest-income countries in Africa have reduced their infant and under-five child mortality rates by at least two-thirds. These findings are especially noteworthy given the comparatively low rate of progress that was achieved in the health sector in low-income countries, including African countries, prior to 2015 (figures 3.5 and 3.6).

"Many countries," according to Dr. Tim Evans, senior director, Health, Nutrition and Population at the World Bank Group, "have made extraordinary progress in cutting their child mortality rates. However, we still have much to do before 2030 to ensure that all women and children have access to the care they need" (World Health Organization, 2015a). The recently launched *Global Financing Facility in Support of Every Woman Every Child,* with its focus on smarter and sustainable financing, will deliver essential health services to an increasingly larger number of low- and middle-income countries (World Health Organization, 2015c). This strategy is expected to bring about major changes in accelerating the pace of improvements in all areas of child health.

Maternal Survival: An Enduring Challenge

Women of reproductive age (fifteen to forty-five years) in both rich and poor countries have always been especially vulnerable to illness, disability, and death associated with pregnancy and childbirth. The threats to life are especially high in low-income countries where large segments of the population reside in rural communities that have few or inadequate health resources.

Experienced midwives are major assets in these communities, and substantial evidence confirms their effectiveness in providing quality prenatal and delivery services (United Nations Population Fund, 2015). Skilled midwives also reduce the high rate of infant deaths and contribute to improving the odds for survival of infants older than one week.

However, midwives, whatever their level of skill, can rarely provide the level of care needed by pregnant women who experience complex pregnancies. Problems such as anemia, malnutrition, malaria, cholera, and HIV/AIDS compound the birthing experience, as does the absence of anesthesia and antibiotics. Maternal deaths from excessive bleeding/hemorrhage, sepsis, and other infections occur all too frequently, even when local midwives are available. On their deaths, mothers often leave behind other children who become the responsibility of grandparents or other family members. The well-known Yoruba proverb that "it takes a village to raise a child" is especially applicable in situations where mothers die from complications of childbirth (Reference, 2017). Nevertheless, optimism exists for believing that solutions for each of these barriers to healthy, safe pregnancies for women in developing countries remain within our reach (box 3.4).

BOX 3.4   Maternal Mortality: Key Facts

- Every day, approximately 830 women die from preventable causes related to pregnancy and childbirth.
- 99 percent of all maternal deaths occur in developing countries.
- Maternal mortality is higher in women living in rural areas and among poorer communities.
- Young adolescents face a higher risk of complications and death because of pregnancy than other women.
- Skilled care before, during and after childbirth can save the lives of women and newborn babies.
- Between 1990 and 2015, maternal mortality worldwide dropped by about 44 percent.
- Between 2016 and 2030, as part of the Sustainable Development Goals, the target is to reduce the global maternal mortality ratio to less than 70 per 100,000 live births.

(World Health Organization, 2016c)

The significant gains that have been achieved in reducing rates of maternal mortality for each major world region over the twenty-four-year period of 1989 to 2013 are reported in figure 3.7. These gains resulted from robust, aggressive international development assistance programs provided by national ministries of health, the United Nations Development Programme, the World Bank, and hundreds of private, voluntary, nongovernmental organizations that have allocated large portions of their resources to helping nations save the lives of mothers and their children. The increasing availability of emergency services, including air evacuations from remote rural communities, also has contributed to the increase in maternal survival rates.

The most significant achievements in reducing maternal mortality rates occurred in the nations of sub-Saharan Africa, South Asia, and Southeast Asia. These gains parallel other broad-based developmental achievements made by the nations of these regions, including access to basic education, transportation, and communication networks; more secure supplies of safe drinking water; and effective systems of solid waste disposal. Figure 3.8 is a vivid portrayal of the death of a single woman during the birthing process. The image appears on a cemetery stone in Dresden, Germany, and depicts a child being taken away as the mother dies. In many other stories, the

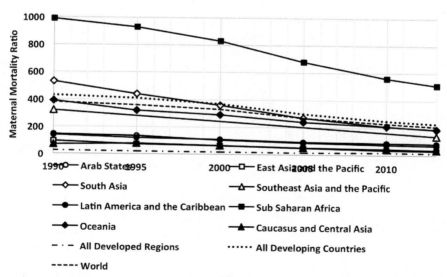

Figure 3.7. Changes in maternal mortality, 1989–2013. *Source*: (Figure 20.10. Changes in maternal mortality [1989–2013], from *The Pursuit of Human Well-Being: The Untold Global History*, 2017, p. 702, Estes, R. J., & Sirgy, M. J. [Eds.], ©Springer International Publishing Switzerland 2017, with permission of Springer)

Figure 3.8.   A mother dies and is taken by angels as her new-born child is taken away. A grave from 1863 in Striesener Friedhof in Dresden. *Source:* **(Photo by Stephen C. Dickson; Creative Commons Attribution-Share Alike 4.0 International license)**

European image reminds us that women everywhere are exposed to the same risks of life and death associated with childbirth. In this case, only one life was saved in the process of childbirth, that of the child.

Early intervention in the form of regular prenatal checkups, the provision of specially prepared prenatal food supplements, and access to skilled personnel prior to and during delivery are responsible for the dramatic drop in rates of maternal deaths that we have reported in this chapter. Still, we have a long way to go in making pregnancy and childbirth a safer experience for both mothers and children. More advanced outreach approaches are needed in remote rural regions of all countries where quality prenatal health care services are difficult to obtain.

Further, more comprehensive approaches to education in public health, improvements in sanitation, enforcement of occupational health laws, and women working together informally on pregnancy and early childhood rearing practices also strengthen the advances of the health care systems in all countries, but especially in those countries where the risk of maternal death is highest. Early detection and rapid intervention in complex pregnancies also would make a major contribution to promoting maternal and child survival rates. These patterns are especially favorable, given that all three subregions at highest risk of maternal deaths are among the world's poorest and the most deprived of quality health care.

The world regions that experienced the lowest levels of net gains in reducing maternal mortality rates were Latin America and the Caribbean, East Asia and the Pacific, and the Arab states of the Middle East and West Asia. Continuing high levels of poverty for some of the countries in these regions, in combination with the absence of skilled health personnel to assist with the birthing process, were the major impediments to reducing the rates of maternal mortality. Inadequate diets, few or no neonatal immunizations, and few or no skilled health care personnel exacerbate the health risks that pregnant women living in impoverished countries experience. Other countries of these regions, though, already had comparatively low levels of maternal deaths, which they achieved and sustained over the long term.

Globally, maternal mortality rates are dropping, especially in countries where maternal death rates were high during the period since the end of World War II. Further gains still need to be made, even within the poorest of nations, in providing safer health environments and more skilled health personnel to assist pregnant women with their deliveries. Clearly, maternal mortality rates are closely associated with changes taking place in the broader sociopolitical environment, and the problem cannot be solved without significant advances across a broad range of social, political, and economic sectors.

Maternal mortality rates remain unacceptably high in the socially least developed countries of Africa, Asia, and Latin America (World Health Organization, 2017a). More than 800 women die each day, or about 303,000 annually, from complications associated with delivery. Most of the maternal deaths that occur in developing countries could have been prevented using available technologies, procedures, and medications. From a positive perspective, rates of maternal mortality in sub-Saharan Africa have improved considerably since 1990. In other regions, including Asia and North Africa, even greater progress has been made because of political independence and at least moderate rates of economic expansion (World Health Organization, 2015a). The global maternal mortality ratio (the number of maternal deaths per 100,000 live births) declined by 2.3 percent per year between 1990 and 2015, but the rate of maternal deaths declined even more rapidly from 2000 to the present. In some countries, because of significant international interventions, the rate declined annually by 5.5 percent between 2000 and 2010 (World Health Organization, 2015b).

The global community should feel an enormous sense of pride in the gains in saving lives that have been realized among all nations since the implementation of the Millennium Campaign (2005–2015) and the SDS (2016–2030). Accomplishing the lifesaving targets specified in each of the bold strategies would not have been possible without the contributions of individual citizens or the robust programs of technical assistance provided by individual governments to one another and by intergovernmental bodies to countries with the greatest needs. Because of this aid, every reason exists for believing that the lifesaving goals associated with the Millennium Campaign and the SDS will be fully realized.

PROVIDING EMERGENCY HEALTH SERVICES TO REMOTE RURAL COMMUNITIES

One component of health care that is frequently absent from discussions of advances in the sector is emergency medicine (Razzak & Kellermann, 2002). These types of services are routinely available to residents of urban centers, including services to pregnant women, through local or regional emergency rooms. In contrast, large numbers of the rural poor have died, given the unavailability of emergency care in their difficult-to-reach communities (World Health Organization, 2013a).

Because of the MDG and the SDG campaigns, emergency medical services have become far more accessible than during earlier decades (Hodkinson & Wallis, 2010). Cell phones and dedicated air evacuation services are being used to bring skilled emergency medicine to even the most remote communities (Lee, 2013). Persons injured in sporting accidents in remote areas are included in the WHO's newly initiated *Emergency Response Framework*. Outreach to these people is included in the MDG and SDG priority lists of persons in need of emergency care. As a result, tens of thousands of people who otherwise would have perished are being saved each year. Miners, construction workers, commercial fisherman, and others who work under high-risk conditions are included in these numbers (World Health Organization, 2013b).

DRIVERS OF HEALTH CARE

The major "drivers" of health care are reflected in figure 3.9 (National Aboriginal Community Controlled Health Organisation, 2013). This figure reflects the major entities that promote improved health care in all societies of the world. The figure also identifies the major contributors to health and health care by health care providers, patients, and their families. The number of these drivers, as depicted in figures 3.1 and 3.9, is large, and each in turn has multiple layers of constituents and special interest groups associated with it. Each of these drivers contributes to advancing health policy with organizations at the local, regional, national, and even international levels. Some of the drivers are *environmental* (quality of physical environment, employment conditions), some are *social* (culture, gender, ethnicity), and others involve the actual *providers and recipients* of health services. All are important to

Figure 3.9. Contributors to health policy and service provision. *Source*: (Figure from the National Aboriginal Community Controlled Health Organisation, 2013, March 25. Reprinted with permission)

policy formation in health, given that the sector consumes as much as one-seventh to one-sixth of the GDP of most nations (World Health Organization, 2017b). In reviewing figure 3.9, readers are encouraged to draw a series of connecting lines between each of the drivers because their relationship with one another is not strictly unidimensional. In doing so, what results is a "spider web" that reflects the complex relationships that exist between the various drivers of health policy and health promotion. The idea, of course, is to portray the dynamic interactions that exist between and among the many drivers that shape health care at all levels of policy formulation. These interactions are numerous, complex, and highly impactful on the health sectors of all societies.

FINANCING HEALTH

Among the major drivers of health policy are the public and private investments made by governments, nongovernmental organizations, business leaders, and consumers. Data pertaining to health investments for major world regions are reported in figure 3.10, which illustrates worldwide variations by major geopolitical regions in financing health services. In reviewing these data, however, readers should be alert to the reality that money alone does not guarantee a higher level of health or even health care (Benton, 2014). The United States, for example, spent approximately 17.9 percent of its GDP in the health sector in 2011 (Fuchs, 2013), but the country's overall rate of years of average life expectancy for the same period lagged 6.2 percent behind that of Japan (83.4 years versus 78.8 years), which spent only 10.3 percent of its GDP on health in 2011. The reason for the lag is a combination of the complex administrative arrangements that exist in the American health sector and the country's persistently high levels of poverty, which deny the poor a high level of continuity of care following emergency room visits. The problem is further compounded by the fact that one in five children in the United States (21 percent) lives in poverty and does not have access to health care on a sustained basis (National Center for Children in Poverty, 2017). Many of the nation's poor children suffer from inadequate nutrition, substandard housing, inadequate schools, and a lack of access to quality health services on a sustained basis (Carroll, 2013; Swartz, 2009). Most economically advanced countries have found childhood poverty to be too expensive a problem to afford (Organization for Economic Cooperation and Development, 2015)

Money and organizational efficiencies are essential to effective health policies everywhere in the world. Figure 3.10, for example, shows that all countries spent approximately 10.1 percent of their total national resources on health and health care services in 2011, including health services to the poor. This percentage has increased significantly from the 4.7 percent of GDP

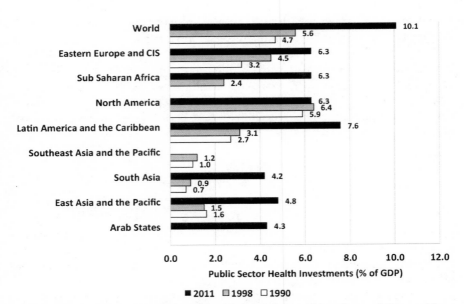

Figure 3.10.   Global investments in health by major world region and the world as a whole. *Source*: (Figure 20.6. Percentages of public sector investments in health: 1990, 1998, 2011, from *The Pursuit of Human Well-Being: The Untold Global History*, 2017, p. 701, Estes, R. J., & Sirgy, M.J. [Eds.], ©Springer International Publishing Switzerland 2017, with permission of Springer)

allocated to the sector in 1990 and from that of 5.6 percent of GDP reported by nations for health expenditures in 1998. Thus, steady and somewhat higher levels of GDP are allocated to health and health services for each period studied and are likely to continue to increase as the world's population continues to age.

Considerable variations exist among the world's major geopolitical regions as to their levels of public and private investments in the health sector (figure 3.10). The region with the highest level of investment in health in 2011 was Latin America and the Caribbean (7.6 percent) followed by Eastern Europe and the Commonwealth of Independent States, sub-Saharan Africa, and North America, each of which invested an average of approximately 6.3 percent of their GDP in health and health care. The United States is an outlier among the region's countries in that it spends somewhat more than 17 percent of its GDP on health care each year. These moderate to high levels of investment in health made by the governments of nations located in selected regions are reflected in the important advances that have been made in all sectors of human progress, especially those related to education and economics. Further, regional performances in health care for 2011 are impressive and are suggestive of additional gains that can be expected in the health and health-related sectors in the future (Organization for Economic Cooperation and Development, 2016).

The geopolitical regions with the lowest levels of investment of national and regional resources in health care also are among the lowest- to middle-performing countries and regions on the United Nations Human Development Index (United Nations Development Programme, 2017), for example, East Asia and the Pacific (4.8 percent) and the Arab states of the Middle Eastern and North African regions (4.3 percent). These comparatively low levels of investments in health care limit development in other sectors of development as well, but especially in the economic and education sectors (discussed more fully in chapters 4 and 5). The most recent data available concerning average annual GDP expenditures for health among the countries of Southeast Asia and the Pacific region (1.2 percent in 1998) suggest a slow rate of development for these nations as well.

The percentages of regional GDP expenditures for health, health promotion, and health services for 1990 and 1998 are significantly lower than those reported for any group of nations in 2011 and beyond. As a result, expenditures for the health sector for all regions are expected to increase exponentially in response to population aging and to the much larger numbers of persons reached through public and private health outreach services. Growth in this sector also reflects increasing rates of inflation and the rapid rates of economic development that are characteristic of the largest percentage of the world's developing countries. Improved access and more sustained continuity of health care services also add to the fiscal increases that are occurring in all the world's nations, including those of the developing countries (World Bank, 2017).

The multilayered, long-term investments that are currently being made in health care significantly advance the health of the world's population and, at the same time, contribute to decreases in rates of premature deaths and add to years of average life expectancy for those children who survive beyond their fifth birthday. Effective outreach services, responsive emergency care, and, most importantly, high-quality primary care are major contributors to health advancement everywhere in the world (Moon & Oluwatosin, 2013).

TECHNOLOGY AND PATIENT-HEALTH CARE PROVIDER COMMUNICATIONS

Technological innovations in the health sector continue to increase in type and impact on improving the quality of life of patients and their families. Indeed, we could have devoted the entire chapter to a discussion of the trans-formational technological advances that have been introduced to improve the quality of patient health care and health well-being just since 1995. Table 3.1 identifies just a few of the most important technological advances that have been made in the early diagnosis of diseases and for use in promoting more timely and complete communications between patients and their health care providers.

Common to these innovations have been significant advances in the devel-opment of complex, highly specialized computer chips and microprocessors in combination with highly sophisticated information and data processing systems. These technologies are now part of the increasing array of min-iaturized electronic devices that are being implanted in growing numbers of patients at risk of potentially serious or even fatal medical events. These devices, for example, are being used to continuously monitor, diagnose, and even initiate lifesaving actions in response to serious life-threatening events, for example, cardiac pacemakers that send a continuous stream of electronic data to correct dangerous cardiac arrhythmias as well as insulin pumps that rapidly adjust the serum glucose levels of patients with diabetes. They also are part of the "smart" technologies that are used in the creation of a new generation of devices, "jewelry" embedded with microchips (e.g., iWatches), and microcomputer-driven prostheses that enable tens of thousands of dis-abled people to walk (using sophisticated bionic limbs), talk (using computer-driven tablets), see (using bionic eyes), and hear (using cochlear implants). These sometimes barely visible microprocessors, many of which fit on a small area of a fingertip, are restoring high qualities of health well-being to

Table 3.1 A partial listing of technological innovations designed to improve patient-provider communication and to improve the quality of health services since 1995

Major Technological Innovation	Description
Electronic Health Record	An electronic health record refers to the systematized collection of patient and population health information that is electronically stored in digital format. An electronic health record system is "designed to store data accurately and to capture the state of a patient across time. It eliminates the need to track down a patient's previous paper medical records and assists in ensuring data is accurate and legible. It can reduce risk of data replication as there is only one modifiable file, which means the file is more likely up to date, and decreases risk of lost paperwork" (Electronic Health Record, 2017). These electronic health records have a wide range of uses in contemporary health practice that, among many others, include (1) for the first time, providing patients and other health care providers full access on a timely basis to the patient's complete medical records; 2) facilitating the collection and storage of vast quantities of health data across a wide range of analytical platforms; (3) recording and rapidly sharing with other health providers patient-specific results of laboratory diagnostic tests, including radiograms and magnetic resonance imaging studies; and (4) compiling, accessing, and analyzing patterns of health and ill-health for people grouped by different levels of social organization.
Implanted Biosensors	Biosensors are computer chips-driven devices that are surgically implanted in patients to both monitor and intervene in potentially life-threatening situations, for example, cardiac pacemakers, defibrillators, loops, insulin pumps.
Smartphones and Tablets for Recording and Reporting Diagnostic Data	Smartphones and tablets have revolutionized the face of medicine. They serve as the mechanism for (1) accessing patient electronic medical records; (2) rapidly sharing diagnostic information with other service providers; (3) rapidly placing service providers in direct contact with one another, often on a face-to-face basis; and (4) contributing to the success of telemedicine and remote medicine, whereby multidisciplinary relationships are created between urban-based practitioners and surgeons and health care professionals in remote rural areas.
Patient Portals	Most hospitals and major medical centers now provide electronic portals through which patients and their families can (1) access medical records; (2) set up appointments; (3) renew prescriptions; and (4) leave messages for service providers, office staff, and others regarding emerging needs.
Medically Sensitive Personal Jewelry	Many consumers wear personal jewelry (neck and wristbands) equipped with sensors that track their heart rates, level of exercise, dietary intake, and the like. These devices alert patients to problematic elements in their health profiles for which corrective action may be needed. They serve as aids to promote healthy behaviors and as diagnostic instruments to identify an emerging health crisis.

(Continued)

Table 3.1 (Continued)

Major Technological Innovation	Description
Miniaturization of Diagnostic Tools for Use in Conducting Internal Diagnostic Examinations	Many specialized disciplines have developed miniaturized camera-based electronic devices that can be ingested by patients to diagnose and, in some cases, prevent serious illnesses including esophageal, stomach, intestinal, colonic, and rectal ulcers, polyps, and cancers. These devices have been shown to be highly effective in providing noninvasive diagnoses as well as to avoid the use of more expensive procedures such as computed tomography, magnetic resonance imaging, and similar technologies. If proper sterilization procedures are followed, these devices can be reused for large numbers of patients.
Augmenting Human Capabilities	The early years of the twenty-first century have witnessed the emergence of many computer-driven aids to enhance or replace human capabilities. These include robotic limbs that function using only the power of the mind and other supersensitive robotic body parts developed to assist patients with quadriplegia and other severe mobility limitations regain limb function using the smallest possible movements of the eyes, jaw, and the like. Though expensive to design and produce, these new aids are being used with great success by profoundly disabled war veterans, persons severely injured in automobile, occupational, and other types of accidents, as well as persons with responsive congenital defects. These technologies are still at an early stage of development, but they are expected to reach tens of thousands or more people in the decades just ahead.
Nanotechnology in Medicine	*Nanomedicine* is a newly emerging specialized field of medical practice that combines medicine, bioengineering, and computer technology. The goal of nanomedicine is to develop and implant highly specialized biosensors and minute portions of medications into the bodies of patients diagnosed with specific diseases or illnesses. Delivery of medication in this way usually reduces the severity of the side effects as well as the toxicity experienced by patients in taking particular classes of medications (Mayo Clinic, 2017b). The products of nanotechnology are extremely small and, in many cases, cannot be seen without the use of a magnifying glass or even a microscope. In time, nanomedicine practitioners hope to use these technologies to replace, or at least share, the functions being performed by the diseased organs. In most cases, "nanomachines" are eventually eliminated from a patient's body in much the same way that other tiny particles of waste are removed.
Gene-based Targeted Treatment of Cancers and Other Potentially Fatal Diseases	The ability to use a patient's own genomic makeup to determine and administer the best possible forms of treatment is one of the major breakthroughs in health care over the past decade. Genomic-based testing and treatment assist in distinguishing between patients who can be expected to benefit substantially from different forms of chemotherapy and radiation and those who likely will not.

Major Technological Innovation	Description
	Genomic-based testing and treatments have improved the health outcomes of whole classes of patients and have contributed to significant reductions in health care costs by using only those approaches to care that are expected to result in the most favorable outcomes. These approaches also prevent patients from having to undergo unnecessary and, often, debilitating treatments.

tens of thousands of patients annually and, in time, to hundreds of thousands. These breakthrough innovations are the result of close collaborations between health care specialists, bioengineers, private sector corporate businesses, private investors, and governments in the form of research support and the legal protections provided by patent laws. They also are the result of the unique wealth of clinical knowledge generated by family and emergency medicine practitioners and, in many cases, that of postmortem pathologists. These experiences have been brought together under the rubric of "translational medicine" with physicians, public health specialists, and others working in concert with private investors and large businesses and corporate enterprises to rapidly bring the steady stream of new innovations into clinical health care practice.

Electronic Health Records

Among the major technological innovations that have taken place since 1995 has been the creation of the electronic health record. Largely funded in the early years of its development by support received from the US central government, these powerful health information systems can store and track incredible volumes of patient notes, diagnostic laboratory results, and the actual images produced by radiography, computed tomography, and magnetic resonance imaging. All the information contained in these health records is of a time-series nature, which permits health service providers to quickly graph changes in a patient's well-being over time (Gartee, 2016).

The stored electronic data can easily be transferred to other health service providers in need of this information and are readily accessible by patients and their family caregivers using a variety of patient "portals." Access to their own health information further empowers patients, together with their families and health care providers, to make more informed data-driven health care decisions. More specifically, access to these records is easily obtained using either stand-alone laptop or electronically networked computers or the increasing array of "smart" handheld electronic devices such as iPads, iPhones, and similar types of equipment. Gone are the days in economically advanced countries of paper recordings of patient clinical histories and treatment interventions. In most cases, complex patient health records can also be downloaded to USB "memory sticks" that patients can take with them to service providers other than those who initially generated the records.

Bioengineering Breakthroughs

Also impressive is the increasing number of bioengineered technological implants (bionics) that are being used to continuously monitor changes in the quality of health of patients and initiate action during crisis situations (Bionics, 2017). In addition to the insulin pumps and pacemakers already discussed, other classes of surgically implanted devices include spinal cord stimulators to reduce chronic pain, robotics in all fields of rehabilitation medicine, and, more recently, the introduction of the first-generation of bionic eyes that are aiding in bringing sight to the blind and others with low vision (Walsh, 2015). The major beneficiaries of these innovations have been disabled persons, stroke patients, severely injured military veterans, as well as police and fireman injured while on duty.

Table 3.1 identifies other major advances in health-focused technological and bioengineering areas, namely, the miniaturization of diagnostic cameras that can be ingested by patients to identify early occurrences of gastroesophageal, bowel, and colon cancers. All of these biomedical engineering advances center around the use of new generations of smaller, more powerful computers that bring patients and health service providers into more rapid contact with one another. Scheduling medical appointments using computers has become routine, as have requests for medication refills. Requests for referrals are easily made using these technologies and often provide patients with biographical sketches of service providers from whom they may seek care. Careful tracking of these interactions is now possible through the extensive archival data systems of most health-oriented information systems.

Yet, we have not seen the end of the second decade of this still young century. New technological innovations are being introduced each year, and, with them, patients and their families are becoming more independent and self-sufficient and are regaining significant functions that have been compromised by disease, illness, old age, accidents, and injuries. Today, the possibilities for such innovations appear to be without limits as each generation of health advances builds on the technological achievements of earlier ones.

CONCLUSIONS

The most dramatic advances in child and maternal survival are taking place in the world's poorest nations. These important gains have been most significant in sub-Saharan Africa (including many nations in the Arab world), South Asia (Bangladesh, India, and Pakistan) and Southeast Asia (Indonesia, Malaysia, the Philippines), Latin America, and the Caribbean (Argentina, Brazil, Costa Rica, the Dominican Republic, Uruguay) and, to a lesser extent, in the economically advanced countries of North America (Canada and the United States) and Europe, where more cost-efficient approaches to health financing are being developed.

Routine health care is rapidly becoming more accessible to people living everywhere in the world, including those living in remote rural communities, for example, the polar ice caps, the desert, jungle areas, and people who consciously have withdrawn from the mainstream of the societies of which they are a part. The advanced levels of heath care are being provided by better trained personnel, including more skilled midwives. The availability of better, more culturally aware and sensitive health personnel has almost totally reversed the negative trajectory that has characterized the history of human health for centuries.

The introduction of effective vaccines and antibiotics to previously underserved populations has profoundly improved the quality of health well-being for untold numbers of people who previously would have perished. Fewer children are dying from infectious diseases than was the case during earlier decades. Rates of exposure to the ravages of pertussis, diphtheria, and tetanus have dropped precipitously in response to the willingness of parents to vaccinate their children against these life-threatening diseases.

The introduction of the Salk and Sabin vaccines in the early 1960s significantly reduced the numbers of new cases of poliomyelitis in developing countries. Consequently, hundreds of thousands of children and adults were spared the crippling effects of and the painful orthopedic operations associated with polio (Right Diagnosis, 2017).

Rates of tuberculosis in both children and adults have plummeted since 1990 in response to new, more effective vaccines (Vynnycky & Fine, 1999). Now, however, more effective vaccines are needed against multidrug-resistant tuberculosis (Mayo Clinic, 2017a).

Smallpox, once a threat to human life everywhere, has been fully eliminated (Baxby, 1999). However, small samples of this deadly disease are being preserved in highly secured laboratories in selected countries in the unlikely event that outbreaks of the disease should recur (Smallpox virus retention controversy, 2017).

The most common forms of sexually transmitted diseases (e.g., syphilis, gonorrhea, and hepatitis C) can now be treated with a single or a few doses of widely available antibiotics. Even HIV/AIDS is being held in check through the administration of a "cocktail" of antiviral medications that enables those afflicted with the disease to carry on as students, parents, workers, and caregivers in activities that contribute to economic growth and improve the competitiveness of their domestic economies.

We identified the unique challenges that confront societies today in response to the changing demographic profiles of their populations. Most developing countries are experiencing dramatic increases in the size of their population aged fifteen years *and younger*—sometimes comprising as much as 30 percent to 40 percent of their total population. Comparable levels of population growth are not occurring in the economically active portions of their populations (fifteen to sixty-four years), and fewer still are experiencing higher than average growth rates of their population aged sixty-five years and older. The population pyramid for Sierra Leone (figure 3.4) illustrates the asymmetric rates of population increase that characterize many developing nations (United Nations Population Division, 2015).

Virtually the opposite situation characterizes patterns of population growth of economically advanced countries: The most rapidly expanding age group of their populations is persons aged sixty-five years and older (United Nations Population Division, 2015). Birth rates are remarkably low in most of the European economically advanced countries, which has been true for all decades since at least 1990. The age pyramid for Japan (figure 3.3) illustrates this trend, although Japan is ahead of the curve with respect to demographic changes occurring in the number of older people as a percentage of their total population. This chapter identified many of the most important health challenges that confront both types of societies in responding to their changing demographic profiles, especially with respect to the economic resources needed to support large numbers of elderly people and exceptionally large numbers of young children and youth. The role of private savings, including their absence, in financing the needs of Japan's aged and Sierra Leone's young populations figures prominently in the respective nation's overall resource mix.

Throughout the chapter, we discussed the significant gains made in helping to advance the years of average life expectancy for adult men and women. Often, these increases have been dramatic and have laid the foundation for projected further increases of 20 percent or more years on average by 2050 and as much as 30 percent more years on average by the year 2100 (Kontis, Bennett, Mathers, Li, Foreman, & Ezzat, 2017). These projected major increases in years of average life expectancy are directly related to expected improvements, frequently dramatic, in health research, especially in DNA sequencing, that may help control the major diseases that afflict mankind today, for example, cancer, heart disease, and respiratory illnesses. Lifestyle illnesses, however, are expected to continue to deny many people more years of life expectancy, given the profoundly negative impact that morbid obesity, type 2 diabetes, tobacco smoking, and high fat in combination with low nutrition diets have on the body. DNA sequencing and similar types of scientific innovations are expected to be the most important contributors to the exceptionally long lives that are projected for the years 2050 and 2100.

Of considerable importance in helping to resolve these endemic and life-style challenges to health status has been the comparatively recent emergence of locally available community health centers (Lefkowitz, 2007). These important components of national and worldwide health systems are found in virtually all nations and regions of the world. Increasingly, they are being staffed by skilled health personnel who have been trained to deal with a wide range of lifestyle and emergency diseases and injuries for which hospitals or other complex health facilities were previously needed. These community health centers can be found in urban and rural communities and, increasingly, have a wide array of basic outreach and treatment services for persons living in remote communities. Many of these centers have personnel with advanced treatment skills who can provide at least first-tier emergency medical services, that is, preparing patients for transport to regional centers that offer higher levels of treatment. The staff also are trained to provide a high level of care for persons who are injured in the workplace or who have other types of accidents. The provision of high-quality pre- and postnatal care to women has become a routine responsibility of these centers. Today, these recently established outreach health services are saving the lives of tens of thousands of previously unserved people each year.

We also have identified some of the major technological advances that have taken place in the health sector since 2000. The innovations we selected for special attention have built on the technologies first developed by the microprocessor industry and in later years on the much-simplified electronic handheld devices first used by engineers but which, today, are essential tools in daily use by a wide range of consumers. Applied engineering, consumer preferences, advanced health education, and skill in being able to use these devices form the four pillars on which the success of these technological innovations is based. Today, a wide array of mass-produced smart electronic devices, for example, iPads, iPhones, and Android-based phones, are used to add information to patients' health records and, in turn, to permit patients, at least those in developed economies, to access that medical information for their own education and action. Comparatively few patients in Western societies would want to be denied access to the medical "portals" that are now a regular part of patient-health care documentation, even if the use of these portals remains limited. These critical technological innovations allow patients and health care providers to work from the same body of diagnostic evidence to plan the most effective approaches to a patient's individual problem.

The major innovations in health, health care, and the health services discussed previously focus on advancing the overall health status of people worldwide. The successful implementation of these efforts adds significantly to contemporary global campaigns that seek to bring an end to the worst vestiges of ill health, including physical and mental disabilities. These efforts, not coincidentally, are linked to efforts designed to bring about major advances in the education and economic sector as well. The approach identified, for example, recognizes the reality that progress in all three of the sectors of human well-being discussed throughout the book—health, education, and economics—is critical to overall advances in human well-being, level of living, and quality of life. Indeed, advances in the health sector contribute significantly to the establishment of a healthy, well-educated, skilled work force that is better prepared to meet the job-related needs of employers. The significant gains made in the health sector have made it possible to train better-educated workers who are prepared to function more effectively in the competitive global market place.

Comparatively few of the strategic advances in the health sector would have been possible without the successful implementation of the World Health Organization's *Health for All* campaign launched in the 1970s, the dramatic health successes realized as part of the United Nations' MDG campaign (2005–2015), or through the just launched fifteen-year SDG initiative that, intrinsic to its seventeen goals, places accelerated improvement in worldwide health and in the sectors that bear directly on health status (e.g., clean water, environmental protection, and safe working conditions) among the most important outcomes to be achieved between now and 2030. The success of these major global initiatives, in turn, would not have been achieved without the receipt of substantial levels of bilateral and multilateral aid flows from economically advanced countries via major intergovernmental bodies, that is, the European Union, the Organization for Economic Cooperation and Development, and the United Nations. Major levels of financial and technical support for these worldwide initiatives also were received from major international nongovernmental organizations (Doctors without Borders, Federation of Red Cross and Red Crescent Societies, Oxfam, Save the Children, World Vision), private foundations (Bill and Melinda Gates Foundation), and other large, mostly religiously based, private charitable organizations (Catholic Charities, Episcopal Community Services). Separate programs of bilateral aid also were provided in support of these dramatically successful initiatives (Organization for Economic Cooperation and Development, 2016). The contributions of these organizations profoundly shaped the new approach to aid for developing countries provided by economically advanced countries. These efforts have and will continue to impact the health well-being of people and nations both individually and collectively.

Finally, access to quality health care is now recognized internationally as a basic human right. Health stands side by side with freedom of expression, freedom of assembly, freedom of religion—including no religion at all if that is the individual's choice—and freedom from discrimination in all its form. As a basic human right, access to quality health care ensures access to a full range of public and private policies that provide access and social protection to others. This right covers comprehensive cradle to grave services. Health as a protected human right also ensures that health and health-related insurance companies and other fiduciary entities make adequate provision for financial coverage using the same principles and guidelines that apply to related classes of consumers.

Global progress in human well-being is rapidly attaining its highest expression globally in the health care arena. Social progress in the sector has been unparalleled since 1990 and reinforces the significant progress being achieved in the economic and educational sectors of all societies worldwide. Significant progress in all three of these sectors of human well-being is expected to continue over the near term at least.

REFERENCES

Alternative medicine. (2017). In Wikipedia, the Free Encyclopedia. Retrieved June 20, 2017, from https://en.wikipedia.org/w/index.php?title=Alternative_medicine&oldid=786494217.

Baxby, D. (1999). The end of smallpox. *History Today, 49*(3), 14.

Benton, E. (2014, April 7). Money doesn't buy health or happiness. *Huffpost United Kingdom*. Retrieved May 1, 2017, from http://www.huffingtonpost.co.uk/elaine-benton/money-doesnt-buy-health-o_b_4731160.html.

Bill and Melinda Gates Foundation. (2017). *Financial services for the poor: A strategy overview*. Retrieved April 12, 2017, from http://www.gatesfoundation.org/What-We-Do/Global-Development/Financial-Services-for-the-Poor.

Bionics. (2017). In Wikipedia, the Free Encyclopedia. Retrieved July 5, 2017, from https://en.wikipedia.org/w/index.php?title=Bionics&oldid=783179342.

Carroll, A. (2013, November 22). Life expectancy and health care spending. *The Incidental Economist*. [Blog]. Retrieved December 24, 2016, from http://theincidentaleconomist.com/wordpress/life-expectancy-and-health-care-spending/.

Cogan, J. F., & Hubbard, R. G. (2011). *Health, wealthy, and wise: 5 Steps to a better health system* (2nd ed.). Stanford: Hoover Institution Press.

Doctors without Borders. (2017). *Our work*. Retrieved April 21, 2017, from http://www.doctorswithoutborders.org/our-work.

Eager, P. W. (2004). *Global population policy: From population control to reproductive rights*. London: Routledge.

Electronic health record. (2017). In Wikipedia, the Free Encyclopedia. Retrieved July 5, 2017, from https://en.wikipedia.org/w/index.php?title=Electronic_health_record&oldid=788717770.

Estes, R. J. (2017). Appendices D and E: Index and subindex scores on the Weighted Index of Social Progress. In R. J. Estes and M. J. Sirgy (Eds.), *The pursuit of human well-being: The untold global history*. Dordrecht, NL: Springer.

Estes, R. J., & Sirgy, M. J. (2017). *The pursuit of human well-being: The untold global history*. Dordrecht, NL: Springer.

Fact of Arabs. (2017). Abu al-Qassim Khalaf ibn al-Abbas Al-Sahrawi: "Father of Surgery." Retrieved April 19, 2017, from http://factofarabs.net/ERA.aspx?id=99.

Fuchs, V. R. (2013). The gross domestic product and health care spending. *The New England Journal of Medicine, 369*:107–109.

Gandhi, M. (n.d.). Health. [Web site]. Retrieved June 25, 2017, from https://www.brainyquote.com/quotes/quotes/m/mahatmagan109078.html.

Gartee, R. (2016). *Electronic health records: Understanding and using computerized medical records* (3rd ed.). London: Pearson Publishing.

Hague Academy of Local Governance. (2016). Local service delivery and the SDGs. Nassaulaan: Hague Academy. Retrieved March 1, 2017, from http://thehagueacademy.com/blog/2016/10/local-service-delivery-2/.

Health for All. (2017). In Wikipedia, the Free Encyclopedia. Retrieved June 21, 2017, from https://en.wikipedia.org/w/index.php?title=Health_For_All&oldid=760692813.

Himmelstein, D. U., Thorne, D., Warren, E., & Woolhandler, S. (2009). Medical bankruptcy in the United States, 2007: Results of a national study. *American Journal of Medicine, 122*(8), 741–746.

Hodkinson, P. W., & Wallis, L. E. (2010). Emergency medicine in the developing world: A Delphi study. *Academic Emergency Medicine, 17*(7): 765–774.

International Fund for Agricultural Development. (2012). Rural poverty portal. Retrieved May 1, 2017, from http://www.ruralpovertyportal.org/country/home/tags/sierra_leone.

Kargbo, P. M. (2012). Impact of foreign aid on economic growth in Sierra Leone: Empirical analysis. WIDER Working Paper 2012/007. Helsinki: United Nations University-WIDER. Retrieved September 13, 2017 from https://www.wider.unu.edu/sites/default/files/wp2012-007.pdf

Kasun, J. (1999). *The war against population: The economics and ideology of world population control*. San Francisco: Ignatius Press.

Kochhar, R. (2014). 10 Projections for the global population in 2050. Washington, DC: Pew Research Center. Retrieved April 21, 2017, from http://www.pewresearch.org/fact-tank/2014/02/03/10-projections-for-the-global-population-in-2050/.

Kontis, V., Bennett, J. E., Mathers, C. D., Li, G., Foreman, K., & Ezzat, M. (2017). Future life expectancy in 35 industrialized countries: projections with a Bayesian model ensemble. *The Lancet*, *389*:1323–1335. doi: http://dx.doi.org/10.1016/S0140-6736(16)32381-9.

Lee, E. (2013, January 24). 5 Ways technology is transforming health care. *Forbes BrandVoice*. Retrieved March 1, 2017, from https://www.forbes.com/sites/bmoharrisbank/2013/01/24/5-ways-technology-is-transforming-health-care/#1953205726c5.

Lefkowitz, B. (2007). *Community health centers: A movement and the people who made it happen*. New Brunswick, NJ: Rutgers University Press.

Mayo Clinic. (2017a). Tuberculosis. [Web site]. Retrieved May 9, 2017, from http://www.mayoclinic.org/diseases-conditions/tuberculosis/diagnosis-treatment/clinical-trials/rsc-20188980.

Mayo Clinic. (2017b). New tumor-shrinking nanoparticle to fight cancer, prevent recurrence. *Science Daily*, May 1. Retrieved June 30, 2017, from https://www.sciencedaily.com/releases/2017/05/170501131753.htm.

Moon, S., & Oluwatosin, O. (2013). *Development assistance for health: Critiques and proposals for change*. London: Chatham House, Centre on Global Health Security. Retrieved June 21, 2017, from https://www.chathamhouse.org/publications/papers/view/190951.

National Aboriginal Community Controlled Health Organisation. (2013, March 25). NACCHO Aboriginal Health News Alert: Download: *Senate report on social determinants deserves cross-party support*. Geneva: World Health Organization. Retrieved June 21, 2017, from https://nacchocommunique.com/tag/health-equity/.

National Center for Children in Poverty. (2017). *Child poverty*. Retrieved January 13, 2017, from http://nccp.org/topics/childpoverty.html.

National Center for Complementary and Integrative Health. (2017a). *Traditional Chinese medicine: In depth*. Retrieved April 8, 2017, from https://nccih.nih.gov/health/whatiscam/chinesemed.htm.

National Center for Complementary and Integrative Health. (2017b). Health. [Web site]. Retrieved March 30, 2017, from https://nccih.nih.gov/.

Office of the United Nations High Commissioner for Human Rights. (2008). *The right to health*. Fact sheet no. 31. Geneva: Office of the United Nations High Commissioner for Human Rights. Retrieved July 6, 2017, from http://www.ohchr.org/Documents/Publications/Factsheet31.pdf.

Organization for Economic Cooperation and Development. (2015). *In It Together: Why Less Inequality Benefits All*. Paris: Organization for Economic Cooperation and Development.

Organization for Economic Cooperation and Development. (2016). *Financing for sustainable development*. Paris: Organization for Economic Cooperation and Development. Retrieved March 3, 2017, from http://www.oecd.org/dac/financing-sustainable-development/.

Popko, K. (2008, Jan–Feb). Developing an aging strategy for the future. *Health Progress, 31*–36. Retrieved June 21, 2017, from https://www.chausa.org/docs/default-source/health-progress/developing-an-aging-strategy-for-the-future-pdf.pdf?sfvrsn=0.

Razzak, J. A., & Kellermann, A. L. (2002). Emergency medical care in developing countries: Is it worthwhile? *Bulletin of the World Health Organization, 80*, 900–905.

Reference. (2017). Q: *What is the origin of the phrase "It takes a village to raise a child"?* Oakland, CA: IAC Publishing. Retrieved January 12, 2017, from https://www.reference.com/education/origin-phrase-takes-village-raise-child-3e375ce098113bb4

Right Diagnosis. (2017). *Statistics about polio*. Retrieved May 10, 2017, from http://www.rightdiagnosis.com/p/polio/stats.htm.

Save the Children. (2017). *What we do*. Retrieved March 30, 2017, from https://www.savethechildren.net/what-we-do.

Shah, A. (2011, September 22). Health care around the world. *Global Issues*. Retrieved April 29, 2017, from http://www.globalissues.org/article/774/health-care-around-the-world.

Smallpox virus retention controversy. (2017, May 22). In Wikipedia, the Free Encyclopedia. Retrieved June 21, 2017, from https://en.wikipedia.org/w/index.php?title=Smallpox_virus_retention_controversy&oldid=781649863.

Swartz, K. (2009). Health care for the poor: For whom, what care, and whose responsibility. *Focus, 26*(2), 69–74.

Tortajada, C., Joshi, Y. K., & Biswas, A. S. (2013). *The Singapore water story: Sustainable development in an urban city-state.* London: Routledge.

Traditional Chinese Medicine. (2017, June 14). In Wikipedia, the Free Encyclopedia. Retrieved June 20, 2017, from https://en.wikipedia.org/w/index.
php?title=Traditional_Chinese_medicine&oldid=785641173.

United Nations. (2015). *The millennium development goals report, 2014.* New York:
United Nations. Retrieved June 30, 2016, from http://www.un.org/millennium
goals/2015_MDG_Report/pdf/MDG%202015%20rev%20(July%201).pdf.

United Nations. (2016). *Sustainable development goals: 27 goals to transform our
world.* Retrieved January 4, 2017, from http://www.un.org/sustainabledevelopment/
sustainable-development-goals/.

United Nations, Department of Economic and Social Affairs, Population Division
(2017). *World Population Prospects: The 2017 Revision.* Retrieved February 28,
2017, from https://esa.un.org/unpd/wpp/Graphs/DemographicProfiles/.

United Nations Development Programme. (2015). *Sustainable development
goals—United Nations.* Retrieved November 27, 2016, from www.un.org/
sustainabledevelopment/sustainable-development-goals.

United Nations Development Programme. (2017). *Human development report,
2016: Human development for everyone.* New York: United Nations Development Programme. Retrieved March 10, 2017, from http://hdr.undp.org/en/content/
download-and-read-latest-human-development-report-2016-human-development-
everyone.

United Nations Inter-agency Group for Child Mortality Estimation. (2015). *Levels &
Trends in Child Mortality: Report 2015* (authored by United Nations Children's
Fund, World Health Organization, World Bank, United Nations Department
of Economic and Social Affairs, Population Division). Retrieved July 6, 2017,
from http://www.childmortality.org/files_v20/download/IGME%20Report%20
2015_9_3%20LR%20Web.pdf.

United Nations Population Division. (2009). *World Population Prospects, 2008 Revision.* New York: United Nations Population Division.

United Nations Population Division. (2015). *World population prospects: 2015
revision.* New York: United Nations Population Division. Retrieved February 28,
2017, from https://esa.un.org/unpd/wpp/Graphs/DemographicProfiles/.

United Nations Population Fund. (2015). *The State of the World's Midwifery, 2015.*
New York: United Nations Population Fund. Retrieved May 1, 2017, from http://
www.unfpa.org/sowmy.

United States Department of Veterans Affairs. (2017). Veterans' health adminis-
tra- tion. *Homepage.* Retrieved May 1, 2017, from https://www.va.gov/health/
about VHA.asp.

Vynnycky, R., & Fine, P. E. (1999). Interpreting the decline in tuberculosis: the role
of secular trends in effective contact. *International Journal of Epidemiology, 28*(2),
327–334.

Walsh, F. (2015, July 21). Bionic eye implant world first. BBC News. Retrieved June 30, 2017, from http://www.bbc.com/news/health-33571412.

Weiss, M. (2017). *Grieving the loss of a child.* Alexandria: American Association of Marriage and Family Therapists. Retrieved March 19, 2017, from https://www.aamft.org/iMIS15/AAMFT/Content/Consumer_Updates/Grieving_the_Loss_of_A_Child.aspx.

Whitlock, J. (2010). *History of surgery: A timeline.* Retrieved April 20, 2017, from https://www.verywell.com/the-history-of-surgery-timeline-3157332.

World Bank. (2017). *World development indicators.* Washington, DC: World Bank. Retrieved March 19, 2017, from http://data.worldbank.org/indicator/SH.XPD.PCAP.

World Health Organization. (1948). *Constitution of the World Health Organization.* Retrieved January 29, 2017, from http://www.who.int/governance/eb/who_constitution_en.pdf.

World Health Organization. (2013a). *Emergency Response Framework.* Geneva: World Health Organization. Retrieved May 1, 2017, from http://www.who.int/hac/about/erf_.pdf.

World Health Organization. (2013b). *World Health Report 2013: Research for Universal Health Coverage.* Geneva: World Health Organization.

World Health Organization. (2015a, September 9). Child mortality rates plunge by more than half since 1990 but global MDG target missed by wide margin. [Joint WHO/UNICEF/World Bank news release]. Retrieved June 6, 2017, from http://www.who.int/mediacentre/news/releases/2015/child-mortality-report/en/.

World Health Organization. (2015b). *Levels and trends in child mortality: Report 2015* (authored by UNICEF, WHO, World Bank, UN-DESA Population Division). Retrieved March 29, 2017, from http://www.who.int/maternal_child_adolescent/documents/levels_trends_child_mortality_2015/en/.

World Health Organization. (2015c). *Global financing facility in support of every woman every child.* Retrieved March 20, 2017, from http://www.who.int/life-course/partners/global-strategy/global-financing-facility/en/.

World Health Organization. (2015d). *Health in 2015: From MDGs to SDGs.* Geneva: World Health Organization. Retrieved February 2, 2017, from http://www.who.int/gho/publications/mdgs-sdgs/en/.

World Health Organization. (2016a). *Global strategy for women's, children's and adolescents' health 2016–2030.* Geneva: World Health Organization. Retrieved March 15, 2017, from http://www.who.int/life-course/partners/global-strategy/en/.

World Health Organization. (2016b). Life expectancy increased by 5 years since 2000, but health inequalities persist. [News release]. Retrieved June 22, 2017, from http://www.who.int/mediacentre/news/releases/2016/health-inequalities-persist/en/.

World Health Organization. (2016c). Maternal mortality. [Fact sheet]. Retrieved June 23, 2017, from http://www.who.int/mediacentre/factsheets/fs348/en/.

World Health Organization. (2016d). *Spending on health: A global overview.* Geneva: World Health Organization. Retrieved February 14, 2017, from http://www.who.int/mediacentre/factsheets/fs319/en/.

World Health Organization. (2016e). *World health statistics 2016: Monitoring health for the SDGs*. [Global Health Observatory Data]. Geneva: World Health Organization. Retrieved June 22, 2017, from http://www.who.int/gho/publications/world_health_statistics/2016/en/.

World Health Organization. (2017a). *Global health observatory (GHO) data*. Geneva: World Health Organization. Retrieved March 2, 2017, from http://www.who.int/gho/database/en/.

World Health Organization. (2017b). *Healthy People: Determinants of Health*. Washington, DC: World Bank. https://www Retrieved May 2, 2017, from https://www.healthypeople.gov/2020/about/foundation-health-measures/Determinants-of-Health.

World Toilet Organization. (2017). *Executive Summary of the 2013 Progress Update on the 2012 High Level Meeting Commitments*. Retrieved June 20, 2017, from http://worldtoilet.org/wp-content/uploads/2014/02/ExecutiveSummary.pdf.

World Vision International. (2017). *Emergencies*. Retrieved March 29, 2017, from http://www.wvi.org/emergecies_archive.

NOTE

1 Of historical interest, the *Schola Medica Salernitana*, situated on the Tyrrhenian Sea in the south Italian city of Salerno, was the first and most important source of medical knowledge during the late medieval period in Western Europe.

Chapter 4

Economic Well-Being

An Essential Element in the Advancement of Well-Being

A secure economy and steady rates of economic growth are critical dimensions of national development that make possible advances in human well-being and, more particularly, in economic well-being (Clark & Senik, 2017; Graham, 2012) (box 4.1). Economic growth, for example, is essential to the establishment of elementary and secondary schools and adult outreach programs in communities of previously underserved populations (United Nations Education, Scientific and Cultural Organization, 2017). Steady rates of economic expansion also make possible the establishment of lifesaving health centers in communities that serve large numbers of infants, children, and pregnant women, but especially women who are experiencing difficult pregnancies that previously resulted in high rates of maternal mortality (World Health Organization, 2016a).

These important advances in developed and developing countries have saved the lives of millions of people who otherwise would have perished from untreated illnesses and diseases. Similarly, national and global progress in economic well-being since at least the 1990s has had a profound impact on housing, infrastructure development, technology development and transfers, the arts, and humanitarian assistance to highly vulnerable people worldwide.

BOX 4.1   Economic Well-Being

Economic well-being is a person's or family's standard of living based primarily on how well they are doing financially. Economic well-being is measured by the government to determine how their citizens are faring, as it is integral in a person's overall well-being.

Among these achievements have been child and adult literacy, the creation of truly remarkable institutions of higher learning, and the protection of historical literature and irreplaceable historical artifacts. Moderate to high levels of economic prosperity also have contributed to improvements in the quality of the dwellings within which we live, including reliable access to clean and safe water, effective systems of liquid and solid waste disposal, and the creation of neighborhoods and communities that support high levels of living and quality of life. Economic growth also has contributed to the political stability of nations and has led to the establishment of participatory forms of governance in most regions of the world (Bloom, Canning, and Sevilla, 2001; Freedom House, 2017). Extraordinary programs of research and development have been financed through economic growth, as have the many and varied products of science and technology that most of us now are able to take for granted, for example, personal computers, the creation of the Internet, and highly protective and incentive-building patent protection systems that provide economic incentives to scientists to create even more wondrous innovations for us (Selian & McKnight, 2017).

Thanks to the critical advances that have resulted from economic investments, average years of life expectancy have increased dramatically. We have medical technologies that most thought not to have been possible just a decade ago. Because of mostly government-sponsored health services, smallpox has now been eliminated worldwide, and effective preventive treatments for polio, diphtheria, pertussis, tetanus, malaria, and cholera are being made available at affordable prices to people everywhere (World Health Organization, 2016a). Similarly, new treatments for drug-resistant tuberculosis are being developed through a wide range of public–private initiatives and are saving millions of people annually who previously would have succumbed to this highly debilitating illness (World Health Organization 2016b).

Advances in all levels of education are associated with patterns of economic growth as well. More children are attending primary and secondary schools at levels not previously experienced. University education is now available to hundreds of thousands of qualified persons who were previously denied access to programs of higher education and even to vocational training opportunities. Women, racial and religious minorities, and others who were not part of the mainstream populations of their countries now have access to a wide range of public and private forms of higher educational that simply were not previously accessible to them.

These steadily improving advances in health, education, science, and technology are improving the quality of life of people everywhere. They are also contributing to the emergence of a better-educated and healthier workforce than that which existed in previous generations. These advances have required major economic investments that, in turn, helped to sustain, even increase, the rate of national, regional, and global economic growth. None of these significant advances in human well-being would have been possible without the partnerships that formed between governments and the private sector, but especially commercial enterprises that provide much of the capital needed to sustain these social growth trends.

This chapter reinforces many of the lessons learned concerning advances in human well-being that were reported in the health and education chapters for the period 1990 through the present. Well-being outcomes also are associated with patterns of local, national, and global economic growth, which, in turn, have a relationship to the economic well-being of persons at all levels of the political and social spectrum (Gourevitch, 2008). The major "drivers" that account for economic growth and advances in economic well-being are covered in subsequent sections of this chapter. These drivers figure prominently in the book's larger narrative and here, as elsewhere, we tread carefully in discussing their origins and methods of functioning vis-à-vis additional advances in human and economic well-being. In this chapter, we use the twenty-five-year period 1990 to 2015 as the primary time frame for our discussion, but we also draw freely on events that occurred earlier than 1990. Some of the findings reported will be surprising to some readers, but they are, nonetheless, critical aspects of the multiple, centuries-long experience in improving the economic well-being of individuals and societies (Piketty, 2013, 2015).

The statistical data reported in this chapter were gathered from a wide range of international organizations, including the International Monetary Fund, the Organization for Economic Cooperation and Development (OECD), the United Nations, the World Bank, and independent think tanks (the Brookings Institution, Freedom House, and others). Taken together, the data reported span three decades following the end of World War II. Whenever possible and practical, we have transposed tables of statistical data into graphical formats to make them more accessible and appealing to the largest possible number of readers. We do, of course, assume all responsibility for any errors or omissions that may have occurred during the process of analysis.

GLOBAL ECONOMIC TRENDS

Economic prosperity has reached historically high levels in virtually all regions and countries of the world. The world's total economic output in 2015 exceeded $73.6 trillion, 12 percent higher than in 2010 ($65.6 trillion) and 80 percent higher than in 2000 ($41.0 trillion) (International Monetary Fund, 2017a). The current rate of global economic growth currently averages 3.4 percent per annum, which suggests that real gross domestic product

(GDP) will likely reach or exceed $100 trillion by the year 2025, 144 percent higher than the sum of all goods and services produced worldwide in 2000. At the same time, world average per capita income levels rose from $4,261 in 1990 to $5,486 in 2000 to $9,511 in 2010 and, in 2015, to $10,093—an increase of 137 percent in just 25 years (Organization for Economic Cooperation and Development, 2016a). These are truly remarkable patterns of economic growth, especially considering the economic collapse that occurred in 2008 and 2009 that impacted most directly the world's already advanced nations (Amadeo, 2017; International Monetary Fund, 2017a).

These contemporary global economic growth rates are unparalleled in modern history and provide substantially more of the resources needed to employ a larger workforce and reduce rates of extreme poverty. The expectation exists everywhere that continuing high rates of economic growth within developing countries[1] will improve the quality of health, education, and economic well-being in poor nations as well and, in time, that of economically advanced countries. This expectation is well founded, given recent economic experiences (International Monetary Fund, 2017b). Almost certainly, global poverty declined by hundreds of millions of people, in part in response to a wide range of global initiatives including the United Nations' Millennium Development Goals and, as well, the United Nations' recently launched Sustainable Development Goals (SDG). These important intergovernmental initiatives, as well as those made by the businesses (World Business Council for Social Development, 2017) and other critical economic actors in the private sector such as foundations, are expected to result in even more dramatic declines in the level of global extreme poverty in the decades just ahead (United Nations Department of Economic and Social Affairs, 2017).

Economic development, especially accelerated rates of economic growth, is expected to continue over at least the near term and to support economic well-being through a variety of approaches: (1) economic growth generates the resources needed to promote advances in all sectors of human well-being (Organization for Economic Cooperation and Development, 2016a); (2) national economic progress serves as the basis for economic growth at the cross-national, regional, and global levels when the outcomes of cross-national economic progress are achieved; (3) economic progress fuels the creation of new jobs, new centers of economic productivity, and even new industries in the most favorable situations; (4) trade organizations between comparable groups of nations enhance their capacity to acquire the resources needed to engage in international trade; (5) nations that are members of major international trade associations are more capable of entering into more profitable trade agreements than other groups of nations; (6) locally organized trade associations are able to accelerate the pace of national and regional development, especially in the areas of health, education, housing, transportation, tourism, and other sectors (United Nations Conference on Trade and Development, 2013); and finally (7) worldwide advances in economic progress contribute directly to advances in human well-being at all levels of social and political organizations (International Monetary Fund, 2017a).

Expected Future Economic Trends

The world economy is projected to grow by a rate of 2.7 percent in 2017 and by 2.9 percent in 2018, remaining below the average world growth rate of 3.4 percent that took place prior to the global financial crisis of 2008 and 2009 (Amadeo, 2017; International Monetary Fund, 2017a). Economic growth rates during the same periods for the world's economically developing countries were higher, however, and confirmed the importance of these nations in world economic development.

In 2016, increases in GDP slowed to 2.2 percent and 1.2 percent, respectively, marking their slowest pace of expansion since the recent economic crisis. Further, the estimate for world economic growth in 2016 has been revised downward by 0.7 percentage points compared to a year ago, due to weaker-than-expected growth rates in the United States, Japan, and in the commodity-exporting countries of developing Africa, the Commonwealth of Independent States, and Latin America and the Caribbean. During the same period, the pace of economic growth slowed for developing (and the sizable group of poorer least developing) countries. Once again, these slower growth rates for poor countries reduce national and regional investments in other sectors of the economy that bear directly on the economic advances of these countries, that is, in the health, education, social welfare, and other sectors that depend on growth in the health sector for their expansion (World Bank, 2016c, 2017b).

Despite an expected slowing of the rate of growth of many global economic indicators, *the world's developing countries remained the major drivers of global growth, accounting for about 60 percent of the increases in world gross product between 2016 and 2018* (World Bank, 2016e, 2017a). This trend is extraordinarily positive and reflects the important contribution that developing countries are making in advancing global health and education as well as other sectors of human well-being. Generous levels of bilateral (country to country) and multilateral (associations of countries to recipient countries) aid from economically advanced countries (Organization for Economic Cooperation and Development, 2017b) and sustained contributions by private charitable organizations promote accelerated rates of growth in developing economies. Foreign direct investments (FDI) in the economies of developing countries play a major role in accelerating the pace of health, educational, and economic well-being (Herzer & Nunnenkamp, 2012).

Nations of the Commonwealth of Independent States[2] and Latin America and the Caribbean have benefited significantly from similar types of sustained programs of international aid and are expected to improve the economic well-being of their citizens during much of 2017 (World Bank, 2017a).

ECONOMIC WELL-BEING

Viewed from its most comprehensive perspective, economic well-being refers *to the level of living and subjective quality of economic life experienced by people based on their position in society, especially in their ability to acquire essential goods and services required to meet their basic "needs" and "wants,"* for example, food, shelter, basic health care, basic education, safety and security, and the ability to access at least minimum levels of credit (Fox, 2012; Italian National Institute of Statistics, 2017; Todaro & Smith, 2012). Each of these areas of economic well-being is essential to living a life of dignity (Paine, 1791/1999). Where possible, many societies can satisfy more than just the basic needs and wants of their citizens, and they often do so at high levels of individual and household consumption. This remarkable capacity of societies to provide for the needs and wants of their citizens is one of the major well-being achievements of contemporary societies.

Achieving Economic Well-Being

The context within which economic well-being unfolds is multifaceted and is rarely achievable without substantial investment on the part of individuals and societal institutions with a relatively "shared" or collective view of economic outcomes, for example, increasingly higher levels of economic productivity, increased job and income security, more reliable means for satisfying basic needs and wants, opportunities to accumulate savings and investments, and the ability to contribute to the income security of the larger communities of which they are a part.

Governments and, more particularly, the for-profit business enterprises that operate within the economies for which governments have regulatory responsibilities place emphasis on increased efficiencies in the production process, the expansion of markets and other opportunities to sell their goods and services, fiscal stability, controlled inflation rates, reliable access to credit needed to finance the growth of their enterprises, the ability to reconcile outstanding debts, consumer confidence, and, of course, setting aside a reasonable share of the enterprises' net income for profits (including payments made in the form of dividends to their investors). Enterprises organized as not-for-profit organizations share all the same economic objectives as for-profit enterprises, with the exception that the profit motivation of these organizations is adjusted for promoting the public benefit through organized philanthropy. Instead, gifts from patrons and sponsors and grants from governmental and other sources fill the profit-making void and make possible the ability of not-for-profit organizations to enrich the range of services they can provide and, at the same time, reach new audiences of "clients."

Economic Well-Being and Relative Deprivation

Economic well-being associated with each type of organization is assessed by the extent to which the aspirations and achievements of individuals, families, communities, and entire societies are consistent with the dominant economic norms that operate within their respective societies. The closer the economic status of a people reflects the values that are implicit in a society's organizing economic principles, the higher the degree of economic well-being that is experienced by the population (Clark & Senik, 2017). Population groups whose economic status are at considerable variance with dominant societal economic norms experience profoundly lower levels of economic well-being. Thus, poor people living in rich societies often feel much poorer than what they would likely experience if they were not surrounded by the high levels of economic consumption experienced by many others in their society. Similarly, economically well-off individuals living in poor societies feel themselves to be the "princes among paupers," given the profoundly high levels of wealth and consumption to which they have access, for example, the poor who live near or even on the streets outside of luxury apartment complexes found throughout poor countries (Dodini, 2016). Poor people living in communities populated almost entirely by other poor people, even though they may be hungry, often feel less of a sense of deprivation than when they are surrounded by people and communities able to engage in higher levels of consumption (Federal Reserve System, 2016; Frank, 2007).

Most people experience levels of economic well-being (box 4.2) somewhere between those of the rich and of the poor, that is, the so-called working or middle classes that make up the preponderance of the populations of most economically advanced societies (Hartmann, 2007). Many members of the working or middle classes undertake a variety of activities designed to improve their economic status, for example, working overtime, seeking employment in higher paying jobs, reducing household expenditures, and, when possible, acquiring new or advanced educational training or degrees or some combination of all the preceding. Some even seek to improve their condition in life through gambling in government-sponsored lotteries, on horse races, or the like. Comparatively few of these people, however, can

---

BOX 4.2   The Economics of Well-Being

Money isn't everything. But for measuring national success, it has long
been pretty much the only thing . . . The specific metric that has pre-
vailed since World War II is the dollar value of a country's economic
output, expressed first as gross national product, later as gross domestic
product . . . And the era of GNP and GDP has been characterized by a
huge global rise in living standards and in wealth.

(Fox, 2012)

---

achieve their planned-for financial goals and may end up deeper in debt than
when they began (especially should the size of their families increase or they
become responsible for caring for financially dependent older parents who
are unable to support themselves). The sudden occurrence of other major life
events—the loss of the major income earner, serious or chronic illness, and
even the loss of employment—adds substantially to the financial pressures
experienced by many members of the working and middle classes. Certainly,
the financial crisis of 2008 and 2009 deprived tens of millions of working and
middle-class people of years of hard-won savings, including major reversals
in the equity value of their homes, on which many depended as an economic
safety cushion to protect them against the extremes of economic fluctuations
(Kimelman, 2017). Former Secretary of the US Treasury Timothy Geithner
discussed the conundrums affecting the working and middle classes in a book
about the major psychological and economic stresses associated with the
recent global financial collapse (Geithner, 2015).

LEVELS OF ECONOMIC WELL-BEING

As is now apparent, the dimensions of economic well-being are multifaceted and are associated with various systems and organizations. For our
purposes, we identify six such societal units around which most economic
activity takes place (box 4.3): (1) individuals, families, and extended kinship
systems; (2) local neighborhoods and communities; (3) states and provinces;
(4) nations; and (5) major world geopolitical regions. (6) The world as a
whole is the sixth unit of economic well-being and is discussed in the pages
that follow. Each of these economic units is multitiered, and each, in turn,
contributes to the economic well-being of the other societal units, that is, the
economic well-being of individuals and families contributes directly to the
economic well-being of communities and the reverse is true as well.

BOX 4.3   Six Levels of Economic Well-Being

- Individuals, families, and extended kinship systems
- Local neighborhoods and communities
- States and provinces
- Nations
- Major world geopolitical regions
- World as a whole

The six levels of economic well-being have a number of crosscutting themes that inform each of the six sectors. These themes, among others, include (1) size, structure, and composition of local and national economies, that is, agricultural versus service-based economies; (2) rate(s) of economic expansion; (3) patterns of wealth distribution within countries and major world regions; (4) degrees of population inclusiveness and exclusiveness in the distribution of local and national wealth; (5) the nature, size, and causes of structural poverty within societies; (6) the contributions made by the nations themselves and the world community to reduce the incidence of poverty and increasing income equality; and (7) local, national, regional, and international efforts designed to improve the economic well-being of disadvantaged population groups.

In this chapter, we discuss as many as possible of the levels and crosscutting themes that inform the personal and societal forces that shape the nature of economic well-being across societies. We also provide illustrations of these dynamics at work for a variety of societal groups. We begin our discussion, though, with a summary of some of the major approaches that have been developed for use in assessing well-being in general and, of course, for use in assessing economic well-being specifically.

Measuring Economic Well-Being

A variety of approaches have been developed to assess economic well-being within and among families and communities, of entire nations, and of the world. Most of these approaches are quantitative in nature, but many draw on both the objective and subjective experiences associated with economic well-being (Veenhoven, 2017). In both sets of situations, work on approaches to economic well-being assessment began in the mid- to late 1970s and reached an almost fevered pace in the years following the conclusion of the United Nations' *First Development Decade* (1981–1990). At that point, it was widely recognized that economic measures alone were not sufficient to capture the richness of the social, political, and economic forces that were at work in shaping the lives of people everywhere in the world (Estes, 2015a, 2015b). Certainly, the traditional measure of gross national product (GNP), long considered the "proxy" indicator for measuring social progress at various levels of economic organization, was no longer judged to be sufficiently comprehensive to adequately reflect the multilayered, highly textured changes that were occurring across all sectors of collective life. Indeed, GDP was no longer considered to be the optimal measure for assessing economic well-being, particularly in heavily nonmonetized and nontechnology-based economies of most developing and nearly all the least economically developed nations (World Bank, 2010, 2014a, 2016d). Though still judged to be a valuable indicator for the "basket" of goods and services that it does measure, GNP alone simply is unable to capture the full spectrum of social exchanges that are taking place in most non-Western countries and that contribute significantly to their economic development, for example, the noncompensated child care provided by grandparents so that their children with children can retain jobs in the labor market (United Nations Development Programme, 2017b).

The growth of contemporary approaches to assessing economic well-being is being enhanced by the inclusion of "happiness" as a major policy outcome associated with economic development in countries with both mature and developing economies (Helliwell, Layard, & Sachs, 2017; Layard, 2017). Substantial levels of resources, in turn, are being made available to foster the further development of more effective methods for assessing national progress in realizing this initiative. Some of the most effective approaches to the assessment of economic well-being predate the current push for knowledge in this area (Estes, 2015b; Organization for Economic Cooperation and Development, 2013), but many emerged during the seven-year period following 2010 (Board of Governors of the Federal Reserve System, 2016; Italian National Institute of Statistics, 2017; United States Bureau of the Census, 2017). We have included some of the most influential of these approaches throughout the chapter, including in the sections that follow.

In addition to the research activities into the nature and dynamics of economic well-being conducted by various governmental agencies and ministries, economic well-being is a major topic of study by large-scale independent research organizations and university research centers, for example, the Brookings Institution, the New Economics Foundation (box 4.4). Major economic scholars in the field of happiness studies devote large portions of their professional efforts to better understanding the subjective and objective components of economic well-being in various regions of the world (Clark & Senik, 2017; Easterlin, 1974; Graham, 2012; Rojas, 2016). In addition, substantive reports

---

**BOX 4.4   The 10 Things Economics Can
Tell Us about Happiness**

- Richer countries are happier countries
- Richer people are happier people
- But money has diminishing returns—like just about everything else
- Income inequality reduces well-being, and higher public spending increases well-being
- Unemployment makes you miserable
- Inflation makes you unhappy, too.
- Working more hours makes you happier . . . until it makes you miserable
- Commuters are less happy
- Self-employed people are happier
- Debt sucks

(Thompson, 2012)

---

concerning this body of research appear regularly as "summaries of research" in the public media, including a recent summary of the major findings on the relationship that exists between economics and happiness published by Derek Thompson (2012), a senior editor at *The Atlantic*.

Economic Well-Being and the Organization for Economic Cooperation and Development

One of the most influential organizations associated with studies of changing patterns of well-being has been the Paris-based Organization for Economic Cooperation and Development (OECD). The OECD's activities in this area began in the late 1970s and gradually evolved to encompass more inclusive approaches to well-being assessment at all levels of political organization (ranging from well-being as perceived by individuals to that of entire nations and groups of nations). The thirty-five-member organization's approach to well-being assessment emphasizes both the objective and subjective conditions of life and covers changes in well-being across all aspects of social, political, and economic development.

The OECD's approach to the assessment of well-being has been reported on extensively (Organization for Economic Cooperation and Development, 2016c, 2017a) and has contributed to the conceptualization of other approaches to assessing economic well-being (Galasso, 2013). An additional strength of this approach is that it has undergone successive development over at least three decades and has helped to advance other innovative approaches to well-being assessment developed by other scholars of the relationship that exists between economics and well-being (Clark & Senik, 2017; Hanushek, 2013; Rojas, 2016). The extensive body of research on changing patterns of personal and collective well-being produced by the OECD is made available to the public in electronic form on its Web site (http://www.oecd-ilibrary.org/). The following reports prepared by the organization may be of interest to many readers: *Measuring Subjective Well-Being* and *How's Life? 2015: Measuring Well-Being* (Organization for Economic Cooperation and Development, 2013).

The US Federal Reserve Board's Approach to Assessing the Economic Well-Being of American Households

The board of governors of the Federal Reserve Bank, the country's central board for monitoring monetary supplies and the safety of banks and the banking system, conducts the most comprehensive studies of the changing nature of the economic well-being of American households (Federal Reserve System, 2016). The board makes use of approximately thirty-two well-tested categories of social indicators to assess changes in national and local economic well-being. The indicators are grouped into nine large categories of economic well-being, which, when taken together, provide a rich picture of the economic lives of the combined population of one of the world's most economically advanced nations: (1) overall economic well-being (N=4); (2) income and savings (N=3); (3) economic preparedness and emergency savings (N=4); (4) banking, credit access, and credit usage (N=4); (5) household and household living arrangements (N=4); (6) automobile purchase decisions and credit lending (N=3); (7) higher education and human capital (N=5); (8) education debt and student loans (N=2); and (9) retirement (N=4).

Though the Federal Reserve Board's categories and indicators are ostensibly objective or quantitative in nature, they reflect Americans' subjective evaluation of their current state of economic well-being. In the overview of their most recent report on the economic status of a survey of 50,000 individuals in American households, the board of governors of the Federal Reserve System (2016) wrote,

> Overall, individuals and their families continue to express mild improvements in their general well-being relative to that seen in 2013 and 2014. However, several groups of adults still indicate that they are experiencing financial challenges, and optimism about the future tempered in 2015. Further, 69% of adult's report that they are either "living comfortably" or "doing okay," compared to 65 percent in

2014 and 62 percent in 2013. However, 31 percent, or approximately 76 million adults, are either "struggling to get by" or are "just getting by." (p. 1)

Similar patterns of economic well-being are reported for most of the world's countries with advanced economies that are almost entirely monetized, based on wage-based employment, function on credit (for homes, automobiles, higher education, consumer purchase), and have strong economic regulatory systems (International Monetary Fund, 2017a; World Bank, 2017a).

The Weighted Index of Social Progress and Assessing Economic Well-Being

The Index of Social Progress and the Weighted Index of Social Progress (WISP) were developed by Richard Estes (2014, 2015a, b) to measure changes in the overall socioeconomic development of nations. The approach uses forty-one social indicators divided across ten sectors of critical importance to the well-being of nations. The contributions of economics and economic growth in fostering overall levels of human development are central to the structure of this approach, although this approach incorporates more sectors than those shown here.

Figures 4.1 and 4.2 summarize the overall pattern of social development, including developments in economic well-being, spanning the forty-year

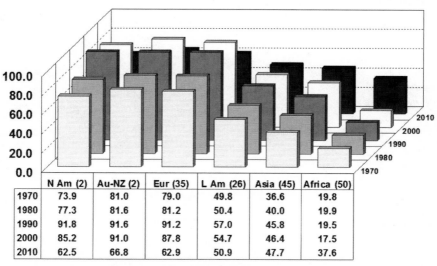

	N Am (2)	Au-NZ (2)	Eur (35)	L Am (26)	Asia (45)	Africa (50)
1970	73.9	81.0	79.0	49.8	36.6	19.8
1980	77.3	81.6	81.2	50.4	40.0	19.9
1990	91.8	91.6	91.2	57.0	45.8	19.5
2000	85.2	91.0	87.8	54.7	46.4	17.5
2010	62.5	66.8	62.9	50.9	47.7	37.6

Figure 4.1. Worldwide distribution of Weighted Index of Social Progress (WISP) scores for countries grouped by "Development Zones," 2010. *Source*: (Figure 2.2 from "Development Trends among the World's Socially Least Developed Countries: Reasons for Cautious Optimism" by R. J. Estes; in *Globalization: The crucial phase* [B. Spooner, Ed.]. © University of Pennsylvania Museum of Archaeology and Anthropology. Used with permission)

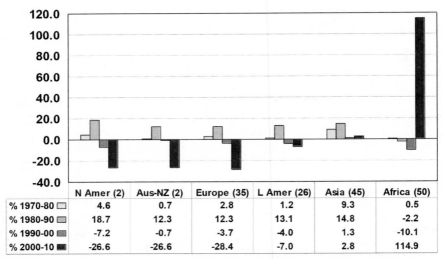

	N Amer (2)	Aus-NZ (2)	Europe (35)	L Amer (26)	Asia (45)	Africa (50)
% 1970-80 ☐	4.6	0.7	2.8	1.2	9.3	0.5
% 1980-90 ☐	18.7	12.3	12.3	13.1	14.8	-2.2
% 1990-00 ■	-7.2	-0.7	-3.7	-4.0	1.3	-10.1
% 2000-10 ■	-26.6	-26.6	-28.4	-7.0	2.8	114.9

Figure 4.2. Percent change in average Weighted Index of Social Progress (WISP) scores by continent (N=160), 1970–2010. *Source*: (Graph from *A life devoted to quality of life: Festschrift in honor of Alex C. Michalos* (F. Maggino, Ed.). Global change and quality of life indicators. 2015, R. J. Estes. © Springer International Publishing Switzerland 2016. With permission of Springer)

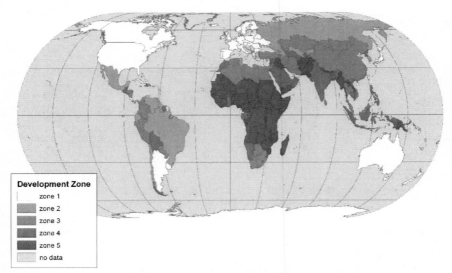

Figure 4.3. Worldwide distribution of Weighted Index of Social Progress (WISP) scores for countries grouped by "Development Zones," 2010. *Source*: (Figure 11.2 from *Globalization: The crucial phase* (B. Spooner, Ed.). Development trends among the world's socially least developed countries: reasons for cautious optimism. 2015, R. J. Estes. © University of Pennsylvania Press, Philadelphia)

period 1970 to 2010 (Estes, 2015a, b). The figures illustrate the dramatic differences that characterize each of the world's major geopolitical regions. Figure 4.2 shows the percentage change that has taken place within each regional grouping of nations for the forty-year period 1970 to 2010. These data show findings for 160 countries included in the global analysis that includes 95 percent of the total global population.

Figure 4.3 presents worldwide findings produced by the WISP in easy-to-understand graphical format. The WISP scores are used to group nations into one of five socio-political-economic "development zones." Countries with the *most favorable* WISP scores in 2015 are grouped into zones 1 and 2 (lighter colors). Countries with the *least favorable* WISP scores in 2015 are grouped into zones 4 and 5 (darker colors). These graphs are generated for each five-year period and, when viewed in color, make it easy to spot changes in objective well-being from each five-year period to the next.

Most Rapidly Developing Countries, 2016

The world's most rapidly developing countries for 2016 as identified by growth rates in gross domestic product are identified in figure 4.4. Most of these countries are emerging markets located in East, South, and Southeast Asia as well as in sub-Sahara Africa. The figure also anticipates the rate and level of economic growth for 2017. Myanmar (Burma), Côte d'Ivoire (Ivory Coast), and Bhutan top the list of countries with the most rapid rates of economic growth, namely, 8.6 percent, 8.5 percent, and 8.4 percent, respectively (Myers, 2016). The combined population of all ten countries identified in the figure exceeds 1.72 billion people, or approximately 23 percent of the world's total. The fact that such a large share of the world's population resides in ten of its economically most rapidly developing countries is especially noteworthy in the context of the positivist orientation of this book. We fully expect that this trend in world economic development will continue over at least the near term and, in time, the countries may well serve as flagship economies for other developing countries to emulate (Kwan, 2002).

Rapid rates of economic expansion make possible increased investments in all sectors of human well-being. Public and private expenditures in the health, education, and housing sectors, for example, are particularly noteworthy since they impact directly on the quality of life of people in every society. Employers, for example, want to hire at least minimally educated, healthy workers. These outcomes are essential to the economics of nations and, fortunately, are expected to be enhanced through the implementation of the social goals of the SDG strategy. As the goals of the strategy are achieved, a substantially larger pool of educated and healthy workers will increase work productivity and earn higher wages than those that currently

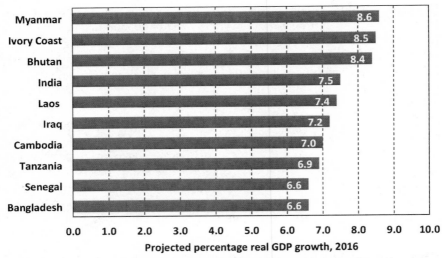

Figure 4.4.   Most rapidly developing countries as measured by gross domestic product growth rates, 2016. *Source*: (Data from Myers, 2016)

prevail. The strategy is expected to improve literacy, reduce the number of worker injuries and sick days, and contribute to an increasingly higher level of work satisfaction that exists among higher-paid workers (Bloom & Canning, 2005).

Other Approaches to Well-Being Assessment in Developing Countries

Other widely used approaches for assessing well-being, including economic well-being, are the *Social Progress Index* and a great variety of even more specialized indexes developed by other economic well-being scholars, for example, Bloom and Canning (2005) and Rojas (2016). Most of these approaches use a combination of objective and subjective indicators of well-being that are applicable to assessing the economic well-being of the 80 percent of that portion of the world's population that resides in developing nations. Still other indexes are entirely subjective in their orientation and provide a complementary assessment of the state of economic well-being along with many of the objective measures used in other approaches to the assessment of economic well-being (Gallup-Shareware, 2016; Sirgy, 2012; World Values Survey, 2015). The Gallup-Shareware polls and the World Values Surveys are international in nature and permit comparisons to be made in economic well-being between nations and major world regions.

Regional Economic Progress

Regional patterns of economic development and economic well-being as reported by the United Nations Development Programme (UNDP), the World Bank, and the International Monetary Fund were uneven during the entire period covered in this chapter, 1990 to 2017 (International Monetary Fund, 2017a). The disparities in growth reported by the World Bank (2014a, 2016d, 2017a) and the International Monetary fund (2016) in figure 4.5 reflect deep fluctuations in the global economy for different groups of countries, including those caught up in the 2008 to 2009 global financial crises that forced hundreds of thousands of people into bankruptcy and more of the near poor into deeper poverty.

The global financial crisis originated in the developed market economies of North America and Europe but quickly spread to the economies of developing nations, including to the poorest nations whose currencies and economies are dependent on aid-granting rich countries. More specifically, the bundling of noncredit-worthy real estate and other mortgages, referred to as "subprime mortgages," weakened the spectrum of investment instruments that were perceived as relatively secure investments, including the value of personal residences and other tangible assets (Subprime mortgage crisis, 2017). These flawed financial instruments, in combination with widespread corruption in

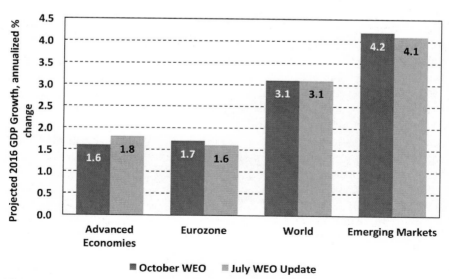

Figure 4.5. International Monetary Fund (IMF) global economic growth forecasts, projected 2016 gross domestic products, annualized percent change by selected grouping of countries. *Source*: (Data from International Monetary Fund, 2016)

some investment houses, resulted in tens of millions of housing foreclosures, dramatic declines in the value of equity-based retirement accounts (e.g., 401Ks, other pensions and annuity funds, market value of personal homes), and hundreds of thousands of bankruptcies among small- and medium-sized businesses. These challenges to economic well-being resulted in sharp declines in the availability of credit to the residents of all countries, but especially to those of developing nations (Kimelman, 2017; United Nations Office of the High Representative for the Least Developed Countries, Land-locked Developing Countries and Small Island Developing States, 2017). At least one international investment house, Lehman Brothers, collapsed, but only a small number of people responsible for the economic crises in Lehman Brothers and other investment houses were prosecuted for the horrendous economic crimes they committed (Reisinger, 2014). The absence of these prosecutions reinforced public sentiment concerning the unequal nature of the justice system in at least the United States—one for the rich and one for the poor with different outcomes for each regardless of the seriousness of the crimes they commit (Rikken, 2016).

Figures 4.5 and 4.6 summarize patterns of economic development for the years 2006 to 2016 for three large clusters of nations and for the world, that is, for advanced economies (N=34), developing countries (N=163), emerging markets (N=34), and countries that use the euro as the exclusive basis of economic exchange, that is, the "Eurozone"[3] (N=12). The figures include comparable data for the world (N=193). Figure 4.5, for example, is based on data from the International Monetary Fund and reflects global economic growth forecasts projected for two different time periods in 2016. For each of the data points, the highest rates of economic growth occur in countries that are classified as emerging markets. The actual and projected growth rates of emerging economies[4] far exceed those reported for all other groups of nations reported in the figure (World Bank, 2016a, c). Similarly, the world is identified as the second "cluster" of nations with the most rapid projected economic growth rates. The higher-than-average growth rates for the world have contributed to significant advances in all sectors of economic activity throughout the world but especially in those sectors of interest to us, that is, health, education, and the economic status of rural populations (Hanushek, 2013; Srinivasan, 2009; World Bank, 2016c).

Figure 4.6 also was prepared using data from the International Monetary Fund (2016) and shows time-series data for the ten-year period 2006 to 2016 with estimated data for 2018. The table includes the same group of countries as those reported on in figure 4.5 but provides statistically more complete information. Analysis of these data reveals that, given prevailing economic conditions, developing countries have become the major drivers of economic growth for the world. Thus, today, following several decades of investments

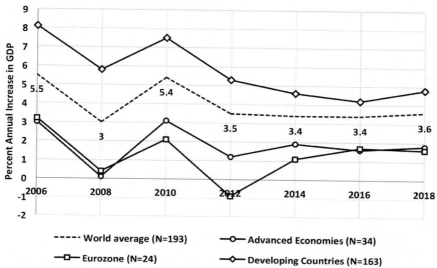

Figure 4.6. Percent annual increases in world gross domestic product for various groups of nations, 2006–2018. *Source*: (Data from International Monetary Fund, 2017a)

and technical assistance in helping to grow their economies, the world is now reaping the yields associated with the investments. Every expectation exists for believing that this macro pattern of global economic development and global economic well-being will continue to unfold well into the future. The projected regional economic growth trends reported in figure 4.6 provide evidence in support of this expectation.

The Weighted Index of Social Progress in Developed Countries

Considerable variation exists in the quality of economic well-being in countries classified as having mature market economies. These variations are associated with unique social, political, and economic forces that characterize each of these countries. In the main, though, national and regional variations in economic well-being are associated with (1) the size, complexity, and structure of the different types of advanced economies that characterize each country or groups of countries, for example, societies that are more market-driven (e.g., United Kingdom) versus those societies that are more democratic-socialist, often referred to as the "Nordic model,"[5] in their orientations (e.g., Denmark, Finland, Norway, Sweden); (2) the comparative youthfulness of many of these economies, especially those of countries that have adopted market-driven economies only since gaining independence from the former Soviet Union in 1991; (3) countries that are experiencing exceptional difficulty in remaining afloat in the presence of major political and economic challenges, for example, Greece, Spain, Portugal; and (4) large economies whose currencies, productive capacity, and leadership dominate the entire group of economically advanced nations, for example, the United States, Germany, France.

These societies are highly stable politically and have secure economic systems. Most have solved the problem of poverty within their borders, albeit some, such as the United States, continue to struggle with nearly 10 percent to 12 percent of its adult population living under established national poverty lines. The United States, unlike nearly all other economically advanced countries, struggles with the problem of child poverty, which amounts to 21 percent of all children aged eighteen years and younger.

International migration is both a solution and a problem when one considers the labor force of most of these countries—a solution in that economic migrants provide critically needed labor to compensate for low and, typically, defining rates of population increase that characterize many of the most economically advanced nations. The pattern is experienced by many nations as they struggle to maintain their cultural identities in the face of large numbers of migrants. The problem is especially acute in France, Germany, Italy, and Spain, but it also manifests itself with street violence in Northern Europe. The United States also has a special and unique set of problems with the country now being home to more than twelve million illegal migrants from Mexico and Central and South America. These countries are finding it difficult to cope culturally with the rapid inflows of new migrants, even though they are essential to the maintenance of the country's labor supply (Essa, 2015; Nations Borders Identities Conflicts, 2017).

In general, residents of economically advanced countries report higher levels of life and economic satisfaction than do residents of economically less-advanced countries (Gallup-Shareware, 2016). This pattern is long-standing. Interestingly, sources of life and economic satisfaction vary between the two clusters of nations, with poorer countries placing greater emphasis on the quality of familial and household relationships as the major prerequisite of quality of life and economic well-being (Gallup-Shareware, 2016; Rojas, 2016).

The Weighted Index of Social Progress in Developing Economies

As reflected in the data reported previously (figures 4.1–4.3), the socio-economic-political well-being situation that exists in countries with developing and least developing economies differs dramatically from that of countries with advanced economies. As a result, the criteria required to assess economic well-being in these countries (and geopolitical regions) differ from those used in determining the economic well-being status of countries with developed market economies. Unlike developed countries, the economies of this latter group of nations are heavily monetized, are based on credit, and engage primarily in the provision of services of value to people rather than in the production of durable goods or other consumables. Credit and its various uses are invested in the productive enterprises themselves. In turn, consumers depend heavily on purchases made using credit to maintain their comparatively high level of living. This model functions well during periods of economic prosperity but can lead to bankruptcies of business enterprises and consumers alike during periods of major downturns in the national and global economies. Individual consumers and their families are vulnerable to economic collapse during periods of extended joblessness, ill health, or the loss of the major family income earner because of divorce or premature death (Estes, 1999). Overconsumption associated with the extension of higher than normal levels of credit, especially for goods whose values steadily decline (almost anything powered by a motor or engine), can compromise the capacity of high consumers to remain afloat in an economy supported primarily through unsecured credit (Durden, 2013). The situation is even worse in developing and socially least developing countries in which even small amounts of purchases made using credit will not be sustainable over the long term. These situations are characterized as economic ill-being and can push many marginally secure people into poverty because of overconsumption (Amadeo, 2017).

Of considerable importance in the trends reported in the preceding figures are the dramatic social, political, and economic changes that are taking place in Africa, including those occurring among the continent's poorest and socially least developed countries (Estes, 2015b). These changes began in the last quarter of the twentieth century and are continuing today. Should improvements of this magnitude persist for another decade or so, many previously least developing countries will probably be reclassified as countries with developing economies. In due course, some may even become "emerging economies," which will attract substantial levels of external capital in support of their more accelerated pace of socioeconomic development. Such a shift would be monumental in scope, indeed, and provide substantial evidence concerning the effectiveness of sustained levels of financial and technical assistance in promoting the development of impoverished nations over the long term. For the near term, though, increasingly higher levels of development assistance will be required to sustain the rapid rates of growth occurring among many sub-Saharan Africa states as well as selected countries located in East and South Asia and in Latin America and the Caribbean (International Fund for Agricultural Development, 2016; Kilmister, 2016).

Under the current growth trajectory, and assuming no further changes in income inequality, nearly 35 percent of the population of developing and socially least developing countries will continue to live under conditions of extreme poverty—a situation that is likely to be reduced appreciably between 2015 and 2030 in response to the SDGs. French economist Thomas Piketty has discussed the conundrums associated with this dilemma in his 2015 book, *The Politics of Inequality*. However, a new approach to reduce the major economic inequalities that exist between the world's richest and poorest nations is the major goal of the newly launched United Nations SDG campaign that has placed the elimination of global poverty as its central objective.

According to Piketty and others, annual economic growth rates of at least 11 percent annually through 2030 will be required to bring about the elimination of extreme poverty in these countries worldwide (World Bank, 2016c). Currently, economic growth rates in the developing and socially least developing countries are averaging 8.9 percent, an impressive rate of economic growth that is expected to continue until at least 2030 because of the successful implementation of the SDSs. Nevertheless, the existing growth rate is below that which is believed to be needed to fully reduce the rate of extreme poverty in developing countries (World Bank, 2014a). We can, though, achieve the higher growth through special development assistance programs that are carried out in cooperation with economically more-developed countries. More specifically, a variety of economic measures exist to make these important economic advancements possible, for example, preferential trade relationships, increases in FDI, debt forgiveness, and subsidized training programs for chronically unemployed workers.

The world's developing and socially least developing countries are expected to grow by 5.2 percent in 2017 and 5.5 percent in 2018—well below the SDG target of at least 7 percent GDP growth set for these countries by the SDGs in 2015 (World Bank, 2017a). However, the economic well-being status that exists at the individual, familial, and community levels differs from that reflected in national trends. In time, both trends will catch up with one another, and the pace of economic well-being will increase dramatically in the decades just ahead. This outcome is almost certainly assured by the launch of the global SDG strategy of the United Nations, which brings together many key actors across sectors in promoting economic well-being development throughout the world (World Bank, 2017a).

To achieve the worldwide goal of accelerated economic growth among developing nations, more substantial international development finance and aid will be needed to fully implement the seventeen goals of the SDG strategy. The additional resources identified are needed to overcome the complex problems associated with chronic poverty in urban centers and in the remote rural communities of developing countries. These initiatives will require significant levels of financial developmental assistance, the forgiveness of international debts, and the identification of poorer developing nations as preferential trading partners (Shah, 2014b).

ADVANCES IN HOUSEHOLD INCOME

Changes in household income are among the most sensitive measures of the capacity of families to participate fully in local markets. Higher income levels bear directly on all three phases of economic activity—production, distribution, and consumption. They also reflect the capacity of nations to meet at least the basic needs of their populations and, in most cases, to satisfy those needs beyond a basic level. Obviously, higher levels of median household income are more desirable than lower levels. This observation is particularly true when household incomes are so low that members of the household continue to live in poverty.

According to a recent poll conducted by the Gallup Organization (Phelps & Crabtree, 2013), median annual household income worldwide in 2013 averaged $9,733 and median per capita income averaged $2,920. These averages are substantially higher than the median household and per capita income levels reported in 1990 (World Bank, 2017a, b). Median household and individual per capita incomes are higher today than those reported for 2013, and the World Bank expects that they will continue to rise appreciably between 2017 and 2030. As these median income levels continue to rise, increasingly larger numbers of the poor will succeed in extricating themselves from extreme poverty. The changes are expected to occur among the poorest nations of East, South, and Southeast Asia—the regions with the largest concentrations of extreme poverty (International Monetary Fund, 2017a, b). The poorest nations of sub-Saharan Africa are expected to benefit significantly from these trends as well. However, significant economic disparities are expected to persist well into the future. Gallup summarizes the extreme nature of these disparities thusly:

> Vast differences between more economically developed countries and those with developing or transitional economies illustrate how dramatically spending power varies worldwide. Median per-capita incomes in the top 10 wealthiest populations are more than 50 times those in the 10 poorest populations, all of which are in Sub-Saharan Africa.
>
> (Phelps & Crabtree, 2013)

Current Household and Per Capita Income Levels

Today, household and per capita income levels in developing countries vary tremendously. Readers are encouraged to visit the Web site of the

BOX 4.5

Over a long period of time, the main force in favor of greater equality has been the diffusion of knowledge and skills.

(Piketty, 2013)

International Monetary Fund (2017b) for detailed information concerning the dynamic nature and projected income patterns currently taking place in each of the world's developing countries.[6] Steady increases in country average income levels since 2013 make clear that per capita average income levels of residents of low-income countries have continued to increase, often substantially (World Bank, 2016d). This pattern is the result of successes that have been realized by national and local poverty alleviation initiatives, including the high levels of aid received from foreign sources. The reality is that many poor people and families are gradually working their way out of poverty to more sustainable levels of living.

Obviously, much work needs to be done to reduce national and global poverty rates. Extreme poverty already has been cut in half since the launching of the Millennium Campaign (2005–2015), and a large share of the remaining population living under conditions of extreme poverty is expected to exit poverty through the initiatives reflected in the recently launched Sustainable Development Campaign (2015–2030). This goal is one that the entire world community is attempting to achieve (box 4.5)

INNOVATIVE APPROACHES TO INCREASING HOUSEHOLD AND PER CAPITA INCOME IN DEVELOPING COUNTRIES

Many approaches to increase the household and per capita income levels and economic well-being of low-income families have been attempted, especially for those living in or on the edges of poverty. These approaches, which include the global initiatives such as the Millennium Development Goals campaign and the Sustainable Development Goals campaign, represent substantial programs of multi- and bilateral development assistance between countries. Major efforts undertaken by international nongovernmental organizations such as Save the Children and Doctors without Borders (*Médecins sans Frontières*) are designed to enhance national and per capita income levels, as are the generous programs of financial and technical assistance provided by major aid-granting foundations including the Bill & Melinda Gates Foundation and the Ford, Carnegie, and Rockefeller foundations, as well as significant aid provided by smaller development assistance foundations, for example, the George Soros Foundation, the Halloran Philanthropies, among hundreds of others. Many individuals also contribute their personal skills to the effort through educational and cultural exchange programs sponsored by the Japanese International Cooperation Agency, the Danish International Development Agency, the US Agency for International Development, the Fulbright Fellowship program, the American Peace Corps, and similar types of formal and informal programs organized by most economically advanced countries. Moreover, a plethora of dynamic "entrepreneurship" and social innovation support programming has blossomed over the past five to ten years, putting the challenges of the "small- and medium-sized enterprise" at the very heart of development finance and social investment activity world-wide. We discuss the contributions made by a selection of these organizations and initiatives later in the chapter.

Public–Private Partnerships in Promoting Economic Well-Being

The most innovative examples of these approaches have been developed to reach the most economically vulnerable populations and have emphasized the use of a combination of tax incentives and private skills training for persons with highly uneven employment histories (Brookings Institution, 2017). Public subsidies of private job training have been among the most commonly used policy approaches and have been among the most effective in promoting sustained levels of well-paying jobs for previously poor people. The use of this approach has a long history in Europe and in North America. Indeed, it continues to be used today to promote more secure levels of economic well-being among workers worldwide in gaining progressively higher levels of job security (Taylor, 2009).

Other types of public–private initiatives frequently exist between governments and business enterprises, for example, in the armaments and munitions industries, in road building, in providing research funds in support of a wide range of research investigations, and as backers of the last resort in student loans and the financing of research laboratories in universities, pharmaceutical firms, and other types of businesses. Similar types of relationships exist between developed and developing countries including the provision of large amounts of critically needed financial assistance to stimulate economic development and economic well-being in developing and least developing countries. The amount of these investments is in the hundreds of billions of dollars each year (International Monetary Fund, 2017a, b; World Bank, 2017a).

Chapter 4

Enhancing Family Economic Well-Being through Private Remittances

A second approach to enhancing the incomes of impoverished families is the migration of adult members of households to foreign countries as contract laborers.[7] This approach has been used for several decades and has proved highly effective in generating substantial sums of income in the form of foreign remittances[8] to families (Organization for Economic Cooperation and Development, 2006). Indeed, both countries of origin and receiving countries make the process of obtaining work visas easier for persons wanting to engage in contract labor. Families receiving foreign remittances, in turn, benefit from the income they receive, which adds appreciably to their living situation and quality of life (Mara et al., 2012).

Many nations depend heavily on the inflows received from foreign remittances to finance a wide range of social, health, educational, and even infrastructure developments (e.g., telecommunications systems, road building). Indeed, most developing countries make it easy for their adult workers to enter into foreign contract labor agreements (Smart & Casco, 1988) and, in turn, have developed sophisticated remittance methods that are easy and inexpensive to use (World Bank, 2014b, 2016a, d). The countries receiving the largest amounts of foreign remittances are reported in figure 4.7 (Migration Policy Institute, 2016). The figure also identifies the countries that are most

Global Overview and Top 10 Countries by the Total Amount of Remittances Received

- Global
  - *Bangladesh*
  - *China*
  - *Egypt*
  - *India*
  - *Lebanon*
  - *Mexico*
  - *Nigeria*
  - *Pakistan*
  - *Philippines*
  - *Vietnam*

Global Overview and Top 10 Countries by Remittance as a Percentage Share of GDP

- Global
  - *Haiti*
  - *Honduras*
  - *Kyrgyz Republic*
  - *Lebanon*
  - *Lesotho*
  - *Moldova*
  - *Nepal*
  - *Samoa*
  - *Tajikistan*
  - *Tonga*

Figure 4.7. Top recipients of international remittances, 2016. *Source*: **(Data from Migration Policy Institute, 2016)**

dependent on foreign remittances to support their economies as reflected in remittances as a share of their GDP in 2011, the most recent year for which we have comparative data.

Unfortunately, on their return home, contract laborers are rarely able to sustain the same level of economic well-being for their families, given the absence of comparable paying jobs for unskilled workers (Pettinger, 2013). This situation typically results in a repetition of the same cycle of economic ill-being that existed prior to seeking employment abroad.

Welfare Assistance to Improve the Well-Being of Economically Vulnerable Populations

Other approaches to raising the median household and per capita income levels of families living in or near poverty involve cash grants to subsidize the ability of poor families to purchase basic goods and services. Cash grants to the poor, however, have not been designed to lift the poor out of poverty but rather to provide only for their subsistence needs. Thus, large sums of money often are spent by national and local governments to support the basic needs of their poor. These expenditures, though large, are rarely sufficient to lift deeply impoverished individuals and families out of poverty. Programs of social support, including improved health and educational services, that are designed to bring the poor into the mainstream of society would be required to achieve that goal (Estes, 1999).

An encyclopedic summary of the major social-welfare approaches that exist in each of the world's nations is presented in the International Social Security Association's *Social Security Programs throughout the World* (International Social Security Association, 2017). This online compendium is continuously updated and offers invaluable insights into the increasingly more comprehensive range of social provisions that are being made for the poor and other income vulnerable population groups, that is, the aged and disabled, the sick, pregnant women, children and youth, unemployed workers, and families with large numbers of children. The sheer breadth and depth of these programs in more than 178 countries are impressive and speak well to the increasing awareness that exists worldwide in recognizing the intertwined nature of social and economic well-being. They also reflect the willingness of countries to make available the financial investments that are needed to implement these critical programs of income support.

Promoting Economic Well-Being through Universal Basic Income Schemes

Among the not-so-recent innovative approaches for improving the economic well-being of poor families is the Universal Basic Income (UBI) initiative, the essence of which is a utopian approach that involves the payment by governments of income to every individual regardless of wealth or other income sources (Vella, 2017). The expectation is that the scheme would solve a host of economic problems that are endemic to every society, for example, chronic joblessness, poverty, and other recurrent economic problems.

The concept of a UBI goes back to the Middle Ages, particularly to economic principles outlined by Sir Thomas More in his book *Utopia* (1516/1967). Variations of the UBI can be found in the writings of Thomas Paine (1791/1999), John Stuart Mill (1848), and Bertrand Russell (1918). Each of these giants in Western philosophy spoke to the advantages of a universal basic income scheme in reducing poverty, preventing crime, and providing an economic ladder for helping recipients of this income to move progressively to higher levels of individual per capita and household income.

In modern times, Martin Luther King was a proponent of this approach to poverty alleviation, as were conservative economists Milton Friedman and Frederick Hayek. In general, political liberals and conservatives embrace the simplicity of the UBI, especially since it would eliminate dozens of administration-heavy federal programs that are specifically targeted to the poor, for example, food stamps, subsidies for health, education, housing, and child and elder care. The expectation is that larger cash payments at regular intervals to the poor and other beneficiaries would significantly enhance efficiencies by eliminating the number and size of federal, state, and local welfare bureaucracies. Funds would be dispensed to eligible recipients each month using the same highly efficient mechanism as that used by the government in making social security payments.

To date, no society has adopted the UBI for ideological and fiscal security reasons, although the advanced welfare states of northern Europe closely approximate the principles associated with the concept of a universal basic income scheme. Most countries, though, are reluctant to implement any version of the UBI, given the absence of a means-test associated with its implementation. The idea of UBI payments going to high-income individuals and families, for example, is ideologically contrary to the goal of many advanced economies, which use demonstrated need as the basis for determining eligibility for entitlement programs.

The Widening Wealth Gap

A major impediment to achieving economic parity among the world's nations is the widening wealth gap between the richest and poorest nations (Collier, 2007; Estes, 2012; World Bank, 2017b). This gap perpetuates poverty and makes it exceedingly difficult for impoverished nations or nations with excessive levels of public indebtedness to achieve more advanced levels of economic development. The extent of this gap is presented in figure 4.8, which uses a champagne glass to depict the amount of wealth to which each of five income groups around the world has access (United Nations Development Programme, 1992). The bowl of the champagne glass shows the highest concentrations of wealth among the top two quintiles, or 40 percent of the global population (94.4 percent), whereas the stem of the glass reflects the resources that are available to the lowest three quintiles, or 60 percent of the global population (5.6 percent). The data reported for all five quintiles reflect the seriousness of the gap that exists in the distribution and consumption of wealth by each quintile of people. The data reported in the figure are illustrative of the wealth gap initially identified in 1992 but which remains current today (United Nations Development Programme, 1992; World Bank, 2017b).

Despite the significant gains that have been achieved in reducing poverty during the period of the Millennium Campaign, in fact, the steep disparities in the distribution of wealth generated by the world community have remained

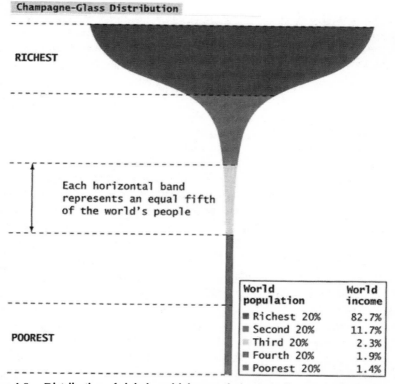

Figure 4.8.   Distribution of global wealth by population quintile. *Source*: (Adapted from United Nations Development Programme, 1992, p. 35)

fundamentally unchanged. The top 20 percent of the population of already rich countries continue to receive somewhat more than 81 percent of the total wealth produced annually, and the top 40 percent of all income earners continue to receive more than 90 percent of all the wealth produced each year from 1990 to the present.

In contrast, nations grouped in the lowest quintiles of income in figure 4.8 have received a little more than 3.3 percent of all the world's goods and services produced each year. Indeed, the bottom 20 percent of income earners worldwide receives just 1.4 percent of the global wealth produced each year (International Monetary Fund, 2017a). Most people living in these nations are already poor, and, despite the introduction of new industries and foreign aid into their economies, they continue to receive a disproportionately low share of the world's total wealth. This pattern, in turn, makes it difficult for the poorest developing economies to advance to higher levels of economic well-being.

The worldwide income inequalities are expected to continue for the foreseeable future, although lifting significant numbers of the poor from abject poverty is expected to continue as well. The economically advanced[9] member states of the OECD[10] are expected to benefit most from high economic growth rates, whereas economically less-developed countries[11] are expected to continue to benefit only minimally from the economic gains that are being realized worldwide. The paradox of high rates of economic growth and development in some countries but not in others is further reflected in the reality that already rich countries consume 80 percent of the world's goods and services but make up only 20 percent of the world's population. Developing countries, by contrast, contain 80 percent of the world's population but consume only 20 percent of global resources! Ironically, many of the basic resources that are needed by economically advanced countries to sustain their already high levels of living flow directly from developing countries to economically advanced countries, for example, clothing and textiles, scarce minerals, low-wage workers, and medium to high-tech production of goods and services in great demand by rich countries. Apple Corporation, for example, produces most of its highly priced electronic products in China, from where they are shipped to people and businesses all around the world, that is, iPhones, iPads, iPods, iWatches. Further, still only rarely can the persons in China and other low-wage countries who produce high-priced goods afford to purchase such items for their own consumption. This situation exists for many goods and services, even comparatively inexpensive ones, as well as for designer-stamped items, textiles, shoes, and other day-to-day goods on which economically advanced countries depend to sustain their high level of living (Collier, 2007; Sachs, 2006; World Bank, 2016c).

Poverty: Still a Major Global Challenge

The preceding discussion makes clear that extreme poverty has proven to be one of the most elusive and difficult problems to solve, especially in nations that have few resources to dedicate to alleviating poverty. In approaching the problem of local and global poverty, however, the World Bank has established a universal standard for measuring poverty, that is, persons living on less than $1.25 per day (purchasing power parity),[12] and moderate poverty is less than $2 a day. The World Bank estimated that, in 2013, 10.7 percent of the world's population lived on less than $1.90 a day (a revised standard based on inflation), compared to 12.4 percent in 2012. In effect, the level of extreme poverty was reduced by 35 percent in 2013 over 1990 levels. On a face-to-face basis, this decline means that, in 2013, 767 million fewer people lived on less than $1.90 a day, down from 881 million in 2012 and 1.85 billion in 1990. These are dramatic declines in rates of human deprivation and are the result of successful partnerships among major international development assistance (ODA) organizations (Roser & Ortiz-Ospina, 2017; World Bank, 2014a).

The gains in poverty reduction reflect high levels of intracommunity and intrafamily cooperation to promote collective well-being. Gone are the ill-being behaviors that have trapped the affected generations of poor people in profound patterns of income insecurity, for example, the absence of basic health and education services combined with the inability of the poor to use those services that are available (Cruz, Quillin, & Schellekens, 2015; Shah, 2014a).

Poverty, though, is not simply an economic problem and is typically compounded by major health and education deficiencies in combination with the lack of access to affordable housing, to accessible transportation, to potable water, and to inclusion in a variety of income security schemes. Further, poverty tends to be an intergenerational phenomenon that is passed on from father to son, mother to daughter, and so on. This situation occurs in developing and developed countries and adds to the complexities that governments experience in solving the problem, especially given the inadequate resources available to them. Large families with many dependent persons, young and old, make efforts to alleviate poverty more difficult. Further, efforts to alleviate poverty are especially complex, given that most poor people live in ghettos and slums that often are resistant to major social changes.

Poverty has a major impact on the economies of societies given that it depresses the capacity of countries to fully utilize the human resources that are available to it. To move forward economically, countries must solve this dilemma. Only then can the society function as an integrated entity. All societies have struggled with finding effective solutions to this challenge and, in so doing, have found many innovative solutions. On the other hand, countries that continue to ignore or minimize the value of these latent human resources deprive themselves of valuable partners who can add to national wealth.

Regional Poverty

Figure 4.9 shows the millions of people living under conditions of extreme poverty for each of the world's major geopolitical regions over a period of twenty years, that is, 1988 to 2008. The figure confirms that the highest concentrations of poor people live in remote rural communities where they are rarely seen and even more rarely are the beneficiaries of ODA. This pattern persists even though most aid-granting organizations seek to reach the extreme poor living in rural communities, but, in fact, most of the aid provided tends to flow to the urban poor who are often living under conditions of even more extreme poverty.

Figure 4.9, in addition to showing the number of rural poor people who live under conditions of extreme poverty, also shows that poverty rates are highest for the developing countries of Latin America and the Caribbean and those of the Middle East and North African regions. The highest declines in extreme poverty rates over the twenty years covered by the figure occurred within

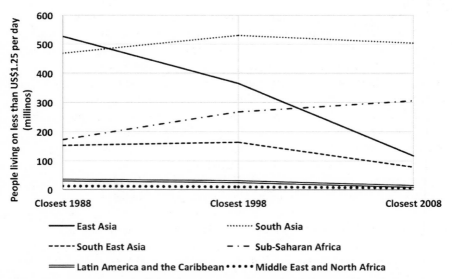

Figure 4.9.   Rural people living in extreme poverty by major world region. *Source:* (Data from International Fund for Agricultural Development, 2016)

the developing nations of East, South, and Southeast Asia. The single largest share of these declines took place in China, where hundreds of millions of the rural poor were lifted out of extreme poverty in response to China's now decades-long rates of double-digit economic growth (Ryder, 2017). Extreme poverty levels declined appreciably in India and other nearby South and Southeast Asian nations (e.g., India, Bangladesh, Pakistan, and Indonesia) but not at the same pace as that which occurred in China. In all cases, these critically important advances in human well-being laid the foundation for even higher levels of social progress through implementation of the Millennium Campaign, other major multinational poverty alleviation initiatives, and the recently launched SDGs campaign (United Nations Department of Economic and Social Affairs, 2017).

Further, rural and urban poverty levels remain especially severe in the socially least developing countries of sub-Saharan Africa. However, impressive progress in the alleviation of poverty has been made among these countries since at least 2000 (International Fund for Agricultural Development, 2016; United Nations Development Programme, 2017a). Therefore, considerable progress is being made worldwide in reducing the incidence of case and structural poverty[13] in all nations of the world (World Bank, 2016c).

Poverty Alleviation Strategies

Successful strategies to alleviate poverty require multiple and nuanced approaches to bring about significant change, for example, increasing household income levels, enhancing consumption patterns including higher food quality and at least a bit higher revenue to pay for housing improvements, school fees, uniforms and to finance nonemergency medical care and transportation costs associated with paid work.

The following are the major strategies that have been used in recent years by either the private or public sector in helping to reduce the incidence of poverty in the world's poorest nations: (1) programs of bilateral aid and development assistance (Zhou, Zhang, & Zhang, 2014); (2) programs of multilateral aid and development assistance (Kilmister, 2016; Organization for Economic Cooperation and Development, 2015, 2016b); (3) international aid and technical assistance provided by nongovernmental organizations (Lawrence and Mukai, 2010); and (d) FDI (Economist, 2013).

The Importance of Foreign Aid in Accelerating the Pace of Economic Development and in Reducing Poverty

Foreign aid, or ODA, has been a topic of considerable controversy since the early 2000s (Development aid, 2017) (box 4.6). Although ODA has increased at a steady pace as countries increase their independence from former colonizing European powers, Zambian-born economist Dambisa Moyo has been a leading critic of the weaknesses of foreign aid. She suggests, for example, that foreign aid is "taxed" at all levels of "management" within aid-receiving countries and suggests that much of what remains often is siphoned off into the private bank accounts of a country's corrupt leadership, including those of the country's military elites (Moyo, 2010). Others have joined with Prof. Moyo to emphasize the limitations of foreign aid and have suggested that such aid is "dead on arrival" (de Rugy, 2015). The many examples of this type of corruption serve as the basis for the argument that the flow of foreign aid between nations must be carefully monitored and controlled to ensure that the aid benefits the intended population. They also argue for the importance of transparency, good governance, and more effective accounting systems to keep track of ODA receipts and the expenditures of donor-assisted recipient countries.

Despite the seriousness of the criticisms heaped on the effectiveness of foreign aid, ODA continues to be an efficient and effective mechanism for transferring large sums of development assistance from rich to poor countries (United States Agency for International Development, 2007). To that end, the OECD has set the goal for all of its members to contribute at least 0.7 percent of the gross national income (GNI)[14] to promote social progress within the world's poorest nations. Only a handful of countries have achieved or exceeded this critical benchmark. Figure 4.10 reports the percentage of GNI allocated by all member states of the OECD to support a broad range of foreign aid activities financed through the Organization for Economic Cooperation and Development (2017a). The ten most generous countries, as measured by the percentage of their GNI allocated to ODA in 2015, are identified in the figure, the majority of which are in Northern Europe. The list is impressive, especially given the comparatively small size of the national economies of

---

BOX 4.6   Official Development Assistance

IN recognition of the special importance of the role which can be fulfilled only by official development assistance, a major part of financial resource transfers to the developing countries should be provided in the form of official development assistance. Each economically advanced country will progressively increase its official development assistance to the developing countries and will exert its best efforts to reach a minimum of 0.7 percent of its gross national product at market prices by the middle of the decade.

(United Nations, 1970)

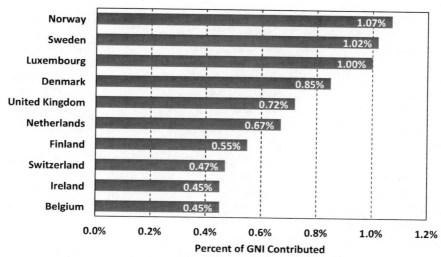

Figure 4.10. Official development assistance in dollars provided as a percentage of donor gross national income (GNI): Organization for Economic Cooperation and Development Top 10 Donor Development Assistant Committee Countries in 2016. *Source:* (Data from Organization for Economic Cooperation and Development, 2017a)

many of these countries, namely, Norway, Sweden, Luxembourg, Denmark, and others. Unlike most intergovernmental associations of nations, however, the world's most generous ODA contributors have strong national social safety nets of their own and, in past decades, were recipients of precisely this type of development assistance especially in the rebuilding decades that followed the end of World War II.

However, the countries that contribute the highest *dollar amounts* to multilateral ODA differ significantly from those that contribute the highest percentage of their total national wealth in helping to accelerate the pace of socioeconomic growth in developing countries (figure 4.10). The highest contributors of actual dollars to ODA are identified. As reflected in this figure, the world's major donor nations to ODA, apart from the combined contributions of members of the OECD, which are counted twice in the figure, are the United States, the United Kingdom, Germany, Japan, and others. Indeed, the total volume of ODA dollars provided by economically advanced countries to developing countries is concentrated in just these four largest dollar donors to ODA. Of interest, too, is that each of the countries identified has a social system that differs appreciably from those countries that contribute the largest share of their national wealth to ODA. The countries that contribute the most dollars to ODA, for example, are large, racially and ethnically diverse states that are characterized by highly competitive and market-driven economic systems. Countries that contribute the highest percentage of their national wealth to ODA, on the other hand, tend to be smaller and more culturally homogeneous nations that have mixed market and semi-socialist economic systems. High dollar donors to ODA also have aggressive programs of international trade with developing countries—mostly in the form of imports of raw materials as well as semiproduced textile, electronic, and other products produced by low-wage workers. The percentages of the GNI of these countries in 2015, and again in 2016, nearly all fell well below the 0.7 percent of GDP goal of ODA established by the OECD, with the highest contributor, the United States, allocating only about 0.17 percent (versus 0.70 percent) to multilateral forms of international development assistance.

As discussed in the next section, nearly all countries have well-developed programs of bilateral development assistance in addition to their support of multilateral aid programs supported by the United Nations and its extensive network of specialized agencies, the OECD, and other major international economic alliances. However, the dollar volume and percent of GNI represented by these dollars tend to fluctuate considerably from one year to the next. Most of these fluctuations occur in response to changing national economic circumstances. The next section identifies some of the most significant changes that have occurred in the bilateral and multilateral aid patterns of individual countries.

Fluctuating Patterns of Bilateral and Multilateral Aid

Overall, net ODA levels increased in seventeen economically advanced countries, with the largest increases recorded for Iceland, Italy, Japan, Norway, and the United Kingdom. Net ODA fell in eleven countries, with the biggest decreases occurring in Canada, France, and Portugal. The G7 countries provided 70 percent of the total net Development Assistance Committee (DAC) ODA in 2015, and the DAC-European Union countries provided 52 percent. Most of the U.S.-financed aid provided was for humanitarian purposes and to fight HIV/AIDS. In contrast, US net bilateral aid to least developing countries fell by 11.7 percent in real terms to $8.4 billion due to reduced disbursements to Afghanistan (Organization for Economic Cooperation and Development, 2017b). Unfortunately, net ODA disbursements to sub-Saharan Africa fell by 2.9 percent to $8.7 billion.

Multilateral ODA (i.e., aid from associations of countries to individual or subsets of countries) from the nineteen European Union countries that are members of the OECD's DAC was approximately $70.7 billion, a rise of 5.2 percent in real terms in 2015 from 2012 or approximately 0.42 percent of their combined average gross national income. ODA increased or decreased in DAC-European countries from 2013 to 2015 as follows and, when available, for the reasons provided (Organization for Economic Cooperation and Development, 2015):

- Austria (+0.7 percent)
- Belgium (−6.1 percent): due to lower levels of debt relief in 2013 compared to 2012
- Czech Republic (−4.7 percent): due to a decrease in bilateral aid to Afghanistan
- Denmark (+3.8 percent): as it increased its bilateral aid
- Finland (+3.5 percent): reflecting an overall scaling up of its aid
- France (−9.8 percent): due to lower levels of loan disbursements and debt relief compared to 2012
- Germany (+3.0 percent): due to a rise in bilateral lending and higher contributions to international organizations
- Greece (−7.7 percent): due to austerity measures
- Ireland (−1.9 percent): despite continued budgetary pressures
- Italy (+13.4 percent): the Italian government had made a firm commitment to increase its ODA allocations to 0.16 percent of GNI in 2013 and reached this target
- Luxembourg (+1.2 percent)
- Netherlands (−6.2 percent): its ODA/GNI ratio fell below 0.7 percent due to overall aid budget cuts
- Poland (+8.6 percent): due to increased contributions to European Union institutions
- Portugal (−20.4 percent): due to financial constraints leading to budget cuts
- Slovak Republic (+2.4 percent)
- Slovenia (−0.6 percent)
- Spain (+3.7 percent): due to debt relief operations in sub-Saharan Africa
- Sweden (+6.3 percent): due to increases in its bilateral aid to international organizations
- UK (+27.8 percent): as it put into place firm budget allocations to meet the 0.7 percent ODA/GNI target (Organization for Economic Cooperation and Development, 2016b).

Changes in Bilateral Aid and Trade Assistance from OECD Members

Elsewhere in the OECD-DAC *Annual Report,* net bilateral ODA among all member states, that is, aid provided by one country to other countries (Kilmister, 2016) rose or fell as follows:

- Australia (−4.5 percent): it delayed expenditure due to reprioritization of its aid program to focus on the Indo-Pacific region. Australia's aid remained stable and on track for an estimated expenditure of A$5 billion in 2013–2014

- Canada (−11.4 percent): due to exceptional payments made in 2012 for climate change and debt relief and to budget cuts affecting 2013
- Iceland (+27.4 percent): it is increasing its aid program
- Japan (+36.6 percent): due to increases in debt forgiveness and bilateral lending
- Korea (+4.8 percent): due to scaling up aid overall
- New Zealand (−1.0 percent): due to an increasing aid program being offset by inflation
- Norway (+16.4 percent): due to planned growth in the development cooperation budget, together with an increase in disbursements to Brazil
- Switzerland (+3.4 percent): reflecting the overall scaling up of its aid to reach 0.5 percent of GNI by 2015

Other donor countries that reported preliminary ODA figures included:

- Estonia (+22.3 percent): due to increases in humanitarian aid and contributions to European Union institutions
- Hungary (−2.1 percent)
- Israel (−6.2 percent)
- Latvia (+12.2 percent)
- Russia (+26.4 percent): due to an increase in bilateral aid
- Turkey (+29.7 percent): continuing the significant expansion of its development cooperation program in recent years; the large increase in 2013 was due in part to the crisis in Syria
- UAE (+375.5 percent): due to exceptional measures to address financial and infrastructure needs in Egypt; its ODA/GNI ratio rose to 1.25 percent, the largest reported share of any country in 2013 (Organization for Economic Cooperation and Development, 2016b)

In 2013, DAC countries' gross ODA (i.e., without deducting for loan repayments) was $151.2 billion, an increase of 9.5 percent in real terms from 2012. Within bilateral gross ODA, nongrant financial instruments rose by 27.3 percent in real terms, representing nearly $18 billion. The largest donors on a gross basis, as in the past, were the United States, Japan, the United Kingdom, Germany, and France (Organization for Economic Cooperation and Development, 2016b).

Patterns of Multilateral Aid and Development Assistance

The World Bank is one of the major leaders in promoting multilateral aid programs of development assistance focused on the elimination of extreme poverty everywhere in the world (World Bank, 2013, 2014a, b, 2016a, b, 2017a,

b) (box 4.7). Other major multilateral actors committed to international development assistance are the United Nations Development Programme (2017a, b), the World Health Organization, the United Nations Office of the High Representative for the Least Developed Countries, Landlocked Developing Countries and Small Island Developing States (2017), the European Union (European Commission, 2017), and the OECD (Organization for Economic Cooperation and Development, 2016b). Nongovernmental and private charitable foundations also play a major role in helping to lift the poor out of poverty.

Since at least 1990, the successes associated with the poverty-reduction programs of these organizations have been remarkable. So, too, have been the contributions made by the previous poor in working collaboratively with these organizations in helping to promote the basic services needed to advance long-term strategies associated with poverty alleviation. Most impressive are the remarkable contributions being made by the previously poor to advancing the economic status of their neighbors and the larger communities of which they are a part.

Such developments were possible only because of the multitiered partnerships that were formed between aid-giving organizations and those who have

---

BOX 4.7   What Is the Difference Between Bilateral and Multilateral Trade Agreements?

Number of Parties:

- A Bilateral Trade Agreement is an agreement signed between two parties or countries.
- In contrast, a Multilateral Trade Agreement is a trade agreement signed between three or more countries.

Purpose

- A Bilateral Trade Agreement is signed in relation to the trade of certain goods, opportunities for the promotion of trade and investment and the reduction of trade barriers.
- The main purpose of a Multilateral Trade Agreement is reducing trade tariffs. Most importantly, Multilateral Trade Agreements guarantee the equal treatment of all nations or parties involved and evenly distribute the risks associated with such Agreements.

(Difference Between.com, 2017)

benefited directly from this aid. The economic gains have been remarkable and most likely would not have occurred without the extensive levels of financial and technical assistance that have been provided to poor people and their families through the carefully thought through strategies adopted by aid-granting organizations. As of 2016, estimates of the level of the financial aid provided to solve global poverty amounted to tens of billions of dollars and, mostly likely, will continue to increase in the future.

Economic Development, Foreign Direct Investment, and Poverty Alleviation

FDI, as described by the New Delhi–based investment firm Fin Gyan (Sehgal, 2017), is, in simplest terms, any investment made by one country in the economy of another.

> FDI usually happens in developing countries by countries that have surplus liquid money in hand. This is a long-term investment whereby corporation of one country makes a major investment to acquire ownership in a commercial venture in another country for control. Further, in cases of FDI, the investor's purpose is to gain an effective voice in the management of the enterprise. For that, at least 10% of equity ownership or voting power of an enterprise is required to qualify an investor as a foreign direct investor. An example of FDI is an Indian company taking a majority stake in a company in America. It includes investment of foreign assets into domestic structures, equipment, and organizations but does not include foreign investment into the stock markets.

FDI investments typically occur between economically advanced and developing countries, albeit many developing countries also invest in the economies of other developing nations who can provide them with critically needed natural resources (box 4.8). The preponderance of FDI inflows are directed to Asia and Latin America and the Caribbean. Substantial FDI inflows, however, also are made into the successor states of the former Soviet Union (to the so-called economies in transition) and to the very large number of developing countries situated in sub-Saharan Africa. FDI flows tend to be highly uneven from one year to the next and depend largely on the financial well-being of the investor countries. In addition to assisting receiving countries in building infrastructure and training their workforce in contemporary approaches to productivity, FDI is intended to serve as a major global policy tool for helping to promote poverty alleviation. Thus, FDI is both a wealth-enrichment approach to economic development for both investor and receiving countries and provides much-needed capital to assist the poor and other chronically unemployed workers to acquire the knowledge and skills to compete successfully in global markets. Apple Corporation's substantial financial and human capital development investments in China, for example, not only help Apple to keep its labor costs in check but also enhance the economic vitality of workers and communities that, otherwise, likely would have been locked out of the mainstream of contemporary economic productivity. FDI in receiving countries is beginning to make possible the ability of line workers to purchase at least a limited quantity of the expensive goods they produce for export. This pattern is consistent with that adopted by Henry Ford in helping to ensure that his assembly line workers could purchase the automobiles that they produced.

In still other countries, FDI approaches to economic development have proven to be highly effective in growing entire industries, creating new jobs, and helping the economies of developing and socially least developing countries to transition from agricultural and extraction industries to urban-based manufacturing and services—the two stable segments of most modern economies. These inflows of foreign investments in developing countries and regions have encouraged the governments of developing nations to allocate a larger share of their resources to research and development initiatives and to support the emergence of more and better health and education systems (Herzer & Nunnenkamp, 2012).

FDI represents a "win-win" strategy for participating nations and for the world at large despite the fluctuations in the levels of new investments that flow from rich to poorer countries. The gains are reflected in the availability of more resources for emerging and developing market economies to grow their economies and for use in promoting increases in national and per capita GDP levels (Al-Sadiq, 2015). Prominent past examples of countries that have benefited from high levels of FDI include Germany, Japan, Singapore, South Korea, Taiwan, and others that have emerged as first-tier economic

---

BOX 4.8   Foreign Direct Investment

Global inflows of foreign direct investment (FDI) fell by 18 percent in 2012 to $1.35 trillion, as the world economy slowed and political uncertainty in some big economies made investors cautious. The European Union alone accounted for two-thirds of this decline. Inflows to developed countries fell by a third to $561 billion, the lowest for almost a decade. Developing countries received 52 percent of global inflows, overtaking rich countries for the first time.

(Economist, 2013)

128

Chapter 4

powerhouses. Today, major beneficiaries of FDI include China, India, Malaysia, the Philippines, Brazil, the Russian Federation, and, in recent years, the newly independent countries of Central Asia, for example, Kazakhstan, Tajikistan, Uzbekistan (International Monetary Fund, 2011).

Along with the other approaches to accelerating the pace of economic growth outlined previously, all nations—rich and poor—are expected to continue to utilize FDI strategies for advancing the status not only of their own but that of other nations as well. Examples of these important economic partnerships include the Association of Southeast Asian Nations, the European Union, the North American Free Trade Association, the Commonwealth of Independent States, and, of course, the World Trade Organization. These economic alliances often exist side by side with important political and military compacts that further foster economic investments in member nations, for example, the North Atlantic Treaty Organization, among many others. A complete list of the memberships of individual countries in regional economic, political, and military partnerships is reported in *The World Factbook* (Central Intelligence Agency, 2017).

DRIVERS OF ECONOMIC ADVANCES IN HUMAN WELL-BEING

There are four major drivers of economic growth: (1) the accumulation of capital stock; (2) increases in labor inputs, such as workers or hours worked; and (3) technological advancements. We have discussed all three of these initial drivers of economic growth throughout the chapter and have provided illustrative examples and evidentiary data that support the inputs, throughputs, and outputs associated with each of these three critical drivers. *Economic well-being*, however, contains a fourth dimension in addition to the three already identified, that is, *people's subjective assessments of their individual economic well-being and that of others with whom they engage*.

In addition to the discussions of the first three drivers of economic growth and economic well-being, we have provided substantial discussions of individual and collective economic well-being. These discussions have taken place within the context of global efforts to improve economic justice and to promote the achievement of progressively higher levels of income equality within and between various groups of income earners. These have not been processes to easily disentangle, but we believe that we have succeeded in doing that. We have drawn extensively for our inspiration in pursuing these topics of national and international social justice and equality on the principles formulated by Paul Krugman (2003), Joseph Stiglitz (2015), Thomas Piketty (2013, 2015), and other leading economists—all of whom deal with economic well-being as a central objective for societies to achieve.

We believe that the rich data presented in this chapter have facilitated our goal toward an improved understanding of the complexities of the many societal forces that are responsible for the economic well-being of their citizens. Ample evidence in support of that objective has been presented in the chapter. Thomas Piketty, a highly influential French economist born after 1960, has provided us with valuable new tools for assessing the extent of global progress in achieving the economic well-being goals that are at the heart of this chapter. The approaches to well-being assessment that he offers also are of great value in understanding the health and education dimensions of well-being as they inform the capacity of consumers to enhance their own economic well-being as well as that of their families, extended kinship systems, communities, and their nations at large. Thus, in our presentation of the major drivers of economic development and economic well-being, we have arrived at a rich understanding of the roles that economic growth, education of the labor force, the health status of the available workforce, and prospective technological developments play in economic well-being.

We have also presented illustrative data covering all aspects of personal and collective well-being, for example, studies focused on individuals and larger collectives of people (Gallup-Sharecare Organization, 2016), national and regional studies of economic well-being (Board of Governors of the Federal Reserve System, 2016; Rojas, 2016), and studies that view economic well-being from a global perspective (Estes, 2015b; Helliwell et al., 2017). Most of these studies have been conducted by research centers located in economically advanced countries, but their findings are equally valid for describing and explaining patterns of economic development and economic well-being in less economically advanced societies as well. These studies draw on the four dimensions of economic well-being as their frame of reference, thereby reflecting a shared understanding of the underlying forces that shape individual and collective economic well-being at all levels of political well-being throughout the world and over a long expanse of human history. These dimensions of economic well-being do not change over time or geographic space. The data provided in this chapter more than amply provide support for these aspects of economic development within different social, political, and economic systems. These dynamics have persisted over long expanses of human history and are likely to continue to do so over at least the near term.

CONCLUSIONS

The world's economy is undergoing profound and rapid changes that are contributing to impressive advances in human economic well-being. These changes are reflected in the high rates of economic growth of many developing countries and in the willingness of already economically advanced countries to assist developing countries in achieving even higher growth rates (International Monetary Fund, 2017b). Progress of this type will add appreciably to the levels of living and quality of life of rich and poor countries, especially as poverty rates in developing countries continue to decline (Cruz et al., 2015; Lozada 2017). The world community has made a commitment to continue strengthening the economic capacity of developing countries and that of poorer countries at a point in history when the economies of developing countries are leading global economic development via increased production, higher levels of consumption, and progressively more equitable patterns of economic distribution for at least some developing countries (International Monetary Fund, 2017a; World Bank, 2014a, 2016a). The world's more economically mature societies are continuing to make even higher financial investments in the economies of developing countries to help them move into fuller economic partnerships among themselves and with economically advanced countries (World Bank, 2014a). This type of assistance is exactly that required by developing nations to bring about increased equity within their borders. Further, the launching of the new United Nations SDGs will serve as a major stimulus in helping the economies of developing countries expand even more rapidly (United Nations Development Programme, 2017b; World Bank, 2017a, b).

A significant portion of this chapter focused on the nature, extent, and complexities of global poverty, especially in its most extreme forms. This focus in a chapter dealing with global economics is justifiable given the hundreds of millions of people worldwide who continue to live in deplorable economic conditions (Collier, 2007; United Nations Development Programme, 2017b). We also concluded that money alone is not the solution to solving the problem of extreme poverty, but carefully targeted capital and resource allocation is a necessary component to any effective effort to alleviate poverty. Today, we are fortunate that many governmental and nongovernmental organizations are investing their financial resources in sustainable approaches to development that recognize the infinitely more complex socioemotional, even cultural, forces that keep the poor trapped in poverty (Theories of poverty, 2017; United Nations Development Programme, 2017a). Thus, the recently adopted approaches to poverty alleviation at the global level make use of financial and sociocultural approaches to the elimination of poverty in all its manifestations. These approaches include subsidized employment opportunities for the poor, bilateral and multilateral aid designed to bring quality health and education services to the poor, international contract labor opportunities, FDI in the economies of developing nations as well as ODA provided by rich countries to economically poorer nations (Sachs, 2006; World Bank, 2016c). Each approach has its own wisdom and levels of effectiveness associated with it, especially when tied to major progress in bringing about fundamental political reform.

Other global actors also are contributing to the growth of developing nations and, in turn, to the elimination of extreme poverty in all its forms but especially through development assistance provided by major international nongovernmental organizations. Business leaders contribute significantly and often can create preferential trade relationships with and between many of the world's socially least developing countries. The combined activities of these aid organizations and business leaders have proven to be essential elements in unraveling the recurrent puzzle of multigenerational poverty (Roser & Ortiz-Ospina, 2017; Shah, 2014a; United Nations Development Programme, 2017a; World Bank, 2013, 2016c).

Though current growth rates are currently lower in economically advanced countries, the growth rates of all nations are expected to increase measurably in response to the increasing numbers of developing countries emerging as full partners with economically advanced countries in the content of current economic arrangements. Growth rates will almost certainly rise in economically advanced countries over at least the near term and are likely to rise even more rapidly over the long term (World Bank, 2016d). Employment levels and the sense of satisfaction that results from secure work are expected to increase everywhere in the world. Savings and investments are expected to rise as well (International Monetary Fund, 2017a) and major technological innovations are expected to increase even more rapidly in response to high investment levels in corporations and a much more skilled workforce. Entirely new industries are expected to emerge in the energy, computer technology, health, and education fields, and more fiscal security for investors will be introduced into global investment markets. Global trade will continue to increase, albeit at a slower than desired pace, but at a high level within and between the economies of developing countries. These innovations will propel rates of economic growth and, at the same time, improve the economic well-being of individual workers, their families, and entire communities. These innovations will be brought about through critical advances in the primary drivers of economic well-being (Vanham, 2015). Major efforts will continue to be needed to steadily increase levels of economic growth for all the world's nations.

Finally, despite the guarded economic prospects that characterize rates of economic growth for some nations, investors and business enterprises remain optimistic that they can contribute to a more positive future for all the world's nations. These more promising prospects for the near term will result in new and important innovations in the productive processes of societies everywhere. Only in this way can we, as a world community, advance the economic status of our own countries and that of others.

We conclude the chapter with the following quote from Thomas Piketty, an economist who is committed to the promotion of social justice through more equitable patterns of economic growth and economic well-being. Piketty wrote in one of his earliest books, *Capital in the Twenty-First Century* (Piketty, 2013):

> Social scientific research is and always will be tentative and imperfect. It does not claim to transform economics, sociology, and history into exact sciences. But by patiently searching for facts and patterns and calmly analyzing the economic, social, and political mechanisms that might explain them, it can inform democratic debate and focus attention on the right questions. It can help to redefine the terms of debate, unmask certain preconceived or fraudulent notions, and subject all positions to constant critical scrutiny. In my view, this is the role that intellectuals, including social scientists, should play, as citizens like any other but with the good fortune to have more time than others to devote themselves to study (and even to be paid for it—a signal privilege).

REFERENCES

Al-Sadiq, A. J. (2015). *The impact of IMF-SUPPORTED PROGRAMS on FDI in low-income countries*. IMF Working Paper WP/15/157. Washington, DC: International Monetary Fund.

Amadeo, K. (2017, March 7). The 2008 financial crisis: Causes, costs and could it reoccur? *The Balance*. Retrieved March 1, 2017, from https://www.thebalance.com/2008-financial-crisis-3305679.

Andersen, T. M., Holmström, B., Honkapohja, S., Korkman, S., Söderström, & Vartiainen, J. (2007). *The Nordic model: Embracing globalization and sharing risks*. Helsinki: The Research Institute of the Finnish Economy. Retrieved June 3, 2017, from http://www.arhiv.svrez.gov.si/fileadmin/svez.gov.si/pageuploads/docs/Strategija_razvoja_Slovenije/The_Nordic_Model.PDF#page=1&zoom=auto,371,608.

Bloom, D. E., & Canning, D. (2005). *Health and economic growth: Reconciling the micro and macro evidence*. UCLA Faculty Working Papers. Los Angeles, CA: UCLA.

Bloom, D. E., Canning, D., & Sevilla, J. (2001). *The effect of health on economic growth: Theory and evidence*. Working Paper 8587. Washington, DC: National Bureau of Economic Research.

Board of Governors of the Federal Reserve System. (2016). *Report on the economic well-being of U.S. households in 2015*. Washington, DC: Board of Governors of the Federal Reserve System. Retrieved May 5, 2017, from https://www.federalreserve.gov/2015-report-economic-well-being-us-households-201605.pdf.

Brookings Institution. (2017). *Briefing book: Tax incentive for the poor*. Tax Policy Center. Washington, DC: Brookings Institution, Tax Policy Center. Retrieved May 20, 2017, from http://www.taxpolicycenter.org/briefing-book/how-does-federal-tax-system-affect-low-income-households.

Central Intelligence Agency. (2017). *The world factbook, 2017*. New York: Skyhorse Publishing. Retrieved July 2, 2017, from https://www.cia.gov/library/publications/the-world-factbook/.

Clark, A., & Senik, C. (2017). *Happiness and economic growth: Lessons from developing countries*. Oxford: Oxford University Press.

Collier, P. (2007). *The bottom billion: Why the poorest countries are failing and what can be done about it*. New York: Oxford University Press.

Cruz, M., Quillin, B., & Schellekens, P. (2015). *The three major challenges to ending extreme poverty*. Washington, DC: World Bank.

de Rugy, V. (2015). Foreign aid is a failure: Throwing good money at bad governments makes poor countries worse off. [Web site]. Retrieved January 30, 2017, from http://reason.com/archives/2014/12/08/foreign-aid-is-a-failure.

Development aid. (2017, June 28). In Wikipedia, the Free Encyclopedia. Retrieved July 2, 2017, from https://en.wikipedia.org/w/index.php?title=Development_aid&oldid=787984076.

Difference Between.com. (2017). What is the difference between bilateral and multilateral trade agreements? [Web-based knowledge hub]. Retrieved July 2, 2017, from http://www.differencebetween.com/difference-between-bilateral-and-vs-multilateral-trade-agreements/.

Dodini, S. (2016, June 29). Findings on relative deprivation from the survey of household economics and decision-making. *Fed Notes*. Washington, DC: Board of Governors of the Federal Reserve. Retrieved April 9, 2017, from https://www.federalreserve.gov/econresdata/notes/feds-notes/2016/findings-on-relative-deprivation-from-the-survey-of-household-economics-and-decisionmaking-20160629.html.

Durden, T. (2013, June 4). The debt of nations. [Blog post]. Retrieved June 20, 2017, from http://www.zerohedge.com/news/2013-06-04/debt-nations.

Easterlin, R. A. (1974). Does economic growth improve the human lot? Some empirical evidence. In P. A. David & M. W. Redder (Eds.), *Nations and households in economic growth: Essays in honor of Moses Abramowitz*. New York: Academic Press, Inc.

Economist. (2013, June 29). Foreign direct investment by major world region, 2007–2012. Retrieved January 13, 2017, from http://www.economist.com/news/economic-and-financial-indicators/21580200-foreign-direct-investment.

Essa, A. (2015, August 6). Migrant crisis a failure of European policy, UN says. *Humanitarian Crisis*. Retrieved July 3, 2017, from http://www.aljazeera.com/news/2015/08/migrant-crisis-failure-european-policy-150806172330199.html.

Estes, R. J. (1999). "Poverties" and "wealth": Competing definitions and alternative approaches to measurement. *Social Development Issues*, 21(2), 11–21.

Estes, R. J. (2012). "Failed" and "failing" states: Is quality of life possible?" In K. Land, A. C. Michalos, & M. Joseph Sirgy (Eds.), *Handbook of quality of life research*. Dordrecht, NL: Springer.

Estes, R. J. (2014). The Index of Social Progress. In A. C. Michalos (Ed.), *Encyclopedia of quality of life and well-being research*. Dordrecht, NL: Springer.

Estes, R. J. (2015a). Global change and quality of life indicators. In F. Maggino (Ed.), *A life devoted to quality of life: Festschrift in honor of Alex C. Michalos*. Dordrecht, NL: Springer.

Estes, R. J. (2015b). Development trends among the world's socially least developed countries: reasons for cautious optimism. In B. Spooner (Ed.), *Globalization: The crucial phase*. Philadelphia: University of Pennsylvania Press.

European Commission. (2017). International cooperation and development. [Web site]. Retrieved March 29, 2017, from https://ec.europa.eu/europeaid/home_en.

Federal Reserve System. (2016). *Relative deprivation from the survey of household economics and decision-making*. Washington, DC: Federal Reserve System.

Fox, J. (2012). The economics of well-being. *Harvard Business Review*, *90*(1–2):78–83.

Frank, R. H. (2007). *Falling behind: How rising inequality harms the middle class*. Berkeley, CA: University of California Press.

Freedom House. (2017). *Freedom in the world*. New York: Freedom House.

Galasso, V. N. (2013). *The drivers of economic inequality: A primer*. Washington, DC: Oxfam USA. Retrieved April 3, 2017, from https://www.oxfamamerica.org/static/media/files/oxfam-drivers-of-economic-inequality.pdf.

Gallup-Shareware. (2016). About the Gallup-Sharecare Well-Being Index. Retrieved May 1, 2017, from http://www.well-beingindex.com/about.

Geithner, T. (2015). *Stress test: Reflections on financial crises*. New York: Broadway Books.

Gourevitch P. (2008). The role of politics in economic development. *Annual Review of Political Science*, 11:137–159.

Graham, C. (2012). *Happiness around the world: The paradox of happy peasants and miserable millionaires*. New York: Oxford University Press.

Hanushek, E. A. (2013). *Economic growth in developing countries: The role of human capital*. Palo Alto: Hoover Institution.

Hartmann, T. (2007). *Screwed: The undeclared war against the middle class—and what we can do about it*. Oakland: Berrett-Koehler Publishers.

Helliwell, J., Layard, R., & Sachs, J. (2017). *World happiness report, 2017*. New York: Sustainable Development Solutions Network.

Herzer, D., & Nunnenkamp, P. (2012, November 26). *FDI and health in developed economies: A panel cointegration analysis*. Working Paper No. 1756. Kiel: Kiel Institute for the World Economy. https://www.weforum.org/agenda/2015/11/5-trends-for-the-future-of-economic-growth.

International Fund for Agricultural Development. (2016). *Reaching the rural poor*. Rome: IFAD. Retrieved from January 23, 2017, https://www.ifad.org/documents/10180/dc9da3d9-b603-4a9a-ba67-e248b39cb34f.

International Monetary Fund. (2011). *Caucasus and Central Asia: Safeguarding the recovery*. Washington, DC: International Monetary Fund.

International Monetary Fund. (2016). *World economic outlook (WEO) update: 2016*. Uncertainty in the aftermath of the U.K. referendum. Retrieved July 1, 2017, from http://www.imf.org/external/pubs/ft/weo/2016/update/02/.

International Monetary Fund. (2017a). *Comparative world economic outlook, 2018*. Retrieved April 4, 2017, from http://world-economic-outlook.findthedata.com/.

International Monetary Fund. (2017b). *IMF data mapper*. Washington, DC: International Monetary Fund. Retrieved April 4, 2017, from http://www.imf.org/external/datamapper/NGDP_RPCH@WEO/OEMDC/ADVEC/WEOWORLD.

International Social Security Association. (2017). *Social security programs through-out the world*. Geneva: ISSA. Retrieved May 16, 2017, from https://www.issa.int/en/ssptw.

Investopedia. (2017). Purchasing power parity (PPP). Retrieved June 2, 2017, from http://www.gallup.com/poll/166211/worldwide-median-household-income-000.aspx.

Italian National Institute of Statistics. (2017). *The 12 dimensions of well-being*. Rome: Italian National Institute of Statistics. Retrieved May 17, 2017, from http://www.istat.it/en/well-being-and-sustainability/well-being-measures/12-dimensions-of-well-being.

Kilmister, M. (2016, October 18). *Development in action. Bilateral vs multilateral aid*. Retrieved April 7, 2017, from http://www.developmentinaction.org/bilateral-vs-multilateral-aid/.

Kimelman, M. (2017). *Confessions of a Wall Street insider: A cautionary tale of rats, Feds, and banisters*. New York: Skyhorse Press.

Krugman, P. (2003). *The great unraveling: Losing our way in the new century*. New York: W.W. Norton.

Kwan, C.H. (2002). *The rise of China and Asia's flying-geese pattern of economic development: An empirical analysis based on US import statistics*. NRI Papers #52. Retrieved June 30, 2017, from http://www.nri.com/global/opinion/papers/2002/pdf/np200252.pdf.

Lawrence, S., & Mukai, R. (2010). International grantmaking update: A snapshot of U.S. foundation trends. IssueLab: A Service of the Foundation Center. New York: Foundation Center. Retrieved June 29, 2017, from http://www.issuelab.org/resource/international_grantmaking_update_a_snapshot_of_u_s_foundation_trends.

Layard, R. (2017). *Making personal happiness and wellbeing a goal of public policy*. London: London School of Economics. Retrieved May 15, 2017, from http://www.lse.ac.uk/researchAndExpertise/researchImpact/caseStudies/layard-happiness-wellbeing-public-policy.aspx.

Lozada, C. (2017). *Economic growth is reducing global poverty*. Washington, DC: National Bureau of Economic Research. Retrieved April 1, 2017, from http://www.nber.org/digest/oct02/w8933.html.

Mara, I., Narazani, E., Saban, N., Stojilovska, A., Yusufi, I., & Zuber, S. (2012, March 25). Analysis of literature on the effects of remittances on education and health of family members left behind. *Regional Research Promotion Programme in the Western Balkans (RRPP)*. Retrieved March 16, 2017, from http://www.analyticamk.org/images/stories/files/2012002.pdf.

Migration Policy Institute (2016). *Remittance profiles: Top receiving countries*. Retrieved January 3, 2017, from http://www.migrationpolicy.org/programs/data-hub/remittance-profiles-top-receiving-countries.

Mill, J. S. (1848). *Principles of political economy*. London: John W. Parker.

More, T. (1516/1967). *Utopia*. In J. J. Greene, J. P. Dolan (Eds.), & J. P. Dolan (Trans.). *The essential Thomas More*. New York: New American Library.

Moyo, D. (2010). *Dead aid: Why aid is not working and how there is a better way for Africa*. New York: Farrar, Straus and Giroux.

Myers, J. (2016). *Which are the world's fastest-growing economies?* Geneva: World Economic Forum. Retrieved July 1, 2017, from https://www.weforum.org/agenda/2016/04/worlds-fastest-growing-economies/.

Nations Borders Identities Conflicts. (2017). *Immigrations conflicts*. UNC Digital Commons. Retrieved June 30, 2017, from http://nbiconflict.web.unc.edu/conflicts/immigration-conflicts/.

Organization for Economic Cooperation and Development. (2006). *International migrant remittances and their role in development. International Migration Outlook*. Paris: Organization for Economic Cooperation and Development. Retrieved April 5, 2017, from http://www.oecd.org/els/mig/38840502.pdf.

Organization for Economic Cooperation and Development. (2013). *Measuring well-being and progress*. Paris: Organization for Economic Cooperation and Development.

Organization for Economic Cooperation and Development. (2015). *Net official development assistance by country as a percentage of gross national income in 2015*. Retrieved April 15, 2017, from https://en.wikipedia.org/wiki/List_of_development_aid_country_donors.

Organization for Economic Cooperation and Development. (2016a). *Gross domestic product (in current US dollars)*. Retrieved February 15, 2017, from http://data.worldbank.org/indicator/NY.GDP.PCAP.CD.

Organization for Economic Cooperation and Development. (2016b). *International development assistance*. Paris: Organization for Economic Cooperation and Development.

Organization for Economic Cooperation and Development. (2016c). *Development cooperation report 2016: The Sustainable Development Goals as business opportunities*. Paris: Organization for Economic Cooperation and Development.

Organization for Economic Cooperation and Development. (2017a). *Development aid rises again in 2016 but flows to poorest countries dip*. Paris: Organization for Economic Cooperation and Development. Retrieved July 2, 2017, from http://www.oecd.org/development/stats/development-aid-rises-again-in-2016-but-flows-to-poorest-countries-dip.htm.

Organization for Economic Cooperation and Development. (2017b). *Economy: Developing countries set to account for nearly 60% of world GDP by 2030, according to new estimates*. Paris: Organization for Economic Cooperation and Development.

Paine, T. (1791/1999). *The rights of man*. UK: Dover Publishers.

Pettinger, T. (2013). *Economic impact of migrants and remittances. Helping to simplify economics*. Retrieved February 12, 2017, from http://www.economicshelp.org/blog/6784/economics/economic-impact-of-migrants/.

Phelps, G., & Crabtree, S. (2013, December 16). Worldwide, Median Household Income About $10,000. World. Retrieved June 2, 2017, from http://www.gallup.com/poll/166211/worldwide-median-household-income-000.aspx.

Piketty, T. (2013). *Capital in the twenty-first century*. (A. Goldhammer, Trans.). Cambridge, MA: Harvard University Press.

Piketty, T. (2015). *The economics of inequality*. (A. Goldhammer, Trans.). Cambridge, MA: Harvard University Press.

Reference. (2017). What is economic well-being? [Web knowledge hub]. Oakland, CA: IAC Publishing Labs. Retrieved July 2, 2017, from reference.com/business-finance/economic-well-being-909c020bab9e11b1.

Reisinger, J. (2014, April 3). Why only one top banker went to jail for the financial crisis. *New York Times.* Retrieved April 16, 2017, from https://www.nytimes.com/2014/05/04/magazine/only-one-top-banker-jail-financial-crisis.html?_r=0.

Rikken, M. (2016). *Two in one: Differences in the US Justice System for the rich and the poor.* Washington, DC: The Sentencing Project.

Rojas, M. (Ed.) (2016). *Handbook of happiness research in Latin America.* Dordrecht, NL: Springer.

Roser, M., & Ortiz-Ospina, E. (2017). Global extreme poverty. [Blog post]. Retrieved April 20, 2017, from https://ourworldindata.org/extreme-poverty/.

Russell, B. (1918). *Roads to freedom. Socialism, anarchism and syndicalism.* London: Unwin Books.

Ryder, H. (2017). The end of poverty in China. *Project Syndicate: The World's Opinion Page.* March 28. Retrieved April 5, 2017, from https://www.project-syndicate.org/commentary/china-end-rural-poverty-by-2020-by-hannah-ryder-1-2017-03

Sachs, J. (2006). *The end of poverty: Economic possibilities for our time.* London and New York: Penguin Books.

Sehgal, N. (2017). What is foreign direct investment? [Blog post]. Retrieved April 2, 2017, from http://www.fingyan.com/what-is-fd/.

Selian, A. N., & McKnight, L. (2017). Technology and the history of well-being. In R. J. Estes & M. J. Sirgy (2017). *The pursuit of human well-being: The untold global history.* Dordrecht, NL: Springer.

Shah, A. (2014a, September 28). Causes of poverty. Global Issues. Retrieved March 8, 2017, from http://www.globalissues.org/issue/2/causes-of-poverty.

Shah, A. (2014b, September 28). Foreign aid for development assistance. Global Issues. Retrieved April 1, 2017, from http://www.globalissues.org/article/35/foreign-aid-development-assistance.

Sirgy, M. Joseph (2012). *The psychology of quality of life: Hedonic well-being, life satisfaction, and eudaimonia* (2nd ed). Dordrecht, NL: Springer.

Smart J. E., & Casco, R. R. (1988). A global perspective on foreign contract labor. *Asian Migrant, 1*(1):8–12.

Srinivasan, T. N. (2009). *Trade, growth and poverty reduction: Least developed countries, landlocked developing countries and small states in the global economic system.* London: Commonwealth Secretariat.

Stiglitz, J. (2015). *The great divide: Unequal societies and what we can do about them.* New York: W.W. Norton & Company.

Subprime mortgage crisis. (2017, July 2). In Wikipedia, the Free Encyclopedia. Retrieved July 2, 2017, from https://en.wikipedia.org/w/index.php?title=Subprime_mortgage_crisis&oldid=788550384.

Taylor, L. (2009). *Growth, development policy, job creation and poverty reduction.* DESA Working Paper No. 90. ST/ESA/2009/DWP/90. New York: United Nations Department of Economic and Social Affairs. Retrieved March 30, 2017, from http://www.un.org/esa/desa/papers/2009/wp90_2009.pdf.

Theories of poverty. (2017, May 28). In Wikipedia, the Free Encyclopedia. Retrieved July 2, 2017, from https://en.wikipedia.org/w/index.php?title=Theories_of_poverty&oldid=782617400.

Thompson, D. (2012, May 31). The 10 things economics can tell us about happiness. *The Atlantic*. Retrieved May 17, 2017, from https://www.theatlantic.com/business/archive/2012/05/the-10-things-economics-can-tell-us-about-happiness/257947/.

Todaro, M. P., & Smith, S. C. (2012). *Economic development* (11th ed.). New York: Pearson.

United Nations. (1970). *Resolution adopted by the General Assembly*. 2626 (XXV). International Development Strategy for the Second United Nations Development Decade. [UN Documents: Gathering a body of global agreements]. Retrieved July 2, 2017, from http://www.un-documents.net/a25r2626.htm.

United Nations Conference on Trade and Development. (2013). *Trade and development report, 2013*. Geneva: United Nations Conference on Trade and Development. Retrieved July 6, 2017, from http://unctad.org/en/PublicationsLibrary/tdr2013_en.pdf.

United Nations Conference on Trade and Development. (2017). *World investment report, 2017*. Geneva: United Nations Conference on Trade and Development. Annex Table 1. Retrieved July 4, 2017, from http://unctad.org/en/Pages/DIAE/World%20Investment%20Report/Annex-Tables.aspx.

United Nations Department of Economic and Social Affairs. (2017). *Sustainable development knowledge platform*. New York: United Nations Department of Economic and Social Affairs.

United Nations Development Programme. (1992). *Human development report, 1992: Global dimensions of human development*. New York: United Nations Development Programme.

United Nations Development Programme. (2017a). *Human development report, 2017: Human development for everyone*. New York: United Nations Development Programme.

United Nations Development Programme. (2017b). *The sustainable development goals*. Retrieved January 10, 2017, from http://www.un.org/sustainabledevelopment/sustainable-development-goals/.

United Nations Education, Scientific and Cultural Organization. (2017). Education. In *Education for all*. Paris: United Nations Education, Scientific and Cultural Organization. Retrieved May 5, 2017, from http://www.unesco.org/new/en/education/themes/leading-the-international-agenda/education-for-all/resources/statistics/.

United Nations Office of the High Representative for the Least Developed Countries, Landlocked Developing Countries and Small Island Developing States. (2017). UN-OHRLLS: UN Office of the High Representative for the Least Developed Countries, Landlocked Developing Countries and Small Island Developing States. [Organization Web site]. Retrieved July 2, 2017, from http://unohrlls.org/.

United States Agency for International Development. (2007). *Foreign direct investment: Putting it to work in developing countries*. Retrieved July 2, 2017, from http://pdf.usaid.gov/pdf_docs/Pnadj943.pdf.

United States Bureau of the Census. (2017). *Well-being*. Washington, DC: Census Bureau. Retrieved July 3, 2017, from https://www.census.gov/topics/income-poverty/well-being.html.

Vanham, P. (2015). *5 Trends for the future of economic growth*. Geneva: World Economic Forum. Retrieved July 3, 2017, from https://www.scribd.com/document/307808653/5-Trends-for-the-Future-of-Economic-Growth-Agenda-The-World-Economic-Forum.

Veenhoven, R. (2017). World database of subjective happiness studies. Rotterdam: Erasmus University of Rotterdam. [Database archive]. Retrieved May 5, 2017, from http://worlddatabaseofhappiness.eur.nl/.

Vella, M. (2017, April 13). Universal basic income: A utopian idea whose time may finally have arrived. *Time*. Retrieved April 24, 2017, from http://time.com/4737956/universal-basic-income/.

World Bank. (2010). *World development report, 2010: Development and climate change*. Retrieved January 12, 2017, from. http://documents.worldbank.org/curated/en/201001468159913657/World-development-report-2010-development-and-climate-change.

World Bank. (2013, June 4). World Bank aims to eliminate extreme poverty by 2030. *The Huffington Post*. Retrieved April 15, 2017, from http://www.huffingtonpost.com/2013/04/02/world-bank-extreme-poverty_n_2999287.html.

World Bank. (2014a). *Ending poverty requires more than growth, says WBG*. Retrieved April 15, 2017, from http://www.worldbank.org/en/news/press-release/2014/04/10/ending-poverty-requires-more-than-growth-says-wbg.

World Bank. (2014b, April 11). *Remittances to developing countries to stay robust this year, despite increased deportations of migrant workers, says WB*. [Press release]. Retrieved April 15, 2017, from http://www.worldbank.org/en/news/press-release/2014/04/11/remittances-developing-countries-deportations-migrant-workers-wb.

World Bank. (2016a). *Latin America and the Caribbean overview*. Washington, DC: World Bank Group.

World Bank. (2016b). *Migration and remittances: Recent developments and outlook. Migration and Development Brief*, No. 26. Washington, DC: World Bank Group

World Bank. (2016c). *Poverty and shared prosperity, 2016*. Washington, DC: World Bank Group.

World Bank. (2016d). *World development indicators*. Washington, DC: World Bank Group.

World Bank. (2016e). *World development report, 2016*. Washington, DC: World Bank Group.

World Bank. (2017a). *Global economic prospects, 2017: Weak investment in uncertain times*. Washington, DC: World Bank.

World Bank. (2017b). *Poverty: Overview*. Washington, DC: World Bank.

World Business Council for Social Development. (2017). *How we drive sustainable development*. [Organization Web site]. Homepage. Retrieved April 15, 2017, from http://www.wbcsd.org/

World Health Organization. (2016a). *World health statistics 2016: Monitoring health for the SDGs*. Geneva: World Health Organization.

World Health Organization. (2016b). *Drug resistant TB: Resources*. Geneva: World Health Organization.

World Values Survey. (2015). *World Values Survey: Wave 7*. (Database). Retrieved July 3, 2017, from http://www.worldvaluessurvey.org/WVSContents.jsp.

Zhou, H., Zhang, J., & Zhang, M. (2014). *Foreign aid in China*. Dordrecht, NL: Springer.

NOTES

1 Developing and socially least developing countries represent the poorest and weakest segment of the international community. They comprise more than 880 million people (about 12 percent of the world population) but account for less than 2 percent of the world GDP and about 1 percent of global trade in goods (United Nations Office of the High Representative for the Least Developed Countries, Landlocked Developing Countries and Small Island Developing States, 2017).

2 The Commonwealth of Independent States is a regional organization formed during the dissolution of the Soviet Union. The current group of members includes Azerbaijan, Armenia, Belarus, Georgia, Kazakhstan, Kyrgyzstan, Moldova, Russia, Tajikistan, Turkmenistan, Uzbekistan, and Ukraine.

3 The Eurozone is a geographic and economic region that includes all of the European Union countries that have fully incorporated the euro as their national currency. These countries currently include Austria, Belgium, Finland, France, Germany, Greece, Ireland, Italy, Luxembourg, the Netherlands, Portugal, and Spain.

4 Socially least developed countries (SLDCs) represent the poorest segment of the international community. These countries contain more than 880 million people (about 12 percent of the world population) but account for less than 2 percent of the world's GDP and about 1 percent of global trade in goods (United Nations Office of the High Representative for the Least Developed Countries, Landlocked Developing Countries and Small Island Developing States, 2017).

5 The Nordic model (also called Nordic capitalism or Nordic social democracy) refers to the economic and social policies common to Denmark, Norway, Iceland, and Sweden that include a combination of free market capitalism with a comprehensive welfare state and collective bargaining at the national level (Andersen et al., 2007).

6 http://www.imf.org/external/datamapper/NGDP_RPCH@WEO/OEMDC/ ADVEC/WEOWORLD/

7 Contract labor refers to someone who is hired to perform a specific job but is not an employee of the hiring agency. The contract laborer is responsible for reporting taxes, carrying insurance, and paying any expenses associated with completing the assigned task.

8 A remittance is a transfer of money by a foreign worker to an individual in his or her home country. Money sent home by migrants competes with international aid as one of the largest financial inflows to developing countries. Workers' remittances are a significant part of international capital flows, especially for labor-exporting countries.

9 "Advanced economies" is a term used by the International Monetary Fund to describe countries that have a high level of per capita income as well as a significant degree of industrialization.

10 The thirty-four member-states of the OECD in 2017 are Australia, Austria, Belgium, Canada, Chile, Czech Republic, Denmark, Estonia, Finland, France, Germany, Greece, Hungary, Iceland, Ireland, Israel, Italy, Japan, South Korea, Luxembourg, Mexico, Netherlands, New Zealand, Norway, Poland, Portugal, Slovak Republic, Slovenia, Spain, Sweden, Switzerland, Turkey, United Kingdom, and the United States.

11 "Emerging markets" and "developing countries" have some characteristics of a developed market but do not meet the standards to be a developed market. These countries may become developed markets in the future or were in the past. The term "frontier market" is used for developing countries with slower economies than "emerging." The economies of China and India are the largest. Brazil and the Russian Federation often are considered part of the emerging market group.

12 Purchasing power parity is a theory in economics that approximates the total adjustment that must be made on the currency exchange rate between countries that allows the exchange to be equal to the purchasing power of each country's currency (Investopedia, 2017). The price for a pound of rice is equalized using purchasing power parity for different countries for which the actual prices for the rice vary.

13 Theories on the causes of poverty are the foundation upon which poverty-reduction strategies are based. Whereas in developed nations, poverty is often seen as either a personal or a structural defect, in developing nations the issue of poverty is more profound due to the lack of governmental funds. Some theories on poverty in the developing world focus on cultural characteristics as a retardant of further development. Other theories focus on social and political aspects that perpetuate poverty; perceptions of the poor have a significant impact on the design and execution of programs to alleviate poverty (Subprime mortgage crisis, 2017).

14 The GNI is the total domestic and foreign output claimed by residents of a country, consisting of GDP plus incomes earned by foreign residents, minus income earned in the domestic economy by nonresidents (Todaro & Smith, 2012).

Chapter 5

Education

Dramatic Gains in Educational Well-Being

Education as a cornerstone of human well-being is perhaps one of the most interesting and dramatic areas of research depicting change over time. This chapter focuses on educational well-being and documents the progress that has occurred in this domain since 1990 (box 5.1). We explore the trends of educational well-being, the causes of these trends, and their effects on other dimensions of well-being such as economic, social, and health well-being. The chapter provides evidence of marked gains in educational well-being worldwide. Furthermore, the evidence suggests that the rate of growth of educational well-being is greater in some world regions than in others. The chapter presents elements of educational well-being throughout history over the long term but especially since the 1970s, given the fact that world data have been gathered reliably and systematically only since then.

The chapter also describes studies of how education is treated as a human rights issue and of the development theories that consider the role of education in improving the quality of life of people and countries. We present an analysis of educational well-being focusing on specific population groups such as women and the disabled. We also discuss public policy issues related to education. Specifically, we present the argument that policies designed to

---

BOX 5.1

When asked how much educated men were superior to those uneducated, Aristotle answered, "As much as the living are to the dead."
Diogenes Laertius (c. 200 AD) (Smith, 1848)

---

improve education, learning, and innovation can enhance the quality of life of people and countries in significant and remarkable ways.

EDUCATION AS A HUMAN RIGHTS ISSUE

Article 26 of the *Universal Declaration of Human Rights*, adopted by the United Nations General Assembly in Paris on December 10, 1948 (United Nations, 1948), states:

> (1) Everyone has the right to education. Education shall be free, at least in the elementary and fundamental stages. Elementary education shall be compulsory. Technical and professional education shall be made generally available and higher education shall be equally accessible to all based on merit. (2) Education shall be directed to the full development of the human personality and to the strengthening of respect for human rights and fundamental freedoms. It shall promote understanding, tolerance and friendship among all nations, racial or religious groups, and shall further the activities of the United Nations for the maintenance of peace. (3) Parents have a prior right to choose the kind of education that shall be given to their children.

In other words, education is considered a human rights issue. Again, in 1952, the *European Convention on Human Rights* declared that education is a human right in its Protocol/Article 2.

> No person shall be denied the right to education. In the exercise of any functions which it assumes in relation to education and to teaching, the State shall respect the right of parents to ensure such education and teaching in conformity with their own religious and philosophical convictions.
> —(European Court of Human Rights, 2010)

In 1966, the United Nations also declared education as an important human right through the inclusion of Article 13 of the *United Nations' International Covenant on Economic, Social and Cultural Rights*. In this context, this declaration of education as a human right is more articulate (United Nations Office of the High Commissioner, 1976):

> 1. The States Parties to the present Covenant recognize the right of everyone to education. They agree that education shall be directed to the full development of the human personality and the sense of its dignity, and shall strengthen the respect for human rights and fundamental freedoms. They further agree that education shall enable all persons to participate effectively in a free society, promote understanding, tolerance and friendship among all nations and all racial,

ethnic or religious groups, and further the activities of the United Nations for the maintenance of peace.

2. The States Parties to the present Covenant recognize that, with a view to achieving the full realization of this right:

(a) Primary education shall be compulsory and available free to all; (b) Secondary education in its different forms, including technical and vocational secondary education, shall be made generally available and accessible to all by every appropriate means, and by the progressive introduction of free education; (c) Higher education shall be made equally accessible to all, based on capacity, by every appropriate means, and by the progressive introduction of free education; (d) Fundamental education shall be encouraged or intensified as far as possible for those persons who have not received or completed the whole period of their primary education; (e) The development of a system of schools at all levels shall be actively pursued, an adequate fellowship system shall be established, and the material conditions of teaching staff shall be continuously improved.

3. The States Parties to the present Covenant undertake to have respect for the liberty of parents and, when applicable, legal guardians to choose for their children schools, other than those established by the public authorities, which conform to such minimum educational standards as may be laid down or approved by the State and to ensure the religious and moral education of their children in conformity with their own convictions.

4. No part of this article shall be construed so as to interfere with the liberty of individuals and bodies to establish and direct educational institutions, subject always to the observance of the principles set forth in paragraph 1 of this article and to the requirement that the education given in such institutions shall conform to such minimum standards as may be laid down by the State.

A world conference on *Education for All* was held in March 1990 in Jomtien, Thailand. One-hundred-and-sixty governmental and nongovernmental agencies were represented at the conference. The conference delegates adopted a declaration that reaffirmed the notion of education as a fundamental human right. In April 2000, the delegates at the *World Education Forum* (convened in Dakar, Senegal) reaffirmed the notion that education is a human right, which means that every child must be provided with a primary school education. At the same gathering, the 1,100 delegates also addressed the issue of inclusion—that all children, including those who are afflicted with disabilities, should be provided with a primary school education. It is a human rights issue (Peters, 2007).[1]

HUMAN CAPITAL THEORY, THE BASIC NEEDS
APPROACH TO INTERNATIONAL DEVELOPMENT,
AND HUMAN DEVELOPMENT THEORY

Many development economists have used *human capital theory* to argue that educational development is a tool of economic growth (e.g., Becker, 1993; Schultz, 1971). Human capital theory (see literature review in Adelman, 2000) states that education contributes to economic development by enhancing workers' knowledge and skill level. Education is not an expense or a consumption element; instead, it is considered an investment for future income. Human capital theory paved the way to the *basic needs approach* of development economists (e.g., Streeten, 1981). "Basic needs are not primarily a welfare concept; improved education and health can make a major contribution to increased productivity" (Streeten, 1981, p. 3). Thus, the basic needs approach to development incorporates education explicitly (captured in terms of literacy and primary school enrollment). Other elements of the basic needs approach include health (captured using life expectancy at birth as a major indicator), food (calorie consumption per person), water supply (infant mortality per thousand births and percentage of the population with access to potable water), and sanitation (infant mortality and percentage of the population with access to sanitation facilities) (Streeten, 1981, p. 93).

Building on the basic needs approach in international development, Amartya Sen (2000, 2002a, 2002b) offered a more all-encompassing perspective of international development, namely, *human development theory* (also known as "the human capability approach"). Based on human development theory, education plays a central role in development. His view on development can be captured succinctly in the following quote:

> Development can be seen, it is argued here, as a process of expanding the real freedoms that people enjoy. Focusing on human freedoms contrasts with narrower views of development, such as identifying development with the growth of gross national products . . . Growth of GNP or of individual incomes can, of course, be very important as *means* to expanding the freedoms enjoyed by the members of the society. But freedoms depend also on other determinants, such as social and economic arrangements (for example, facilities for *education* [italic added for special emphasis] and health care) as well as political and civil rights (for example, the liberty to participate in public discussion and scrutiny).
> —(Sen, 2000, p.3)

In other words, human freedom is a direct function of three factors of development: educational, health, and economic arrangements. Human freedom can be achieved by the *ability* to realize one's own well-being. Educational arrangements enable the individual to improve his or her own well-being. Sen makes the distinction between "functioning" and "capability." Well-being is viewed as a goal of development and is judged through functioning. A *functioning* is essentially a choice that the individual makes designed to enhance his or her well-being. It can be construed as an achievement—what the individual manages to do or be. A capability is a choice made to achieve functioning. Education is a form of capability to allow the individual to improve his or her functioning, thus his or her state of well-being. Educational attainment is indeed one of the three dimensions in the Human Development Index (HDI), an index devised from Sen's theory, namely, human development theory (United Nations Development Programme, 1990, 1992). Indicators used to capture educational attainment are primary school enrollment, secondary school enrollment, and tertiary school enrollment.

EDUCATIONAL WELL-BEING FRAMEWORK

Figure 5.1 shows a framework we use to study and organize our thoughts concerning educational well-being. This framework delineates an important distinction between educational well-being outcomes, antecedents, and consequences. Educational well-being outcomes (the middle box) essentially represent the desired state of education around the world. That is, outcomes are goals reflecting the final state of an educational system in a country or world region. These educational outcomes can be viewed in terms of two dimensions: quantity and quality. The quantity dimension of educational well-being refers to the number of people who are counted as "educated" based on schooling standards. In this vein, average years of total schooling (age fifteen plus) may be treated as a good "quantity" indicator of educational well-being. A variation of such an indicator is average level of education achieved. For example, an average of twelve years may signify that the average person in each country has achieved a high school diploma; an average of fourteen years may signify a two-year college degree; sixteen years may reflect a four-year college degree, and so on. Other quantity indicators may include the number of people who have completed primary school (ages six to nine), lower secondary school (ages ten to thirteen), upper secondary school (ages fourteen to eighteen), and tertiary school (ages eighteen plus). Tertiary education refers to postsecondary schools such as vocational/trade schools, community colleges, and universities offering bachelor, master, and doctoral degrees. Of course, more refined measures of tertiary education are further broken down in terms of associate degrees, bachelor degrees, master degrees, doctoral degrees, and other postgraduate degrees. In this instance, a country or world region registering high levels of school completion is viewed as having higher levels of educational well-being outcomes compared to those registering lower levels of school completion.

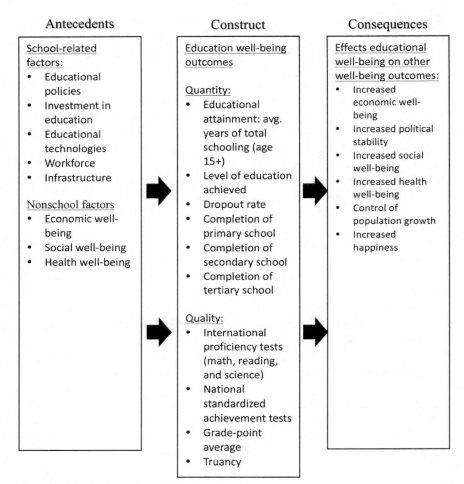

Antecedents   Construct   Consequences

Figure 5.1.   Educational well-being framework

The second dimension of educational well-being (figure 5.1, middle box) focuses on quality rather than quantity. Quality, as an indicator of educational well-being, reflects learning. In this context, quality education is viewed in terms of mastering levels of proficiency in mathematics, reading, and science. Countries or world regions that register higher levels of learning proficiency in mathematics, reading, and science are considered to have higher levels of educational well-being outcomes compared to those registering lower levels of learning proficiency. It should be noted that statistics for quality indicators of educational well-being are collected at both national and international levels. International agencies that administer educational achievement tests (mathematics, reading, and science tests) include the Programme for International Student Assessment (PISA), Trends in International Mathematics and Science Study (TIMSS), and the Progress in International Reading Literacy Study. Additionally, most countries around the world have their own standardized achievement tests.

As shown in figure 5.1, the "quantity" dimension of educational well-being is influenced by a host of school-related factors as well as nonschool factors. *School-related factors* include educational policies, investment in education, educational technologies, workforce issues, and school infrastructure. Quantity and quality of education (and the factors influencing them directly) are influenced by *educational policies* of all types. There are policies regarding compulsory education, discrimination against certain groups, admission standards, caps, funding, recruitment of instructors, instructor evaluations, and many others. These policies affect the educational landscape in many ways. They must be accounted for in comparing educational well-being across countries and world regions. Some policies are specifically designed to enhance the opportunity, the ability, and the motivation to enroll in educational institutions, resulting in higher levels of educational attainment. These policies must be identified, and countries having these policies may be rated higher in educational well-being than countries not having these policies. Similarly, policies are formulated to enhance the opportunity, the ability, and the motivation to learn content and enhance language, mathematics, and science proficiency. These policies must be identified too, and countries having these policies may be rated higher in educational well-being than those not having those policies.

Investment in education is another major school-related factor impacting the quantity and quality dimensions of educational well-being. For example, for many reasons, countries that invest higher levels of gross domestic product (GDP) (per capita) in education are likely to score higher on both the quantity and quality dimensions of educational well-being. A country that spends increasingly more of its government budget on education probably provides greater opportunities for its students to enroll in educational institutions and attain higher levels of schooling than countries that have allocated decreasing amounts to the education sector. Such investment in education is likely to result in higher levels of educational attainment.

Educational technologies are another significant factor affecting the quality and quantity of educational well-being. Countries that are increasingly invested in providing students with personal computers and Internet connectivity are likely to have an edge in educational well-being compared with countries who are less invested in educational technologies. Today, both educational attainment and learning are dependent on students having their own personal computers, being computer literate, and having the connectivity that allows them to access the Internet.

Workforce is another school-related factor. Many issues related to teachers and educational staff affect both the quantity and the quality of education. Countries that have more qualified, well-performing teachers are likely to register higher levels of educational attainment and learning excellence. Quality teachers make a huge difference in both educational attainment and learning. Countries that have a high level of teacher attrition are likely to suffer. For example, teacher attrition is symptomatic of problems related to opportunity, ability, and motivation to learn, which in turn affects the quality of education. Of course, there can be other reasons for teacher attrition such as lack of support from the administration, standardized test pressure, and inappropriate student behavior.

Another important school-related factor is school *infrastructure*. In many developing countries, schools have deficient infrastructures. Some may operate with frequent power outages and perhaps no electricity at all. Many schools may not have toilets and sanitation systems. Some schools in war-ravaged countries may not have physical classroom facilities. Infrastructure matters a great deal. Countries with ill-equipped school infrastructures are likely to be at a major disadvantage in educational well-being. Inadequate school infrastructure adversely affects the opportunity, ability, and motivation to enroll in desired curricula and to learn the desired subject matter.

Figure 5.1 provides a set of *nonschool factors* that have a direct effect on the quality and quantity of education. These include economic well-being (e.g., poverty), social well-being (e.g., neighborhood crime, teenage pregnancies), and health well-being (e.g., disease incidence).

The box to the far right in figure 5.1 reflects a set of consequences of educational well-being. That is, both quality and quantity of education play a vital role in contributing to other well-being dimensions of a country: increased economic well-being, increased political stability, increased social well-being, increased health well-being, control of population growth, and increased happiness. Specifically, high levels of both quality and quantity education contribute to economic development. Countries with high levels of quality and quantity education are likely to register high levels of GDP per capita, have higher numbers of patents and copyrights per thousand persons, and have a more educated workforce than countries with low quality and quantity education. Similarly, countries with higher levels of quality and quantity education are likely to register lower levels of income inequality than countries with lower levels of education. This finding is due to the possible effects of education in inflating the ranks of the middle class. A country in which most of its citizenry is educated is a country that may experience high levels of political stability compared to countries whose citizens have a low level of education. Countries with a more educated public are likely to be more engaged in fighting social ills such as crime, suicide, and teenage pregnancies. They work hard to decrease social ill-being. They work hard to increase social well-being too (e.g., have more social organizations that bring people together in fellowship). The same can be said of issues of health ill-being and well-being. Countries with a more educated public are likely to allocate more resources to fight disease (i.e., reduce health ill-being) and to practice preventive medicine (i.e., increase health well-being). Countries with high education levels are likely to control population growth. Educated people tend to invest in their children's future, and having too many children would not be affordable. Finally, education contributes to happiness. A major source of happiness comes from the achievement of lifetime goals. Education is extremely instrumental in goal achievement.

Educational Well-Being Outcomes

Let us now focus on educational well-being as an end state, a desired state, by documenting gains and capturing trends in well-being outcomes in various world regions. Education is a critical sector necessary for progressive advances in human well-being. Progress in this sector is needed to ensure inclusive and quality education for all and to promote lifelong learning. Education is also crucial to the good life. Learning skills necessary to cope with modern life and to be a productive citizen is imperative to a good life. Education serves an important role in enhancing the economy at large, helping a population manifest its full potential and achieve overall quality of life in every country in every walk of life.

We make the distinction between "quantity" indicators of education well-being and "quality" indicators. A key quantity indicator of educational well-being is *average years of total schooling (age fifteen plus)*. The assumption is that a country with citizens with more schooling is a country considered high on educational well-being (compared to a country having citizens with little schooling). Hence, we believe that educational attainment is a quantity measure of educational well-being. We refer to indicators of educational attainment such as average years of total schooling (age fifteen plus) as "quantity" because these indicators do not signal quality of learning per se. For example, people can achieve a high level of schooling (in terms of number of years of formal education) with little learning. They simply get by to get the required passing grade but not much learning takes place. Hence, the distinction between quantity and quality education is important. Quality education in its formal sense is typically captured through proficiency tests in language, mathematics, and science. We must also recognize that learning (quality) is inherently related to educational attainment (quantity) and that the process underlying this relationship is extremely complex. For a better appreciation of this complexity, the reader is encouraged to read Hattie (2008) and Hattie and

Yates (2014). It is beyond the scope of this chapter to discuss the interrelationship between quality and quantity indicators of educational well-being. Suffice it to say that they are certainly interrelated but different.

Educational Well-Being Outcomes: Quantity

Quantity education refers to the average years of total schooling that adults (aged fifteen plus) have accrued (van Zanden et al., 2014, p. 89). Conceivably, the range is zero schooling (no formal schooling at all) to twenty-two plus (doctoral degrees and other postgraduate education). However, statistically speaking, the range of country averages is 1.5 years of schooling to 12.4 (figure 5.2). It should be noted that we selected average years of total schooling that adults (aged fifteen plus) have accrued as our "quantity" measure of educational well-being. That is not to say that there are no other "quantity" indicators of educational well-being. Examples include high school dropout rate, high school completion rate, and level of education achieved. We chose average years of total schooling mainly because the World Bank provides

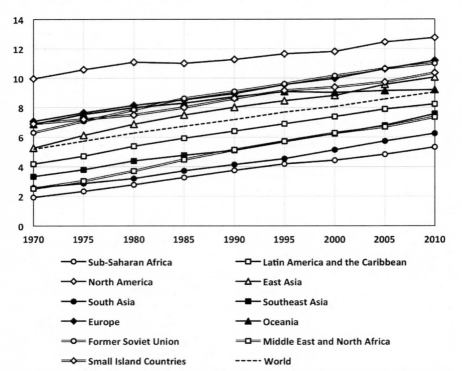

Figure 5.2. Average years of total schooling, age fifteen plus, total. *Source*: (Data from World Bank, 2017)

such statistics worldwide. Statistics pertaining to the other indicators are sparse and intermittent at best.

Focusing on the period between 1970 and 2010, figure 5.2 shows positive trends. As shown in the figure, the world trend (dotted line) is indeed positive. The gains are remarkable, especially in sub-Saharan Africa, Latin America, East Asia, South Asia, Southeast Asia, Europe, the Middle East/North Africa (MENA) region, Oceania, and the former states of the Soviet Union. Even in North America, the trend is positive but not as pronounced as in the other world regions. In North America, the average years of total schooling in 1970 were about ten, surpassing all the world regions. Hence, the rate of change in North America is not as marked as those of the other regions, given that educational attainment was already significantly higher than that in other world regions.

To examine the rate of change between the developed and the developing countries in terms of educational attainment and gender disparity (figure 5.3), we have divided the world into two groups, the developed and the developing countries, and in terms of gender, males and females. The positive trend in educational attainment (between 1970 and 2010) is pronounced in both developing and developed countries. Gender disparity in educational attainment is also narrowing—women are catching up with their male counterparts in both developed and developing countries. This development is, of course, very positive news.

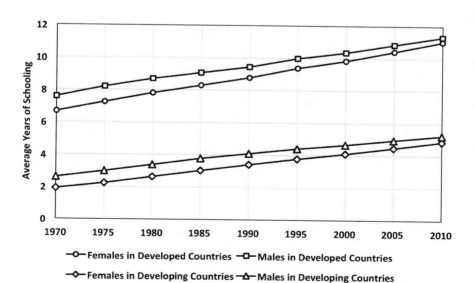

Figure 5.3.   Average years of total schooling, age fifteen plus, males vs. females, developed vs. developing countries. *Source*: (Data from World Bank, 2017)

We can further analyze gender disparity in terms of world regions. Figure 5.4 shows the world trend for both men and women between 1970 and
2010. The world trend is positive and highly pronounced. Gender disparity
is indeed narrowing. In 2010, educational attainment hovered around nine
years of total schooling for both men and women. Again, good news! This
world trend is replicated in all world regions. If we look for world regions in
which there is a significant gender disparity, these might be South Asia and
the MENA regions. Even in those regions, the gap in gender disparity is narrowing significantly.

Despite the good news, the road ahead remains long and challenging;
today, for example, more than 57 million children in the most socially vulnerable subregions remain out of school (United Nations Children's Fund, 2015)
and are, therefore, unable to participate fully in the world's global international labor markets. Most of these children are concentrated in sub-Saharan
Africa and in other war-ravaged and conflict-affected areas of the world. The
United Nations estimates that 103 million youth lack basic literacy skills
worldwide with most them being female (United Nations, 2015a). However,
we need to focus on the good news, not the gloom-and-doom news hyped in
the media. There is significant human progress in educational well-being in
every sense of the word. We need to focus on those factors that have pro-
pelled educational well-being to greater heights and ensure that policies are
in place to maintain and further enhance this progress. Much more about the

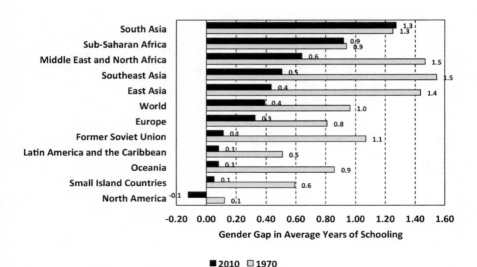

Figure 5.4. **Average years of total schooling, age fifteen plus, gender gap by world
region.** *Source*: (Data from World Bank, 2017)

factors that may account for this progress and the policies underlying those drivers are discussed later.

Educational Well-Being Outcomes: Quality

The quality dimension of educational well-being is captured in terms of actual learning or what education experts refer to as learning proficiency. We selected proficiency in language, mathematics, and science as three key indicators of "quality." Examples of other quality indicators include self-reported academic performance, grade point average, grade repetition, and possibly missed days (truancy). We chose the proficiency indicators mainly because proficiency statistics are now collected by international agencies worldwide. Statistics pertaining to the other indicators are difficult to obtain if they are even collected at all by national governments.

At least three internationally recognized organizations administer proficiency tests across the globe, namely, the PISA, TIMSS, and the Progress in International Reading Literacy Study. PISA is a worldwide study by the OECD in member and nonmember nations of fifteen-year-old school pupils' scholastic performance in reading, mathematics, and science. Educational assessments of reading, mathematics, and science were first performed in 2000 and then repeated every three years (Programme for International Student Assessment, 2017). For example, countries such as Finland and Singapore have gained a reputation of outperforming most other countries using PISA and TIMSS achievement tests. Figures 5.5 to 5.10 show progress in learning proficiency in mathematics, language, and science.

As shown in figure 5.5, the rate of improvement in learning mathematics in the developed countries, although high, remained flat between 2000 and 2012. In contrast, the improvement in mathematics proficiency in the developed world to that in the developing world is remarkable. The trend shows that students in the developing world are becoming increasingly proficient in mathematics. Nevertheless, they have a long way to go to catch up with students in the developed world. The figure shows almost no disparity between men and women in proficiency in mathematics in the developing countries. However, there is a slight disparity in the developed world, namely, male students seem to have a slight edge over female students in mathematics proficiency. Analysis of the TIMSS data (2000–2012) reveals a similar pattern.

Examining mathematics proficiency by gender disparity by world region (figure 5.6), we note that mathematics proficiency for the world at large was stable in 2000, 2003, 2006, and 2009 but rose markedly in 2012 for both male and female students. Focusing on the world regions, we note that mathematics proficiency is higher than the world average in East Asia, followed

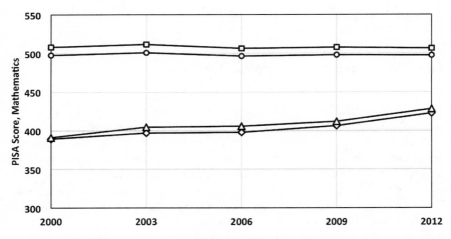

Figure 5.5. Mean performance on the Programme for International Student Assessment mathematics scale, developed vs. developing countries, males vs. females. *Source*: (Data from World Bank, 2017)

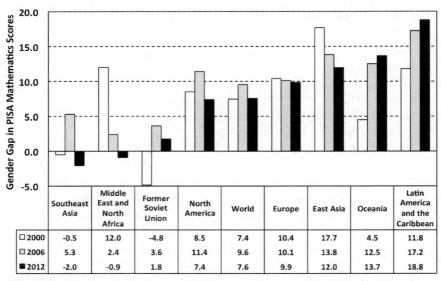

	Southeast Asia	Middle East and North Africa	Former Soviet Union	North America	World	Europe	East Asia	Oceania	Latin America and the Caribbean
☐ 2000	-0.5	12.0	-4.8	8.5	7.4	10.4	17.7	4.5	11.8
☐ 2006	5.3	2.4	3.6	11.4	9.6	10.1	13.8	12.5	17.2
■ 2012	-2.0	-0.9	1.8	7.4	7.6	9.9	12.0	13.7	18.8

Figure 5.6. Mean performance on the Programme for International Student Assessment (PISA) mathematics scale, world regions, gender gap. *Source*: (Data from World Bank, 2017)

by Oceania, North America, and Europe. Regions below the world average are the former states of the Soviet Union, MENA, Southeast Asia, South Asia, sub-Saharan Africa, and Latin America, in that order. We also note that mathematics proficiency is increasing among both male students and female students in East Asia (with male students doing better than female students but females catching up in 2009 and 2012). In Oceania, mathematics proficiency seems to be declining for both male and female students (with female students doing worse). In North America, progress in mathematics proficiency seems flat (for both male and female students, with male students doing slightly better than female students). A similar trend is evident in Europe (progress is flat with males doing slightly better than females). In the world regions scoring below average—South Asia, Southeast Asia, the former Soviet Union, MENA, and Latin America—there are marked fluctuations for both male and female students.

When we analyze the PISA data in relation to language proficiency (i.e., reading) (figure 5.7) from 2000 to 2012 in developed and developing countries for males versus females, we see similar patterns in terms of the rate of improvement. The rate of improvement in language proficiency among students in the developing countries is positive and significant compared to the rate of change of those in the developed countries—the rate of change in

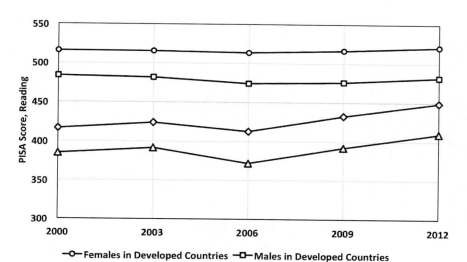

Figure 5.7. Mean performance on the Programme for International Student Assessment (PISA) reading scale, developed vs. developing countries, males vs. females. *Source:* (Data from World Bank, 2017)

language proficiency among students in the developed countries seems flat. Again, this is good news in terms of acknowledging gains in educational proficiency in the developing countries. Nevertheless, the discrepancy between language proficiency among students in the developing versus developed countries is high—that is, students in the developed countries outperform students in the developing countries by a significant margin in language proficiency. Turning our attention to gender disparity, we note a reverse phenomenon. In contrast to mathematics proficiency, in which male students seem to outperform female students in the developed countries, the opposite seems evident in relation to language proficiency. That is, female students slightly outperform male students on the reading proficiency tests in the developing countries, but much more markedly in the developed countries.[2]

Examining language proficiency by gender disparity by world region (figure 5.8), we note that reading proficiency for the world at large was stable in 2000, 2003, 2006, and 2009 but rose markedly in 2012 for both male and female students. Focusing on the world regions, we note that reading proficiency is higher than the world average in East Asia, followed by Oceania, North America, and Europe—a profile highly like that for mathematics proficiency. Regions below the world average are the former Soviet Union, MENA, Southeast Asia, South Asia, sub-Saharan Africa, and Latin America, but not necessarily in that order. Note from the figure that there are marked fluctuations among those world regions. Examining gender disparity in the various world regions, we observe that reading proficiency is increasing

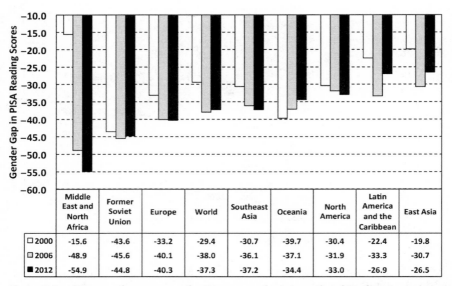

	Middle East and North Africa	Former Soviet Union	Europe	World	Southeast Asia	Oceania	North America	Latin America and the Caribbean	East Asia
☐ 2000	-15.6	-43.6	-33.2	-29.4	-30.7	-39.7	-30.4	-22.4	-19.8
☐ 2006	-48.9	-45.6	-40.1	-38.0	-36.1	-37.1	-31.9	-33.3	-30.7
■ 2012	-54.9	-44.8	-40.3	-37.3	-37.2	-34.4	-33.0	-26.9	-26.5

Figure 5.8. Mean performance on the Programme for International Student Assessment (PISA) reading scale, world regions, gender gap. *Source*: (Data from World Bank, 2017)

among both male and female students in East Asia. In Oceania, reading proficiency seems to be declining for both male and female students. In North America, progress in language proficiency seems flat (for both male and female students). A similar trend is evident in Europe (progress is flat with female doing slightly better than male students). For the world regions scoring below average—South Asia, Southeast Asia, the former Soviet Union, MENA, and Latin America—there are marked fluctuations for both male and female students.

Figure 5.9 shows learning proficiency data in relation to science. Again, the difference between developed and developing countries is huge, but the trend is consistent with those for mathematics and reading proficiency. That is, the rate of improvement is much more pronounced among students in the developing than in the developed countries. Of course, this finding is consistent with the main theme of this book—that gains in human well-being are much more evident among the developing than developed countries. With respect to gender disparity, the figure shows hardly any disparity at all in either developing or developed countries. This result is, of course, still good news. Female students have made significant strides in science education, and now there is no notable difference between male and female students in science proficiency. It should be noted that an analysis of the TIMSS data (2000–2012) reveals a pattern like the one discussed previously.

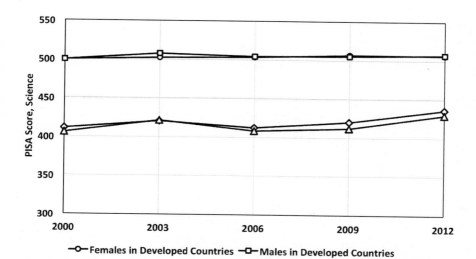

Figure 5.9.   Mean performance on the Programme for International Student Assessment (PISA) science scale, developed vs. developing countries, males vs. females. *Source*: (Data from World Bank, 2017)

Examining science proficiency by gender disparity by world region (figure 5.10), we note that science proficiency for the world at large was stable in 2000, 2003, 2006, and 2009 but rose markedly in 2012 for both male and female students. Focusing on the world regions, we note that science proficiency is higher than the world average in East Asia, followed by Oceania, North America, and Europe—a profile highly like that for mathematics and reading proficiency. Regions below the world average are the former Soviet Union, MENA, Southeast Asia, South Asia, sub-Saharan Africa, and Latin America but not necessarily in that order. Note from the figure that there are marked fluctuations among those world regions. Examining gender disparity in the various world regions, we note that science proficiency is increasing among both male and female students in East Asia (but much more so for male than for female students). In Oceania, science proficiency seems to be declining for both male and female students. In North America, progress in science proficiency seems flat (for both male and female students). A similar trend is evident in Europe (progress is flat with female doing slightly better than male students). With respect to the world regions scoring below average, South Asia, Southeast Asia, the former Soviet Union, MENA, with Latin America (being the exception), there are marked fluctuations for both male and female students. In Latin America, science proficiency is increasing with female doing better than male students.

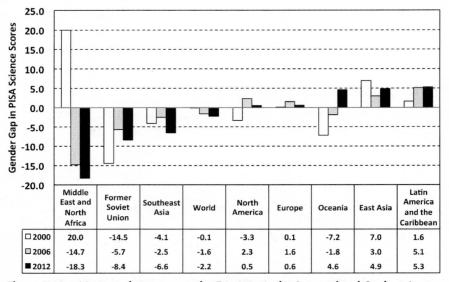

	Middle East and North Africa	Former Soviet Union	Southeast Asia	World	North America	Europe	Oceania	East Asia	Latin America and the Caribbean
☐ 2000	20.0	-14.5	-4.1	-0.1	-3.3	0.1	-7.2	7.0	1.6
☐ 2006	-14.7	-5.7	-2.5	-1.6	2.3	1.6	-1.8	3.0	5.1
■ 2012	-18.3	-8.4	-6.6	-2.2	0.5	0.6	4.6	4.9	5.3

Figure 5.10.   Mean performance on the Programme for International Student Assessment (PISA) science scale, world regions, gender gap. *Source*: (Data from World Bank, 2017)

SCHOOL-RELATED FACTORS AFFECTING EDUCATIONAL WELL-BEING

In this section, we explore certain factors that may account for educational well-being outcomes, both quantity and quality outcomes, specifically, educational policies and their impact on educational well-being. Government investment in education is considered a major factor impacting educational well-being. We also examine the effects of educational technologies, workforce in education, and infrastructure issues.

Educational Policies

One major educational policy that may account for educational well-being outcomes is compulsory education (box 5.2).[3] The World Bank defines compulsory education as the "number of years that children are legally obliged to attend school." Many countries mandate a school-leaving age of twelve, but most countries enforce a school-leaving age of sixteen. Some countries (or states) are considering raising the school-leaving age to eighteen. The rationale for compulsory education is that society benefits collectively from compulsory education because education in general promotes good citizenship and economic development. Some evidence in the educational policy literature suggests that compulsory education is correlated with educational attainment and other well-being factors at the country level (e.g., Acemoglu & Angrist, 2002; Angrist & Krueger, 1991; Dee, 2003; Lleras-Muney, 2002; Lochner & Moretti, 2001; Milligan, Moretti, & Oreopoulos, 2003, 2006). For example, Professor Philip Oreopoulos at the University of Toronto in Canada concluded the following:

BOX 5.2

Society has suffered so cruelly from ignorance, that its riddance is a matter of necessity, and by the universal diffusion of knowledge alone can ignorance and crime be banished from our midst; in no other way can the best interests of society be conserved and improved than by this one remedy—the compulsory enforcement of this great boon—the right of every Canadian child to receive that education that will make him a good, loyal subject, prepared to serve his country in the various social functions which he may be called on to fill during his life; and prepare him, through grace, for the life to come.

(Annual Report of the Ontario Teachers' Association, 1875, as cited in Prentice & Houston, 1975, p. 176)

Education levels rose dramatically in Canada between 1920 and 1970. The national grade attainment average increased from 8.1 to 11.3. Provinces also implemented or tightened many compulsory school limits. I estimate changes in these limits had a significant impact on the rise in grade attainment, accounting for about 13% of the rise. Those affected experienced a 14% increase in their annual income. Compelling would-be-dropouts to take additional education also lowered the chances for unemployment, decreased the chances of working in a manual occupation, and raised the fraction reporting speaking both English and French.

—(Oreopoulos, 2003; p. 24)

Figure 5.11 shows the trend in duration of compulsory education in years broken down by developed versus developing countries. Compulsory education in the developed countries is more than ten years of formal schooling, whereas the average in the developing countries hovers around seven years. However, it should be noted that the trend of compulsory education in the developing countries is positive (i.e., an increasing trend). Compulsory education was registered at 5.8 years of formal schooling in 1999, increasing to around eight years in 2014. The trend in the developed countries increased slightly, from ten years of formal schooling to around 10.3.

Figure 5.12 shows the trend in duration of compulsory education in years broken down by world region. The trend for the world overall is positive

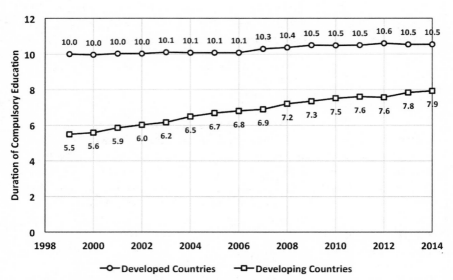

Figure 5.11. Duration of compulsory education (years), developed vs. developing countries. *Source*: **(Data from World Bank, 2017)**

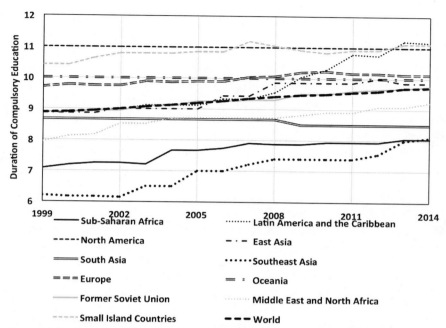

Figure 5.12.   Duration of compulsory education (years) by world region. *Source*: (Data from World Bank, 2017)

(dotted line). In 1999, the world average hovered close to 8.8 years. This figure climbed to 9.7 in 2014. World regions above the average are North America, Europe, East Asia, Oceania, and Europe. Regions below the world average are Latin America, South Asia, Southeast Asia, the former states of the Soviet Union, and MENA. It should be noted that the positive trend is most marked in those regions below the world average, with the highest rate of increase in Latin America, Southeast Asia, and the MENA region. Only East Asia is among the above average regions that witnessed a marked increase.

We conclude that compulsory education as an educational policy has been a resounding success. As such, it should not only be maintained but should also be reinforced.

Investment in Education

Unlike during past decades, governments today invest significant resources in advancing the educational status of their citizens. They are joined in these efforts by private citizens, nongovernmental organizations, businesses/

social enterprises, and private charities committed to the advancement of public education. These efforts are directed at preschool (K–12) and primary school education (grades 1–6) as well as at education and career training for youth pursuing academic and technical training tracks (grades 7–12). Virtually all countries currently make substantial investments in postsecondary education, especially in national college and university systems. They also make major investments in technical education that are especially critical to the development of countries whose economies depend primarily on manufacturing. In most countries, girls and women have equal access to formal education at the same levels as do boys and men, including posttertiary technical and university education. Indeed, in many countries, the percentage of university students who are women is substantially larger than that who are men (Ratcliffe, 2013; United Nations Educational, Cultural and Scientific Organization, 2015). These changes are fundamental and reflect substantial contributions to the well-being of the students involved as well as to society (box 5.3)

Professor George Psacharopoulos, an education economist at the University of Athens, has long conducted studies to estimate the results of investment in education (Psacharopoulos, 1985, 1994; Psacharopoulos & Hinchliffe, 1973; Psacharopoulos & Patrinos, 2004). Some of the pertinent findings include the following:

- Overall, the average rate of return to another year of schooling is 10 percent;
- Overall compared to men, women receive higher returns on their schooling investments, especially in relation to secondary education;
- The highest returns on investment are strongest for low-income and middle-income countries;
- Average returns to schooling are highest in Latin America and in sub-Saharan Africa; and
- Average returns on schooling are lowest in the MENA region.

This analysis corroborates the observation that investments in education produce a good rate of return, especially for developing countries, for women,

---

BOX 5.3

We are not the sources of problems. We are the resources that are needed to solve them. We are not expenses, we are investments.

(Arrieta & Cheynut, 2002)

and for impoverished world regions such as sub-Saharan Africa. The same analysis strengthens the case for combating child labor in terms of not only the moral argument (i.e., minimizing the physical hazards to children) but also economic investment.

We conducted our own analysis using data from the UNDP and the World Bank. Figure 5.13 reflects the major investments in education made by countries grouped by geographic region and the world for the following periods: 1990, 1995–1997, and 2005–2013. The investment trends in education reflected in these figures are impressive and confirm that dramatic shifts have taken place on the part of all national regional governments since 1950 to invest in the human capital resource profiles of their population, although the investment levels differ by each region. Of special interest is the fact that the most dramatic shifts in education have occurred in the countries of North Africa and West Asia and the sub-Saharan countries of Africa whose entire educational systems have expanded in response to the needs of their countries for a more technically educated workforce. Even so, these latter groups of countries, located principally in Africa, have invested progressively higher levels of their public resources in pre- and postsecondary education. These investments mark a dramatic departure from past educational investment

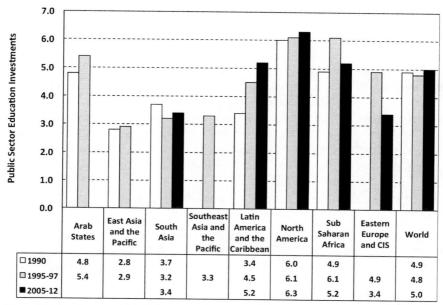

	Arab States	East Asia and the Pacific	South Asia	Southeast Asia and the Pacific	Latin America and the Caribbean	North America	Sub Saharan Africa	Eastern Europe and CIS	World
☐ 1990	4.8	2.8	3.7		3.4	6.0	4.9		4.9
☐ 1995-97	5.4	2.9	3.2	3.3	4.5	6.1	6.1	4.9	4.8
■ 2005-12			3.4		5.2	6.3	5.2	3.4	5.0

Figure 5.13. Percent of public sector investments in education, 1990, 1995–1997, 2005–2012. *Source*: (Data from United Nations Development Programme, 2013; World Bank, 2015)

patterns and suggest that educational well-being can be expected to increase steadily as the investment in education continues. One of the most significant outcomes is that adult literacy is now widespread in the countries and subregions of Africa and in the developing nations of Asia and Latin America, such that literacy, rather than illiteracy, has become the norm in the contemporary globalized world (Irogbe, 2014).

The most central patterns regarding public investments in education as captured in figure 5.13 reflect the fact that public expenditures for education for the world remained constant between 1990 and 2012. However, the nations of Latin America and the Caribbean made more substantial investments in education during the twenty-two-year period than any other world region—from 3.4 percent in 1990 to 5.2 percent in 2012. These investments closely parallel the overall advances in well-being reported for the region during the same period and for the years following 2012. Substantial public investments in education also were made by the Arab States of North Africa and West Asia (4.8 percent and 5.4 percent, respectively) and, to a lesser extent, by the nations of North America (from the world's highest in 1990 of 6.0 percent to 6.3 percent in 2012).

Ironically, the nations that experienced the most serious ideological struggles for which re-education was the most needed—those of Eastern Europe and the Commonwealth of Independent States—allocated the lowest levels of public expenditures to education—a substantial decline from 4.9 percent of total central government expenditures in 1990 to a low of 3.4 percent of public investments in 2012. The public-sector expenditures of the nations of Eastern Europe and Central Asia declined appreciably following the restoration of their independence after the collapse of the former Soviet Union in 1991. The results of these declines are reflected in the considerably shortened life expectancy of men, the failure of much of the physical infrastructure, and the emergence of a governmental sector that was neither able to govern nor to provide for the most basic needs of widely dispersed populations. Not surprisingly, people's self-assessed satisfaction with life plummeted during this period.

It should be noted that investigating the link between investments in education and educational well-being outcomes is a slippery slope. On an intuitive level, one expects that countries that score highly on education investment should register better outcomes. Not necessarily! The evidence is convoluted. A team from the National Bureau of Economic Research in Cambridge, Massachusetts (Glewwe, Hanushek, Humpage, & Ravina, 2011), reviewed most of the empirical studies published from 1990 to 2010 and concluded that the amount of investment in education is not directly linked with student and learning outcomes. What does this mean? The implication is rather obvious. It is not how much money one spends on education that matters; it is what one spends it on. For example, spending money on school libraries is a worth-while investment. Sufficient evidence suggests that a strong library program can lead to higher student achievement (Lonsdale, 2003).

Educational Technologies

Let us examine information and communication data from the World Bank. Figure 5.14 shows Internet users (per 100 people) for 1990, 2002, and 2014. The figure shows a clear world trend of increased usage of the Internet beginning in 1994 (box 5.4). The trend seems exponential, with North America registering the highest, followed by Europe. Figure 5.15 shows the use of personal computers (per 100 people). A similar trend should be noted with a slight variation. The use of personal computers in North America was highest, followed by Europe, Oceania, and East Asia. Other studies from the OECD (Organization for Economic Cooperation and Development, 2010) show that the highest percentage of households possessing a personal computer is in Denmark (63 percent), the United States and Australia (50 percent), and Italy (20 percent). Some 400 million people use the Internet, representing only 7 percent of the world's population (United Nations Educational, Cultural and Scientific Organization, 2004, p. 8). This figure reflects what education scholars call "the digital divide." This digital divide contributes to educational inequalities in terms of access, opportunity, process, and outcomes

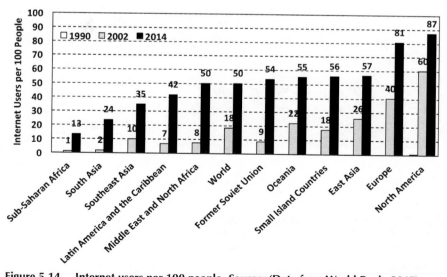

Figure 5.14.   Internet users per 100 people. *Source*: (Data from World Bank, 2017)

BOX 5.4

Technology such as Information and Communication Technology (ICT) is a potent force in driving economic, social, political and educational reforms. Countries, particularly developing ones, cannot afford to stay passive to ICT if they are to compete and strive in the global economy. The health of the economy of any country, poor or rich, developed or developing, depends substantially on the level and quality of the education it provides to its workforce. Education reform is occurring throughout the world and one of the tenets of the reform is the introduction and integration of ICT in the education system. The successful integration of any technology, thus ICT, into the classroom warrants careful planning and depends largely on how well policy makers understand and appreciate the dynamics of such integration.

(Jhurree, 2005, p. 467)

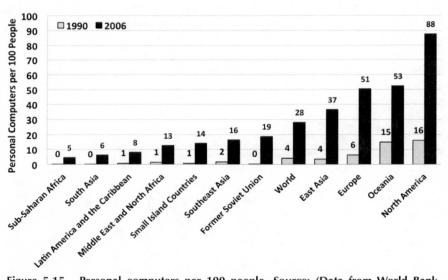

Figure 5.15. **Personal computers per 100 people. *Source*: (Data from World Bank, 2017)**

(United Nations Educational, Cultural and Scientific Organization, 2004, p. 92; Zajda, Biraimah, & Gaudelli, 2008a; Zajda, Davies, & Majhanovich, 2008b). The people who suffer from this digital divide are of course the poor in each country and in the poor countries of the world (e.g., China, India, Pakistan, Philippines).

Many education scholars claim that information and communications technology (ICT) is changing the educational landscape now and way into the future and that such change will engender a profound increase in learning and educational attainment. Professor Vikashkumar Johore of the Mauritius Institute of Education in Mauritius has long argued that ICT provides many benefits to learning and education (Jhurree, 2005). Among the most salient benefits are the following:

- A tool for learners that motivates learning through constructive engagement
- A tool to help teachers enhance their instruction in the classroom
- A tool for both teachers and administrators to carry out their administrative responsibilities such as student record keeping, lesson planning, and preparing slides
- A tool to help schools promote equal access to education, especially to students with disabilities
- A tool to help students, teachers, and administrators to communicate, exchange knowledge and concerns, brainstorm and collaborate in many ways
- A skill for students to acquire that would give them a competitive advantage in the labor market

Given the fact that mobile phones are the most prevalent type of ICT in the developing world and that the rate of penetration is increasing exponentially, Valk, Rashid, and Elder (2010) reviewed the evidence of the effectiveness of mobile phone–facilitated mobile learning (mLearning) in improving educational outcomes in the developing countries of Asia. They examined the findings from six mLearning pilot projects in the Philippines, Mongolia, Thailand, India, and Bangladesh. They found evidence suggesting that the use of mobile phones improved educational outcomes by improving access to education. However, the study findings also provided no concrete evidence that mobile phones promoted new learning. Furthermore, some evidence (Goldberg, Russell, & Cook, 2003) suggests that students in classrooms in which all students are provided with laptop computers tend to do better than students without laptops—in terms of:

- collaborating with other students;
- registering a higher level of participation in project-based instruction;
- producing higher quality reports;
- having greater access to information from the Internet;
- spending more time doing homework on computers;
- directing their own learning;
- using active learning strategies, engaging in problem solving and critical thinking;

- scoring higher on proficiency tests in language and mathematics; and
- having a higher overall grade point average.

We conclude that the rise of educational technologies has contributed significantly to educational well-being. Although we have a digital divide, all signs point to the likelihood that the digital divide will shrink soon, further contributing to educational well-being, especially in the developing world. Again, good news!

Workforce

Much evidence in the literature indicates that teacher quality is positively related to student performance (box 5.5). Students who are taught by experienced teachers do better than those taught by inexperienced teachers (e.g., Hedges, Laine, & Greenwald, 1994) and students' attendance is higher at schools with high-quality teachers than at schools with low-quality teachers (e.g., Bryk & Thum, 1989).[4] For example, based on PISA scores, students from Finland are strong performers. Mr. Pasi Sahlberg, former minister of education in Finland, attributes the success of Finnish students to teacher quality. He notes that, in Finland, teaching is considered a popular profession. Most teachers in Finland believe that teaching is a calling, a social mission. Finnish teachers must have a master's-level education to qualify to teach. The educational system in Finland provides teachers with less classroom time and more time for preparation and other life activities. Finnish teachers are not micromanaged by the school administration; they have much professional autonomy. School administrators such as school principals are also involved in actual teaching. Further, there is trust in the system. That is, parents of students trust schools to deliver a quality education (Wiseman, 2015, p. 60).

BOX 5.5

It is only now that people are starting to listen to those who saw the shortage of qualified teachers as a major impediment to national development and that national and international authorities are beginning to realize that the achievement of the Millennium Development Goals and the Education for All objectives depends on the training of professionals capable of the long-term effort to promote education effectively, in particular through the training of teachers and managerial staff in the education system.

(Teacher Training Initiative of the United Nations Educational, Scientific and Cultural Organization, 2005, page 2)

Significant problems with the educational workforce exist in various parts of the world. Perhaps the significant disparity between the educational well-being of students in the developing and the developed countries may be explained (at least in part) by workforce problems. There are problems recruiting and retaining young, qualified teachers; problems related to recruiting and retaining teachers with expertise in specialist subject areas such as mathematics and science; problems of teacher absenteeism. In some countries in sub-Saharan Africa, the shortage of teachers is a national crisis.

Dr. Bob Moon, Professor of education at the Open University in the United Kingdom, provided a detailed analysis of the global issues dealing with teacher recruitment and retention in a working paper commissioned by the United Nations Educational, Scientific and Cultural Organization's (UNESCO) Section for Teacher Education in 2006 (Moon, 2007). The following is a synopsis of his analysis: In Europe, there are wide disparities between countries in relation to supply and retention of teachers. For example, in France and Germany, the number of teacher candidates preparing to qualify to teach exceeds the number of positions available. In other countries such as Finland and Ireland, the supply of teachers is also strong. In countries such as Austria, the number of newly qualified teachers exceeds the number of available positions, and many teacher graduates wait a long time to find a position. A shortage of teachers is most evident in relation to some specialist secondary subjects such as physics. A major issue for Europe is "the graying" of the teaching profession. For example, in France and Germany, more than a third of the teachers are expected to retire within the next five years. Furthermore, although the official retirement age is sixty-five in most countries in Europe, only a small fraction of teachers (around 6 percent) work to the retirement age—most quit in their early fifties.

What factors play a role in teacher recruitment and retention in Europe? One negative factor is the strengthening of the economy. Potential teachers become attracted to employment opportunities in other sectors of the economy (e.g., the growing knowledge-based sector) that pay better than the teaching profession. In contrast, in many countries in Europe, teaching is a "civil service," which is good because civil service jobs provide an additional layer of job security—protecting people against the ups and downs of economic cycles. Another positive factor in teacher recruitment and retention in Europe is the rise in the status of teachers.

Much data from sub-Saharan Africa have pointed to the large numbers of unqualified teachers in schools and the difficulty of attracting new recruits. Estimates show that one-third of the existing primary teachers are untrained. Worse than ever, this shortfall in trained teachers is rising and is expected to rise significantly soon. For example, Ghana has only a quarter of the teachers it needs and Lesotho only one-fifth. Two major factors seem to account for this teacher shortage. First, the salaries of teachers are significantly deflated relative to other comparable professions. Alternative employment opportunities are increasingly available. Second, the spread of HIV/AIDS is another impediment to teaching recruitment and retention. Estimates show that nearly a million children a year lose their teacher to HIV/AIDS. The scale of the HIV/AIDS pandemic is no doubt influencing the working conditions of teachers significantly. There is also corruption in the public service sector, which is rampant. In Kenya, for example, some evidence indicates bribery is involved in teacher placements and transfers. Sub-Saharan Africa also suffers from teacher migration. Many of the best and most qualified teachers in this world region are migrating to Europe and North America. Yet another problem in sub-Saharan Africa is the fact that millions of recruited teachers are paraprofessionals (i.e., they lack teaching credentials). Because the need is so great, "parateachers" (with some training lasting only a few months or even weeks) are recruited in force. The consequence of the influx of parateachers is a marked decrease in salaries and wages and deterioration of working conditions. Adding insult to injury is the mandatory early retirement of the more experienced, and often more expensive, teachers. Enforcing early retirement has helped governments cut costs but at a significant detriment to educational well-being.

South and West Asia are also facing the problem of teacher shortages in the drive to provide every child with at least a primary education. Of course, there is variation in teachers' shortages across countries in South and West Asia. For example, in Afghanistan, the current pupil–teacher ratio is 65:1 and is climbing at an accelerating rate. There are similar problems in Pakistan. One estimate is that today 34 percent of primary-age children are out of school because of teacher shortages. As pointed out for sub-Saharan Africa, South Asia and West Asia also suffer from unqualified teachers—large numbers of teachers do not meet national requirements (e.g., in Nepal, 25 percent of teachers are not certified). Like sub-Saharan Africa, HIV/AIDS also impacts the teaching workforce.

World regions such as North America are not exempt from the problems of recruiting and retaining teachers. Teacher shortages have been endemic in the United States for many years. A major problem leading to teacher shortages may be the attractiveness of alternative job opportunities. Compensation plays a major role. Other factors include significant increases in student enrollments and the lowering by regulation of pupil–teacher ratios. Another big problem in the United States is the fact that teachers leave the teaching profession long before retirement. That is, teaching has a higher turnover rate than comparable professions such as nursing. For example, evidence suggests that after five years of teaching, between 40 percent and 50 percent of qualified teachers leave the profession. Why? Again, evidence suggests job dissatisfaction and the lure of other, more desirable occupations. Another source of job dissatisfaction and turnover is teachers being required to teach subjects outside their area of specialty.

Although educational attainment is on the rise worldwide, the problems associated with the educational workforce may account for the lower levels of educational well-being in some countries, especially the less-developed ones. The problems of the workforce include the following:

• Retention of qualified teachers (i.e., qualified teachers seek greener pastures in other sectors of the economy)
• The age profile of teachers (i.e., a significant portion of the teacher population is retiring or retiring early)
• Teaching outside one's area of specialization (i.e., teachers are forced to teach in areas they do not feel qualified to teach)
• The gender balance issue (lack of female teachers in mathematics and science)
• The migration issue (i.e., qualified teachers in countries that have the greatest educational needs migrate to other countries for better pay and better working conditions)

Given the magnitude of the problems with the educational workforce, what are possible solutions? Professor Moon suggests the following policy initiatives to solve the problems of the educational workforce:

• Allowing schools to recruit individuals without formal training in education provided that these individuals can be trained through a customized educational training program
• Allowing unqualified individuals to enter the teaching profession for a two-year period in the field (e.g., using the "peace corps" model)
• Developing flexible forms of teacher training to attract native individuals into the teaching profession (e.g., school-based training accompanied by distance-learning courses)

The workforce seems to be a significant factor that may account for much of the variation in educational well-being across countries and world regions. In the developed countries such as Finland (in Europe), where educational well-being is very high, teacher quality is also high. Conversely, in developing countries such as Kenya (in sub-Saharan Africa), where educational well-being is low, we see big problems with teacher quality. The obvious policy implication is to formulate policies directed at enhancing teacher quality.

Infrastructure

Much has been documented on the effects of school infrastructure (or lack of infrastructure) on educational well-being outcomes. The World Bank collects data in sub-Saharan Africa on the availability of toilets and sanitation in schools as well as on the frequency and extent of electric power surges in schools. These types of infrastructure issues take a toll on educational well-being in terms of classroom attendance and learning outcomes. What happens if a school's infrastructure is damaged but not restored because of lack of funding? How does the damage affect educational well-being outcomes? Studies have been conducted on such topics, and the evidence clearly shows that the quality of school infrastructure has a significant effect on school attendance and dropout rates (e.g., Branham, 2004). That is, students are likely to feel highly discouraged about participating in schools (and school learning activities) that need structural repairs, schools that use temporary structures, and schools that have understaffed janitorial services.

Jonathon Kozol (1991), in his classic book *Savage Inequalities*, has described the effects of dilapidated schools in urban America on students' educational well-being. He observed that many schools in the poor urban districts have flooded cafeterias, basements used as classrooms, classrooms without books, laboratories without equipment, classrooms that are overheated, walls that are rotted, ceilings that are leaking, classrooms that are overcrowded, and so on. These schools register low levels of student school attendance and lower levels of student achievement. Based on an extensive review of the research literature, Higgins, Hall, Wall, Woolner, and McCaughey (2005) concluded that extreme environmental elements (e.g., poor ventilation, excessive noise) have adverse effects on students and teachers. Improving these elements would have significant effects on educational well-being.

Apart from the extreme environmental elements, improving the infrastructure of school buildings seems to have a positive effect on educational well-being outcomes if it is done as a design process involving students, teachers, and administrators. In other words, the positive effect of improvements in the school building is likely to produce the most positive outcomes with engagement of the various stakeholder groups.

NONSCHOOL FACTORS AFFECTING EDUCATIONAL WELL-BEING

The administration of President Lyndon B. Johnson (United States) released a two-volume report on July 2, 1966, titled "Equality of Educational Opportunity." This report has come to be known as the "Coleman Report" because the report was produced by the American sociologist James S. Coleman (professor of sociology at Johns Hopkins University). Professor Coleman was commissioned to study school and nonschool factors affecting educational well-being in the United States (e.g., Cain & Watts, 1970; Meier, 2000). He undertook an unprecedented nationwide survey of education in the United States involving 600,000 students, 60,000 teachers, and 4,000 public schools. The report described US schools that were deeply segregated with huge economic inequalities among the schools. Most importantly, Coleman's study determined that educational outcomes in the United States are more related to nonschool than school factors. School factors such as quality of facilities, programs, and teachers did not matter that much compared to nonschool factors such as the proportion of students with encyclopedias in their home and the extent to which students' parents had high aspirations for their children. In other words, students' family backgrounds and the socioeconomic makeup of the school's community were the best predictors of student achievement.

Economic Well-Being

It seems obvious to us that poverty plays an important role in educational well-being outcomes, both in terms of educational attainment and learning. But what is the evidence? The relationship between poverty and children's academic performance has been well documented in relation to both primary and secondary schools (e.g., Campbell, Pungello, Miller-Johnson, Burchinal, & Ramey, 2001; Entwisle, Alexander, & Olson, 2005; Murnane, 2007). Children from poor families are more likely to leave school without graduating compared to children from families in higher-income brackets. For example, a major study conducted by the National Institute of Child Health and Human Development Early Child Care Research Network (2005) has provided evidence that children of poor families in the United States have lower cognitive and academic performance than children who are not of poor families. The same findings are not only evident in developing countries but much more pronounced (EFA Global Monitoring Report Team, 2006). Children growing up in poor families are exposed to a variety of risk factors such as disease, crowding, family stress, lack of psychosocial stimulation, and limited resources. Most poor families use language dominated by commands rather than by explanations and elaboration. Parents of poor families use a harsh style of parenting rather than an interactive style that promotes emotional development and social competence. Children in poor families are less likely to be read to, an important factor in the development of phonemic comprehension. Poor parents usually do not invest in their children's education by buying them books to read.

Policies designed to reduce the way that poverty affects children's educational well-being have been tried in various developing countries. An example of a successful program is a monthly cash transfer of small amounts of money to mothers who send their children to school and ensure that their children are properly fed and immunized (Behrman & Hoddinott, 2005).

So far, we have focused on the effect of poverty on educational well-being and glossed over the relationship between affluence and educational well-being. Much evidence in the literature suggests that children and youth residing in high socioeconomic neighborhoods tend to excel on school achievement measures compared with their counterparts in low socioeconomic neighborhoods (see literature review by Leventhal & Brooks-Gunn, 2000). The effects of neighborhood affluence on a variety of quality and quantity educational well-being measures are undeniably strong. The positive effects include high levels of IQ, verbal ability, reading achievement, mathematics achievement, basic skills tests, grade point average, chances of completing high school, attending college, and years of schooling completed. Research also shows that institutional resources can make a difference. Specifically, the availability, accessibility, affordability, and quality of community-related institutions (i.e., services related to learning, recreational, and social activities; child care; schools; medical facilities; and employment opportunities) can enhance educational well-being outcomes for children and youth. Community learning institutions are equally important such as libraries, family resource centers, literacy programs, and museums. Parents can draw on these institutions to stimulate their children's learning, which, in turn, contributes significantly to children's development in relation to school readiness and educational achievement. Additionally, institutions related to organized social and recreational events (e.g., parks, sports programs, art programs, theater programs, community centers, children and youth groups) help promote children's physical and emotional well-being, which play a vital role in educational well-being.

The economic well-being of children, as a nonschool factor, plays an important role in education. The obvious implication of the research on the effects of economic well-being on educational well-being is that policy makers should formulate policies to help schools in low socioeconomic districts within both developing and developed countries. Those policies should focus on providing support to families of low socioeconomic levels to adopt behavioral strategies that can motivate children to excel in school. Policies should also focus on changes in the neighborhood environment most likely to enhance educational well-being.

Social Well-Being

Much research on social well-being and ill-being has looked at this concept in terms of "social capital." Social capital refers to sociability, social networks, social support, trust, reciprocity, community, and civic engagement (Bourdieu, 1986; Coleman, 1994; Putnam, 1995). In a study of "at risk young," Furstenberg and Hughes (1995) examined how different types of social capital of the family (i.e., parents' resources within the family, the social network of the parents, and the parents' embeddedness in the community) impact the academic success and psychological well-being of children. Furthermore, much evidence has accumulated showing that young people who experience social ill-being (i.e., who are not engaged with their peers and teachers, have poor relationships with their parents and relatives) are likely to use drugs, become disruptive in class, experience anxiety and depression, and fail to complete secondary school (e.g., Blum & Libbey, 2004; Libbey, 2004; Marcus & Sanders-Reio, 2001).

The obvious implications of this research are that policies should be directed at enhancing the social capital of students, especially in districts and neighborhoods where social capital is lacking. An example of an institution designed to enhance social capital that has worked well over the years in the United States is the Parent-Teacher Association (Parent-Teacher Association, 2017). This organization typically supports school and family interactions in many ways, thus fostering social capital for a given school. Now there are Parent-Teacher Associations in many countries worldwide, both in developing (e.g., India) and developed countries (e.g., United States, United Kingdom, Australia, New Zealand).

Health Well-Being

Does better health lead to better education? Conversely, do sickness and disease detract from educational well-being? The effect of health on educational well-being is widely accepted by the public health community. The public health literature has documented this effect in both developing and developed countries (Taras & Potts-Datema, 2005a–2005d).

Figure 5.16 shows the prevalence (measurement of all individuals affected by the disease at a time) of HIV among individuals aged fifteen to forty-nine in selected regions. The prevalence of HIV is most profound in sub-Saharan Africa. The World Bank data show significant increases in individuals with HIV between 1990 and 2000 and modest decreases from 2000 to 2015. The same figure also shows similar surges in the spread of HIV in Latin America and Southeast Asia, but nowhere as drastic as the spread in sub-Saharan Africa.

Because the trend of educational attainment in sub-Saharan Africa (see figure 5.2) is upward, we cannot infer that the spread of HIV has adversely affected educational attainment in this region. One would expect that the spread of this disease would hamper educational attainment, but this appears not to be the case.

Marc Suhrcke and Carmen de Paz Nieves (2011) developed a theoretical framework to explain much of the evidence linking health and educational

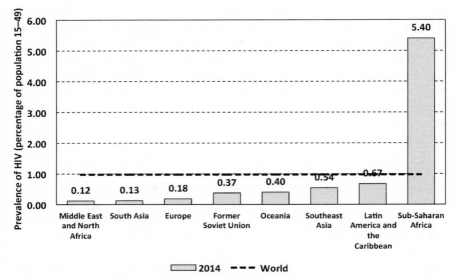

Figure 5.16.   Prevalence of HIV, total (percentage of population ages fifteen–forty-nine).
Source: (Data from World Bank, 2017)

well-being. They viewed educational well-being in a manner consistent with our view of the concept. That is, educational well-being can be viewed in terms of quantity as in educational attainment (e.g., total number of years of schooling, dropping out, college enrollment) and quality as in academic performance (e.g., grade point average, grade repletion, truancy). These two dimensions of educational well-being are influenced by children's health conditions (e.g., sleeping disorders, mental problems, asthma) and health-related behaviors (e.g., substance abuse, smoking, nutritional deficiencies, obesity and overweight, physical activity). These health conditions and health-related behaviors influence educational well-being outcomes through a set of mediating factors (e.g., development of cognitive abilities, discrimination in classroom, self-confidence, learning skills, physical energy, interaction with teachers and classmates).

Obviously, policies should target children's health conditions and health-related behaviors. Many school programs can be designed to deal with children's health issues. For example, many schools in the United States have school-based obesity prevention programs, health and nutrition programs, programs designed to reduce substance abuse, programs related to sports and recreation to increase students' physical activity, among others. Health care institutions operating at a local level could be more involved in addressing children's health problems within the community. Governments can assist by ensuring that families with children (especially poor families) have access to the health care system. Governments can sponsor social marketing campaigns targeting specific health issues among children and youth such as substance abuse.

EFFECTS OF EDUCATIONAL WELL-BEING ON OTHER WELL-BEING OUTCOMES

Education plays an important role in human well-being in a wide variety of ways, serving to increase economic well-being, political stability, social well-being, control of population growth, and happiness (box 5.6).

Increased Economic Well-Being

Consider literacy skills (box 5.7). At a mundane level, people buy goods and services in the marketplace. Most commercial transactions assume that consumers are literate and have basic information about how the marketplace operates. The implication here is obvious: Education plays an important role in *consumer well-being*.

BOX 5.6

Why learning matters. For individuals, learning will help everyone acquire the new skills and qualifications needed for employment and advancement. Learning will increase our earning power. In addition, it will help older people to stay healthy and active, strengthen families and the wider community and encourage independence. Opportunities to learn will lead us to greater appreciation of art, music, poetry and literature, and develop our potential as rounded human beings.

(Department of Education and Employment, 1998)

BOX 5.7

The estimated long-term effect on economic output of one additional year of education in the OECD area is generally between 3 percent and 6 percent.

(Organization for Economic Cooperation and Development, 2006, p. 27)

Population literacy is typically operationalized in terms of the percentage of the adult population in the country that has achieved a minimal level of language proficiency to allow them to read and write. Similarly, primary education attainment can be operationalized in terms of percentage of children aged six to nine in the country who graduated from a primary school. Secondary education attainment can be operationalized in terms of the percentage of children aged ten to eighteen in the country who graduated from a secondary school.

A popular definition of literacy is that of UNESCO: "People aged over 15 who have the ability to read, write, and understand a short, simple statement about everyday life" (van Zanden et al., 2014, p. 91). An alternative measure is "people aged 15 and older who have attained at least some basic education"—enrolled in formal education (van Zanden et al., 2014, p. 93). The world has made huge progress in achieving significant gains in literacy. More than 80 percent of people aged fifteen years or older were reported as literate in 2010 compared to 12 percent to 18 percent in 1820 (van Zanden et al., 2014, p. 94).

Organizing the data by world region, we know that in 1870, the world population registered a 23.9 percent adult literacy rate that increased to 81.5 percent in 2010. In 1870, Western European and Western offshoots registered the highest literacy rates: 60 percent and 82 percent, respectively. In contrast, sub-Saharan Africa registered a low of 2 percent in 1870. This picture changed dramatically over the decades: In 2010, literacy had increased to almost 100 percent in Western countries and their offshoots, whereas sub-Saharan Africa climbed more than 65 percent. These are indeed remarkable gains. In other words, in 1890, 60 percent to 70 percent of the population aged fifteen years and older in Europe and 20 percent to 40 percent outside of Europe were estimated to be literate (United Nations Educational, Scientific and Cultural Organization, 1953, pp. 169–71).

Most jobs necessitate a minimal level of literacy and education. People who are illiterate or who have a low level of education are disadvantaged in every way. Because they cannot easily function, their well-being becomes severely compromised. Much research has documented the effects of education on *economic well-being*. Education plays an important role in economic development. An educated workforce is more productive because workers become better socialized and trained to use technology to produce more goods and services of higher quality (e.g., Romer, 1990). Education contributes to economic growth through the invention of new technologies and the adoption of existing technologies to spur productivity (e.g., Petrakis & Stamatakis, 2002; Van Leeuwen & Foldvari, 2008).

Our analysis of the World Bank data reveals significant correlations between average years of total schooling (age fifteen plus) and GDP per capita—that is, the higher the level of schooling, the greater is the GDP per capita. Figure 5.17 shows this relationship for developing and developed countries. Both groups show a marked, positive correlation. However, the positive correlation is much more pronounced in the developed than in the developing countries. One explanation may be the fact that the developing countries are besieged by many problems besides poverty, such as bad governance, war and civil strife, crime, and poor health. These problems prevent education from making a direct, impactful contribution on the standard of living. The same pattern is evident when one compares the average years of total schooling (age fifteen plus) and unemployment (figure 5.18). Figure 5.18 shows that people who are more educated are more likely to be employed than unemployed, and this pattern is more evident in the developed than developing countries. Figure 5.19 shows the relationship between average years of schooling (age fifteen plus) and patent applications per 100,000 capita (residents). The relationship, as expected, is positive.

Developed countries have many more patent applications than the developing countries, also expected. Figure 5.20 shows the relationship between average years of schooling (age fifteen plus) and income inequality (as captured by the Gini index—a measurement of the income distribution of a country's residents). This number, which ranges between 0 and 1 and is based on residents' net income, helps define the gap between the rich and the poor, with 0

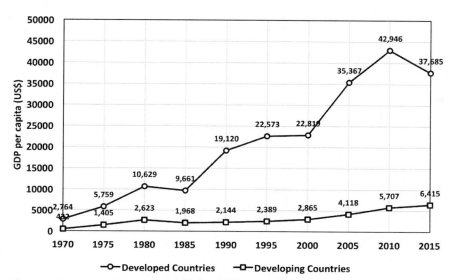

Figure 5.17. Gross Domestic Product (GDP) per capita (current US$), developed vs. developing countries. *Source*: (Data from World Bank, 2017)

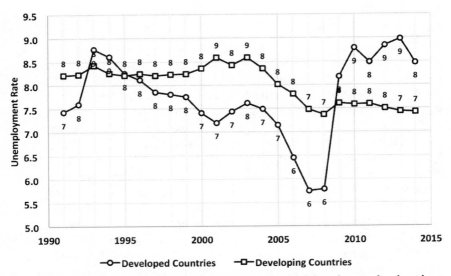

Figure 5.18. Unemployment, total (percentage of total labor force), developed vs. developing countries. *Source*: (Data from World Bank, 2017)

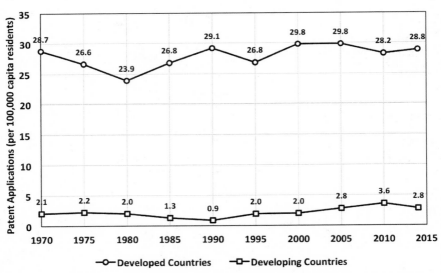

Figure 5.19. Patent applications per 100,000 capita. *Source*: (Data from World Bank, 2017)

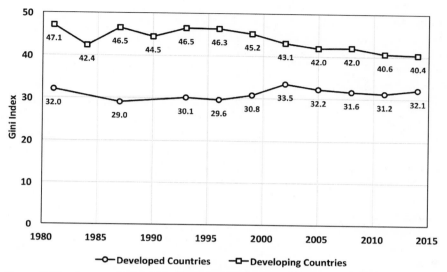

Figure 5.20. Income inequality, developed vs. developing countries. The Gini index is an established metric of income inequality captured at the country level. It varies between 0 and 100, with higher scores signifying more inequality. *Source*: (Data from World Bank, 2017)

representing perfect equality and 1 representing perfect inequality. Note that income inequality is much more marked in the developing than in the developed countries. Within the developing countries, those countries with more education tend to register higher-income inequality than countries with less education. Perhaps this result is a sign of social mobility. As people become more socially mobile and acquire more education, their standard of living improves, creating more variance in income inequality in the developing countries. This pattern is less evident in the developed countries.

We conclude by a quotation from an education expert affiliated with Statistics Canada: "The well-being of modern society is dependent not only on traditional capital and labor but also on the knowledge and ideas possessed and generated by individual workers. Education is the primary source of this human capital" (Crocker, 2002, p. 1).

Increased Political Stability

Other societal-level well-being effects include increased political stability and health and decreased crime, income inequality, and poverty. Education serves to increase *political stability* (e.g., Alesina & Perotti, 1996). Educated people are more likely to find their place in society. They take on jobs that are more meaningful to them. They are likely to become engaged in their work, become successful, and experience satisfaction in work life. They are more likely to make decent wages to support themselves and their families. Financial resources play an important role in enhancing the sense of well-being in other life domains. An increased sense of well-being in work life, family life, leisure life, community life, spiritual life, and so on contributes to political stability. It is dissatisfaction with one or more life domains that lays the foundation for political instability. For example, a country with a high rate of youth unemployment is a country ripe for political instability. Young people who are unemployed or stuck in jobs that heighten their sense of frustration is a recipe for social and political unrest.

Education serves society by increasing political stability and contributes to human productivity. In other words, educated people tend to be more productive and to contribute to society, much more so than those who are less educated. Those who contribute to society feel they are a part of society and its corresponding political system, which they seek to strengthen. In contrast, those who are less educated may feel alienated from society. They may feel that the political system has failed them. Such sentiment may lead to social unrest, to civil strife, and, in large numbers, to political instability.

Increased Social Well-Being

A similar argument can be made regarding the effects of education on *crime* (e.g., Sabates, 2008). People who are not educated are not likely to generate the level of income that can support themselves and their families satisfactorily. Hence, many engage in criminal behavior such as theft, embezzlement, burglary, mugging, extortion, trading goods on the black market, and tax evasion. Many criminals justify their behavior based on lack of education and skill that would allow them to maintain gainful and legal employment. They turn to crime out of desperation.

Education is again the answer. Having more people who are educated is likely to increase their social well-being, which in turn may alleviate many of the society's problems related to social ill-being.

Increased Health Well-Being

Education serves to improve *health* (Organization for Economic Cooperation and Development, 2010). Much research has shown that education is strongly associated with improved health. Education helps people make informed decisions about their health. Education helps people adopt healthier lifestyles and better manage illness. Through primary and secondary schools, education offers an environment for children to develop healthy habits. Nutritiously balanced school meals help children develop healthy eating habits. Through proper schooling, children become better informed about how to maintain a well-balanced diet. Most importantly, education adds to life expectancy.

Wigley and Akkoyunlu-Wigley (2006) conducted a longitudinal study that tracked the health of the same individuals for the years 1990, 1995, and 2000. The results of their study showed that increased educational attainment had a substantial effect on life expectancy. Research has also shown a strong association between education and *infant mortality rates* (e.g., KC & Lentzner, 2010). Educated women are in a better position to care for their infants and to use contraceptives to ensure that they have fewer children (e.g., Bongaarts, 2010; Skirbekk, 2008).

Controlling Population Growth

Education also plays a significant role in the control of *population growth*. Research has shown that education motivates women to have fewer children (Lutz & Samir, 2011). These scholars have estimated that the population could reach 10 billion by 2050; however, if a greater effort is made to educate more women, the results could be closer to 8.9 billion.

To further appreciate the notion that education can help to control population growth, we need to understand the role of technology in economic development and how increases in technology influence population demographics. In 1798, the great demographer Thomas R. Malthus made a strong argument that was accepted by much of the scientific community at that time—when a given population (i.e., in a specific country) is small, most of the people are likely to experience a high standard of living. Increases in the standard of living increase the "passion between the sexes," which results in increases in the population. Demographers traditionally refer to this phenomenon as "the positive check." However, when the size of the population reaches levels beyond the carrying capacity of the country (the ability of the country to feed itself and to take care of its young), fertility is then reduced. The reduction of fertility in conjunction with increases in malnutrition, disease, and famine all converge to reduce population growth—a phenomenon referred to as "the preventative check." According to economists Oded Galor and David N. Weil, the Malthusian hypothesis applies only to developing economies (i.e., primarily agrarian societies) (Galor & Weil, 2000). When economies change from agrarian to industrial, increases in technology result in a shift where the relative level of skills rises, which in turn leads families to have fewer children (i.e., emphasis shifts to quality of children and away from quantity of children). Output per capita increases with proportional increases in the rate of population growth. However, further increases in technological change (i.e., societies moving into the information age) prompt fertility rates to decline. *Education plays an important role in this process.* Increased technological changes require increases in education of the labor force. Increases in the use of technology in the labor market prompt parents to ensure that their children receive more schooling. More schooling further accelerates the rate of technological progress.

To escape the Malthusian trap in developing countries, public policies should be devised to increase the level of technology, which in turn necessitates education. That is, more emphasis is needed to increase educational attainment in the developing countries to ensure economic development and control of population growth.

Increased Happiness

After reviewing ninety American studies, Witter, Okun, Stock, & Haring (1984) concluded that educational attainment accounts for 1 percent to 3 percent of the variance in subjective well-being. This observation was reinforced by Layard (2005, p. 62), who wrote that "education has only a small effect on happiness, though of course it raises happiness by raising a person's income."

However, Alex Michalos, a guru of social indicators research, highlighted the fact that most of the studies linking education with happiness tend to focus on direct effects. He asserts that indirect effects are more realistic (Michalos, 2008). He believes that education plays a significant role in reducing discrepancies between what one has and several referent states, such as what one wants, what relevant others have, what one had in the past, what one expected to have three years ago, what one expects to have in five years, what one deserves to have, and what one needs to have. This idea is the basis of his multiple discrepancies theory (Michalos, 1985). That is, life satisfaction increases when an individual engages in actions that produce outcomes serving to decrease multiple discrepancies (decrease discrepancies between what one has and what one wants, between what one has and what other relevant others have, etc.). Hence, education comes into play when it helps the individual reduce these multiple discrepancies, which it certainly does.

EQUITY ISSUES IN EDUCATIONAL WELL-BEING

In this section, we address equity issues in educational well-being in relation to two major segments of the population: girls/women and the disabled.

Advances in Educational Well-Being of Women

The well-being of women has improved significantly during the past fifty years, but more needs to be accomplished. There have been significant increases in female literacy as well as in the number of girls completing primary and secondary school. Even the increase in tertiary education among women has been dramatic (United Nations Development Programme, 2013, p. 159) (box 5.8).

Gender discrimination in education has been gradually dismantled from ancient times to the present—from the gender equitable Chera Dynasty of the Sangam Age in India (300 Before the Common Era–400 Common Era) to the United Nations Millennium Development Goals campaign of 2015. Major strides toward the reduction of gender disparities in education are evident.

However, even in 2015, total gender equality remains an elusive dream in some countries. In the least developed countries, the number of women with at least a secondary education remains at 17.9 percent compared with men at 27.1 percent. The equivalent values worldwide are 53.3 percent for women and 62.9 percent for men (United Nations Development Programme, 2013, p. 159). Gender inequality is most pronounced in the least developed countries and is concentrated in the Arab states of North Africa and West Asia, South Asia, and, still, in wide expanses of sub-Saharan Africa (United Nations Development Programme, 2013, p. 159).

Figure 5.21 illustrates the public's attitude toward education for girls and women. In Kuwait and Egypt, 36 percent of respondents to the World Values Survey strongly agreed or agreed with the statement: "A university education is more important for a boy than a girl." In contrast, 15 percent of Japanese respondents and only 2 percent of Swedish respondents strongly agreed or agreed with the same statement.

Because of continuing gender disparities, but building on past and recent successes, in 2015 the United Nations restated the goal of gender equality at the 2015 Summit on Sustainable Development: *Goal 5: Achieve gender equality and empower all women and girls* (United Nations Development

---

BOX 5.8

A mother's education is more important to her child's survival than is household income or wealth.
(United Nations Development Programme, 2013, p. 89).

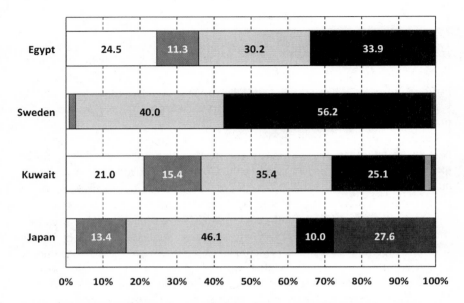

□ Agree Strongly ■ Agree □ Disagree ■ Stongly Disagree ■ No Answer ■ Dont Know

Figure 5.21. World Values Survey: "A university education is more important for a boy than for a girl." Responses by country (Egypt 2012, Japan 2010, Kuwait 2013, Sweden 2011). *Source*: (Data from World Values Survey, 2010–2014)

Programme, 2014). The United Nations Web site regarding the attainment of this goal states the following:

> Gender equality is not only a fundamental human right but a necessary foundation for a peaceful, prosperous and sustainable world. Providing women and girls with equal access to education, health care, decent work, and representation in political and economic decision-making processes will fuel sustainable economies and benefit societies and humanity at large.
>
> — (United Nations, 2015b)

As reported in specialized studies conducted by the United Nations (UN Women, 2015), considerable progress has occurred worldwide in achieving gender parity between men and women, especially because of the gains made through implementation of the Millennium Development Goals campaign focused on women (which include equal access to primary and secondary education for both girls and boys).

Considerable progress in education for girls and women has been documented. Education has been recognized to change women's lives and to improve gender equality in all walks of life. Educated women assume leadership positions in politics, administration, and the economy.

Since 1990, the good news is that female literacy and the number of girls completing primary, secondary, and even tertiary educations have increased dramatically. The bad news is that the number of women in developing countries that offer some secondary education remains low compared with that of men (United Nations Development Programme, 2013). This situation does not mean that things cannot change for the better. Professor Liz Eckermann at Deakin University in Australia, an expert on gender studies, points to the example of the state of Kerala in India (Eckermann, 2017). Government initiatives in education have been successful, producing rapid, dramatic results. These initiatives have produced the best health and well-being outcomes in all of India even though Kerala is one of the poorest, most densely populated Indian states. Improved female literacy rates have had a positive effect on health, employment, and subjective well-being.

We conclude by stating the following:

- Although gender inequality persists in schools in some of the developing countries, there is significant progress in gender parity. One can easily state that gender equality in the twenty-first century pervades the educational system in every nation around the globe.
- Much of the progress in gender parity in society is linked with the progress evidenced in the school systems. In other words, gender parity in education is leading to gender parity in society.
- The traditional norm that boys are assigned to labor-market-oriented courses (e.g., mathematics, science, engineering, business) whereas girls are assigned to domestic life courses (e.g., history, language, home economics, nursing) is no longer a tradition. Gendered curricula are no longer the norm.
- The "gender pipeline" argument[5] is increasingly recognized around the world. That is, parents are increasingly recognizing that occupational opportunities for their female children are linked to attending school, doing well in school, and taking the courses that would lead to prestigious, well-paying occupations.
- Evidence suggests that female students believe that their active participation in formal schooling and success in education are linked to their future prosperity.

Advances in Educational Well-Being of the Disabled

Education for the disabled has been a difficult issue because significant resources are required to deal with this issue (box 5.9). It is an issue referred to as "inclusive education . . . which means more than physical integration, so that in addition to accessible classrooms and facilities, students with disabilities must be afforded adequate instructional systems. These supports may include flexible curriculum (for some students), adequately prepared teachers, and a welcoming school community culture that goes beyond tolerance to acceptance" (Peters, 2007, p. 99). Inclusive education was endorsed by ninety-two governments and twenty-five international organizations at the 1994 World Conference on Special Needs Education in Salamanca, Spain. This document is known as the "Salamanca Statement" (United Nations Educational, Scientific and Cultural Organization, 1994).

Peters (2007) traces the movement for inclusive education to 1960 when the UN General Assembly adopted the landmark *Convention against Discrimination in Education*. Before 1960, inclusive education was treated as a welfare issue, not a human rights issue. Significant progress has been made in the development of inclusive educational policies since 1960. The 1960 convention obligated signatories to eliminate and prevent discrimination in education. The convention also required signatories to promote equal opportunity. However, the convention also stated that higher education should be made equally accessible to all based on "individual capacity." Individual capacity was operationalized in terms of IQ tests. The 1971 UN *Declaration on the Rights of Mentally Retarded Persons* introduced the concept of "maximum potential," shifting policy away from "individual capacity." The declaration states "such education, training, rehabilitation and guidance as will enable him to develop his ability and *maximum potential* [emphasis added]." The 1975 UN *Declaration on the Rights of Disabled Persons* defined a person with a disability "as one who is unable to ensure the necessities of normal social life due to deficiency." The goal was further articulated in the declaration as the right "to enjoy life as normal as possible" and "to promote integration in normal life." The focus of education in this context

---

BOX 5.9

A dominant problem in the disability field is the lack of access to education for both children and adults with disabilities. As education is a fundamental right for all, enshrined in the Universal Declaration of Human Rights, and protected through various international conventions, this is a very serious problem. In a majority of countries, there is a dramatic difference in the educational opportunities provided for disabled children and those provided for non-disabled children. It will simply not be possible to realize the goal of Education for All if we do not achieve a complete change in this situation.

(Lindqvist, 1999, p. 7)

is to develop the abilities, capabilities, and self-reliance of the disabled. The 1981 UNESCO *Sundberg Declaration* went further by addressing education as "lifelong," not simply primary and secondary education. The declaration put the disabled on an equal footing with the nondisabled by stating, "Persons with disabilities must be given the opportunity to utilize their creative, artistic, and intellectual potential to the full, not only for their own benefit, but also for the enrichment of the community." The 1982 UN *World Programme of Action Concerning Disabled Persons* went further by adding language related to location and responsibilities, stating that education of disabled persons should take place in the general school system and should be "compulsory" in the same way that the nondisabled are treated (United Nations Enable, 2003–2004). The 1989 UN *Tallinn Guidelines for Action on Human Resources Development* recommended strategies to promote education and training such as "special education teachers as consultants to regular education teachers, resource rooms with specialized personnel and materials, special classrooms in regular schools and interpreters for deaf students." Another strategy: "General-teacher-training curricula should include a course of study in skills for teaching disabled children and young persons in regular schools" (United Nations, 1989). The 1990 UNICEF *Convention on the Rights of the Child* stressed children's right to "full and harmonious development of personality and preparation to live a responsible life in a free society" went further by treating disabled students equally to nondisabled students. Specifically, policy statements reflected a change of perspective: Instead of helping disabled children to fit into society, society should change to welcome their inclusion. Also in 1990, UNESCO sponsored the *World Declaration* ratified by 155 countries. This declaration stresses universal access and equity in education for the disabled. In 1993, the United Nations developed *standard rules on the equalization of opportunities* for persons with disabilities. These rules expanded the scope of rights to access in terms of cultural activities, recreation and sports, and religious participation. In 1994, the Salamanca Statement set the policy agenda for inclusive education on a global level by recognizing individual differences in learning and identified gifted and talented students in that mix (United Nations Educational, Scientific and Cultural Organization, 1994). This policy forced a shift in thinking: from learning "deficiencies" to learning "abilities." In 1995, the World Summit for Social Development established specific links between education, poverty, and disability. In other words, participants in this summit recognized that people with disabilities are too often forced into poverty, unemployment, and social isolation. That is, poverty is a significant barrier to education for the disabled. In 2000, UNESCO developed a framework for action that made "the care and education of children with special needs" a priority. More recently in 2004, UNESCO developed a flagship document (*The Right to*

Education for Persons with Disabilities: Toward Inclusion) that addresses specific challenges in achieving educational goals.

Of course, developing countries, strapped for resources, have not made significant strides to address this fundamental human rights issue. Estimates of the percentage of children and youth with disabilities who attend school in developing countries are extremely low: 1 percent to 4 percent (Habibi, 1999; United Nations Educational, Scientific and Cultural Organization, 1994, Section 10).

PUBLIC POLICY AND EDUCATIONAL WELL-BEING

In this section, we argue that successful educational policies and programs applied in one country cannot and should not be applied in another country without considering the "context." We also argue that education is an important factor in globalization. For countries to compete in the global marketplace, education must be a priority in policy making. We discuss specific strategies to enhance education in a global economy and make the point that education plays an important role in the making of global citizens.

Context Is Important

In formulating public policy, *context is key*. That is, one cannot use large data sources (data provided by the World Bank, TIMSS, PISA) to rank order countries to identify top performers and laggards. Implicit in our attempt to rank order countries is the notion that we can identify "best practices" countries; if we do, then we can simply study these best practices educational systems and mimic them in countries with low educational well-being. The problem with using best practices educational systems is "context." Can we, for example, use Finland's educational system to formulate educational policies in a laggard country such as Ghana? The answer is clearly *no*. Finland's success story is not only due to school-related factors such as type and level of investment in education, workforce issues, the use of educational technologies, and the like; Finland's success is complicated by nonschool factors, that is, factors in the schools' environment or outside the school. Nonschool factors cannot be changed easily by educational policies because such policies are inherently directed to school-related factors. Nonschool factors include the culture of the community housing the targeted schools, the socioeconomic status of the families of the school children, the religions of these families, income inequality, family relationships, and family circumstances that may affect students' performance in the classroom such as whether the student got enough sleep or whether she or he comes to school hungry. In most countries, an understanding of nonschool factors and the implications of these factors for learning should be part of the public discourse. Policy makers who push for across-the-board reforms (e.g., hold teachers accountable through merit pay, abolish the tenure system for teachers, and provide more funding for computers in the classroom) should step back and recognize the role of the nonschool factors on the effectiveness of policies that are in place and those that are proposed. The educational policy that has gained much publicity in the United States, namely the "No Child Left Behind" policy of President George W. Bush's administration (United States Department of Education, 2004), does not consider nonschool factors. It is administered through an accountability standard called Adequate Yearly Progress (AYP). For the federal government to provide funds to a given school district, that district must demonstrate significant progress in standardized achievement tests. This educational policy has forced schools in the United States to focus on helping students attain higher scores on standardized achievement tests. Teachers are forced to teach not to achieve a higher level of educational well-being by taking the context into account; they teach to ensure that students score well on the standardized achievement tests. School administrators evaluate a teacher's performance based on the extent to which students pass their standardized achievement tests. That is not say that we should give up "big data" (standardized achievement testing). Such data are important to allow policy makers to monitor the level of educational well-being of their constituencies. However, big data also contain much information about the context of the schools and the school districts. Such information must be part of the equation in policy formulation. Policies must be designed to promote educational well-being by addressing both school-related and nonschool factors. It is not an easy task, but it can be done. Educational researchers must play a major role in this endeavor.

Education in the Global Economy

Much of progress in standard of living and quality of life can be attributed to technology (Schumpeter, 1943; Solow, 1957). Joseph E. Stiglitz (2001 Nobel laureate in Economics) and Bruce C. Greenwald, in their seminal book, *Creating a Learning Society* (2014), have effectively argued that technological progress, or what they call "learning how to learn or learning to do things better" is pivotal to improvement in human productivity, living standards, quality of life, and ultimately societal progress. What separates developed from less-developed countries is the knowledge gap, not resource deficiencies. Hence, policy development should focus on closing the knowledge gap—that is, on enhancing learning. Government policies have played a significant role in the speed of technological progress (e.g., public investments in education, government-funded research, legal protection of intellectual property). These authors are persuasive in their argument: Much of the difference in per capita income among countries can be accounted for by learning and learning spillovers. Policies do transform countries and their economies into "learning societies," which in turn serve to enhance the quality of life and well-being of citizens. The authors posed two key questions: (1) Do markets, on their own, result in efficient learning and innovation? (2) If not, what are the government policies that help in the creation of learning and innovation? The answer to the first question is that markets, left to their own devices, are inefficient in creating learning and inducing innovation. Modern industrial policies seek to promote industries and technologies with greater learning capabilities and greater spillover effects on other sectors of society. For example, well-designed trade restrictions, government subsidies to support sectors, and exchange rate interventions can play an important role in creating and accelerating learning.

The traditional theory of comparative advantage assumes that knowledge is fully available. If this theory is so, countries develop their economies by taking advantage of their relative endowments (e.g., Portugal exports wine because it is endowed with weather conducive to growing wine; Germans are endowed with a history and tradition of good automotive engineering, allowing them to be competitive in the automobile market). Stiglitz and Greenwald argue that the most important "endowment" that a country has is its learning capacity (i.e., knowledge it can learn to gain a comparative advantage) vis-à-vis competitors. Countries that gain a comparative advantage are those that have learned how to increase productivity (i.e., more output that can be produced with the same or less input or more output produced per worker with the same or decreased levels of input).

Countries can increase their rate of economic growth by creating a learning society. Firms in the developed countries learn quickly how to improve their productivity[6] by filling in the gap between current and best practices (i.e., moving toward the frontier) and moving the best practices forward (i.e., moving the frontier forward). The former is done through education and training, the latter through research and development. In contrast, firms in developing countries enhance their productivity by closing the gap between their firms' current practices and best practices in the advanced industrial countries.

What Is to Be Learned and How to Foster Learning?

Stiglitz and Greenwald (2014) identified three types of learning that serve economic growth, quality of life, and societal progress: (1) learning about comparative advantage, (2) learning to manage organizations and societies, and (3) learning capacities and learning to learn. *Learning about comparative advantage* is about identifying what "products" organizations can market widely and globally with greater efficiency and effectiveness, that is, entrepreneurship. *Learning to manage organizations and societies* refers to management knowledge—knowledge about managing large organizations and large projects with minimum negative externalities (i.e., with little pollution, without endangering the safety of the public, and causing little harm to other stakeholders). *Learning capacities and learning to learn* refer to the ability of individuals, firms, and countries to discover knowledge that might be relevant to establishing a comparative advantage and the management of large organizations and projects. This approach may entail using trial-and-error learning or using feedback to make corrections. It may entail the design of institutions that foster innovation and creativity.

The same authors identify six strategies: (1) learning capabilities, (2) access to knowledge, (3) the catalysts for learning, (4) contacts, (5) creating a creative mind-set, and (6) the context. *Learning capabilities* refer to the individual's capacity to learn. For example, much has been said about how young people tend to learn better than older people. Perhaps this observation is the case because the young are not invested in old ideas. The young absorb information much more readily than the old. They are more motivated to learn the skills and knowledge that would enable them to succeed, but this trait does not mean that only the young have better learning capabilities. Programs and institutions could be designed to enhance learning capabilities. For example, making learning personally relevant to one's goals (or demonstrating how this learning could be used to help the individual or firm perform better) is a strategy to enhance learning capabilities.

Access to knowledge is another way to enhance learning. New knowledge is difficult to acquire without old knowledge. That is, all knowledge builds on preexisting knowledge. Access to knowledge is important in that regard. One needs to access knowledge to build new knowledge. Access to knowledge is a major problem for the developing countries. Universities and other institutions of learning play a central role in providing access to knowledge. The open access movement is dedicated to this goal.

Catalysts are methods designed to spur people to learn. Ideas build on other ideas; old technology spurs new technology. For example, a person looking at a patented device may think of new ways to improve the device. Thus, catalyst policies could be designed to provide incentives for people and organizations to focus on technologies, the goal being to improve these technologies.

Learning can occur through *contact* with other people and institutions. Learning can occur through observation. One can formulate policies designed to encourage contact among institutions. Encouraging firms in developing countries to visit best-practices firms in developed countries is an example of such policies.

With respect to creating a creative mind-set Stiglitz and Greenwald mean a set of beliefs grounded in science that enhance societal progress. People must believe that their standard of living and quality of life can be improved through solutions found in science and technology. The belief that science and technology, not religion alone, is the basis for societal progress and is foundational to economic prosperity and quality of life. Such a belief is inculcated through an educational system that teaches students the basic tenets of science and technology and the notion that the use of science and technology is the ultimate approach to improving the quality of life. As such, policies designed to instill more science and technology in educational curricula in primary and secondary schools are essential.

Finally, the *context* is equally important to fostering a learning society. Some environments enhance learning, others stifle it. A learning environment is one that can help create learning capability, a learning mind-set, a network of contacts that encourages learning, and catalysts to learning. For example, employees working in a hostile environment who can barely make ends meet are not likely to have the mental energy to devote to learning, innovation, and creativity. A safe, collegial, nurturing work environment is needed to induce learning and enhance productivity.

Market Structure, Government Intervention, and Learning

Proponents of classical economic theory have long argued that competition provides a spur to innovation, whereas monopolies stifle competition and, by default, learning and innovation. However, large enterprises have distinct advantages in innovation. Large firms can fund innovation efforts that smaller firms cannot. On the other hand, large firms tend to be more bureaucratic and rigid, which puts them at a disadvantage in some sectors of society where the pace of technological innovation is rapid. Stiglitz and Greenwald argue that the relationship between competition and innovation may be U-shaped.

A strong welfare state can absorb some of the risks of small businesses, which in turn may encourage small businesses to engage in innovation. More generally, the authors advocate the Nordic model, in which government plays a larger role in formulating an array of policies that are conducive to learning and innovation (see also p. 105). Government intervention provides the substitute for capital markets in subsidizing research and development and education. The Nordic model encourages investments in education, allows less reliance on private financing of higher education, reduces the adverse effects of bankruptcy due to student loans, and promotes the use of income-contingent loans. Government-subsidized education is complementary to private investments in innovation. Government investments in education tend to increase the returns to private investments in innovation. Government policies that promote education ensure that society benefits from innovations. That is, the Nordic model does better in disseminating knowledge throughout the economy, which is pivotal for enhancing societal productivity. The US model, which is based on ruthless competition, encourages firms to keep their ideas secret and to keep whatever knowledge they acquire to themselves. The Nordic model maintains a high rate of economic growth not only in productivity but also in quality of life. The Nordic model advocates the use of institutional and policy reforms that promote greater innovation, reducing insecurity associated with innovation and openness, and providing more support for those displaced by innovation through retraining and additional education—to ensure that the displaced can remain productive members of society.

In other words, government can correct market failures endemic in a learning economy. Government provides educational opportunities that enhance individuals' capacity and motivation to learn. Government can also provide social protection that would allow entrepreneurs to offset the risks associated with new ventures. Government supports basic research, which is foundational for technology improvements. Finally, government can also help offset the excesses in financial markets associated with macroeconomic volatility.

The reader should also be cognizant of the trade-offs of popular policies such as intellectual property rights, legal protection against patent and copyright infringements, and legal restraints on workers' mobility. Although some may argue that such policies provide stronger incentives for investments in learning and innovation, others argue that they reduce the flow of knowledge, which in turn may result in less learning and perhaps less investment in learning.

To do this, government must do a better job of linking schools to jobs. In many instances, there is a disconnect between schools and the rapidly changing labor market. In other words, there is a gap between education and the economy. Professor Alexander Wiseman of Lehigh University, an expert in comparative education, advocates "competency-based education" (Wiseman, 2015). Competency-based education is not about vocational education; it is about what students can do when they complete their formal education. Conventional formal education places much more emphasis on knowledge than on skills. Students become competent at knowing facts and figures but not necessarily at using those facts and figures in a job context. Business leaders often complain that many schools (secondary schools as well as post-secondary schools) produce students with knowledge but no job-related skills, especially soft skills—skills that make workers successful in the workplace, such as interpersonal skills, teamwork skills, decision-making skills, presentation skills, organizational skills, and information technology skills. One strong remedy to this disconnect between knowledge and skills is apprenticeship. Apprenticeship programs encourage employers to apply industry standards to help students transform their knowledge into skills highly relevant to industry. The good news is that apprenticeship programs are becoming increasingly popular in many of the developed countries such as the United States, Austria, and Denmark. Besides apprenticeship programs, many countries have adopted competency-based education (sometimes called National Qualifications Frameworks). Competency-based education combines skills and knowledge as part of the educational curricula in both secondary and post-secondary schools. The focus of competency-based education is on industry standards rather than on subject-based curricula. Japan is a good case in point. The Japanese secondary schools tend to be more involved in helping workforce-bound students enter the labor force upon high school graduation. Japanese employers maintain strong relationships with high schools and teachers through semiformal contracts that allow employers to cull the best students of the noncollege bound youth. Similar programs have been developing in colleges globally. Academic knowledge is no longer sufficient. Industry is increasingly involved with higher education to guide curriculum matters. Additionally, the norm is now established in many large firms for job training. For example, over the past several decades, about two-thirds of company training dollars in the United States were spent on college graduates entering the job market. Furthermore, much more emphasis is now placed on vocational training at trade schools. The popularity of trade schools and vocational training is taking hold, which is another remedy to the knowledge–skills gap.

Education Amounts to Nation Building

Comparative education scholars have increasingly recognized that education is an important tool for nation building (Gutmann & Ben-Porath, 1987). Education is an indispensable tool for national political and economic development. Political leaders have long used their national educational systems to create loyal, productive citizenry. Schools are key components in the political socialization of youth. Perhaps, therefore, responsibility for education is spelled out in the constitution of most nation states.

Professor Alexander Wiseman, mentioned previously, argues that formal education is a strong socialization agent (Wiseman, 2015). This socialization effect is derived from several educational sources. First, there is civics education. Schools play a role in citizen development through civics education. Good citizenship is achieved partly through direct instruction using a civics-education curriculum. Consider civic education in China. It is called "moral education," "character education," or "values education." Second, in addition to the educational institution, citizenship development is also influenced by other socialization agents such as the family institution, mass media institutions, religious institutions, political institutions, and the like. Nevertheless, the educational institution is at the top of this list of socializing institutions. People who have higher levels of educational well-being tend to be good citizens. They have strong values reflective of social justice, human rights, and a sense of civic duty, and they care about their fellow citizens and the country at large, not only the country at large but also the world at large! In other words, education fosters national citizenship and global citizenship as well (Rauner, 1998). Much evidence suggests that there is a shift away from national civics to global civics—citizenship as a global and universal state. Furthermore, these civic values reflect a global trend in democratic attitudes among youth, which may account for many of the democracy movements in countries characterized by a history of autocratic regimes. Professor Wiseman puts it this way:

> The impact of formal mass schooling around the world is that political socialization into local and national communities is now increasingly normal. The result is that students increasingly claim the rights (and responsibilities) of global citizens rather than citizens of specific or limited communities.
>
> —(Wiseman, 2015, p. 105)

Students around the world are increasingly becoming global citizens. Students identify with others around the world because they all share a common experience—formal schooling. Shared norms, values, and culture are achieved through formal schooling. Global citizenship is increasingly becoming part of the curricula in many schools around the globe. Consider Oxfam International (https://www.oxfam.org/), a nongovernmental organization established in 1995 to help reduce poverty and social injustice worldwide. Part of its mission is to introduce a global citizenship curriculum in schools worldwide. Oxfam's global citizenship curriculum is designed to teach students universal concepts such as social justice, equity, diversity, globalization, sustainability, and world peace. Furthermore, part of the curriculum involves imparting specific skills such as critical thinking; advocacy for social justice, equality, respect, and upholding dignity for all people; cooperation; and conflict resolution. Values embedded in the curriculum include social identity, empathy, respect for diversity, sustainable development, and concern for the environment. Oxfam provides schools with professional development training, resources for teaching global citizenship, and support for projects related to global citizenship.

Other programs and institutions designed to propagate global citizenship in schools exist around the globe. For example, International Baccalaureate (IB) (International Baccalaureate, 2017) is essentially a nongovernmental organization, created in 1968, that offers four programs of international education aimed at developing intellectual and social skills that help students succeed in a globalized society. Students in an IB program are exposed to world literature, world languages, and world history. Many colleges and universities have increasingly adopted the IB program, hence becoming IB schools.

CONCLUSIONS

We close the chapter by stressing that education is imperative for human well-being, having reviewed the range of ways it contributes to the quality of life of individuals, families, states, and the world at large. Policies designed to improve education, learning, and innovation can enhance the quality of life of people and countries in significant and remarkable ways. Societies that must deal with accelerating technological change must create a learning society, and, as discussed previously, education plays an important role in creating a learning society. Societies must adapt to technological change, and such adaptation must be planned and executed by educators, educational researchers, and public policy makers who deal with educational issues. These change agents can further enhance educational well-being through programs and policies designed to enhance learning capabilities. Programs and policies can be designed to increase access to knowledge and create catalysts for learning. Educational policies cannot be simply formulated based on the "best practices" of a few good countries in the developed world. The context must be considered in policy formation. Doing so requires close and effective collaboration among agencies that collect big data on educational well-being (e.g., the World Bank, UNESCO, OECD, and ministries of education in every country), educational researchers who use big data, educational policy makers, educational administrators, and teachers. Such close collaboration is essential to the further advancement of educational well-being and, ultimately, human well-being in a global context.

We began by discussing education as a "human rights issue," providing much documentation concerning treaties, declarations, and articles of international agencies and country articles of constitution that education is an inalienable right, a human right to all—that no person should be denied the right to education regardless of gender, disability, or social status. We discussed how education is a tool of economic development—a tool that enhances workers' knowledge and skill level. As such, we must view education as an investment in our future growth and prosperity, not an expense or a consumption element.

We then provided the reader with an analytical framework to guide the remaining discussion. The framework shows that we can break down the discussion by describing how comparative educational researchers have conceptualized and measured educational well-being in terms of a set of "quantity" and "quality" indicators. The framework also shows the factors that influence educational well-being, both school-related (i.e., educational policies, investment in education, educational technologies, workforce issues, and school infrastructure) and nonschool related (i.e., economic well-being, social well-being, and health well-being). The consequences of educational well-being are also captured in the framework. That is, educational well-being influences other dimensions of societal well-being—such as economic well-being, social well-being, health well-being, political well-being.

Focusing on quantity indicators of educational well-being (e.g., average years of total schooling for adults aged fifteen plus), we demonstrate the significant gains in educational attainment worldwide. We showed that the growth rate of positive change in educational well-being is much more pronounced in relation to the developing countries compared to the developed countries. The disparity between men and women is disappearing too, especially when one looks at the trend in global educational well-being. With respect to quality indicators of educational well-being (learning proficiency in reading, mathematics, and science), we observed that there is a marked difference between the developing and developed countries in terms of reading, mathematics, and science. Students in the developed countries outperform students in the developing countries by a significant margin. However, the good news is that students in the developing countries are quickly picking up the pace. We believe that they will catch up with students in the developed countries in a few decades. Also good news is that the disparity between male and female students is negligible.

We then shifted focus to address factors deemed influential in educational well-being: school-related and nonschool-related. With respect to school-related factors, we started out by discussing the impact of educational policies on educational well-being. We specifically focused on compulsory education, a very important educational policy, and we showed that this policy has contributed significantly to the noted progress in educational well-being. Addressing the impact of investment in education, our analysis shows that this factor does make a big difference in educational well-being. That is, countries and world regions that invest a greater portion of their GDP per capita in education tend to register higher levels of educational well-being than countries and world regions that invest a lesser amount. Most striking is the fact that the highest returns on investment seem to be strongest for the developed rather than for the developing countries. Again, further good news reinforcing the overall theme of this book, that is, advances in human well-being are not only significant but also more evident among the developing than the already-developed countries. With respect to educational technologies, we have seen an exponential use of personal computers and the World

Wide Web in education, in both developing and developed countries. Of course, the use of educational technologies was first widespread among the developed countries, but the developing countries are catching up rapidly. There is also much evidence suggesting that educational technologies play an important role in educational well-being. Again, this development is good news for educational well-being and human well-being at large. Focusing on workforce issues, we explained that the disparity between the developed and the developing world might lie in the use of teachers in schools. There are significant problems of teacher training, recruitment, and retention in both the developed and developing countries, but much more so in the latter. One significant workforce issue is the shortage of qualified teachers and the use of paraprofessionals. Using paraprofessionals has allowed governments to save much money in educational expenditure and deal with the teacher shortage problem. However, such a solution has taken a toll on educational well-being. The outcomes are not as positive as they should be. Many scholars point to Finland as having a "best practice" educational system and argue that Finland's success is partly attributed to the proper credentialing of teachers, who are highly qualified and respected as professionals in society at large and well paid. Of course, to emulate Finland requires shifting priorities at the national level. For many countries, this course may translate into investing more in education than in other sectors of society. Infrastructure plays a significant role in educational well-being too. Much evidence suggests that educational well-being is adversely affected in schools with dilapidated infrastructures compared to schools with good infrastructures. Again, infrastructure issues may partly account for the disparity of educational well-being between the developed and developing countries. In many places in sub-Saharan Africa, schools lack basic water, sanitation, and electricity to function regularly. To deal with this problem, governments must give more priority to education compared to other sectors of the economy. Nonschool factors include economic well-being, social well-being, and health well-being. Much research has shown that schools in high socioeconomic districts produce students with high levels of educational well-being, compared to schools in low-socioeconomic districts. This phenomenon is worldwide. It is not all about money and wealth or lack of wealth—it is the culture and mindset associated with poverty. Much research has shown that students raised in high socioeconomic status neighborhoods have a different culture compared to their poor counterparts. High socioeconomic parents socialize their children with a different set of values—treating education as an important life goal that should be pursued with passion. As such, children from high socioeconomic backgrounds fare much better in educational well-being than their counterparts from low socioeconomic backgrounds. The same phenomenon applies at the national level in the sense that developed countries share a progress-prone culture, in which education plays a central role. The policy implications of this fact are profound. Policies must be formulated to educate the poor that education is pivotal to success in life and that education requires hard work, sacrifice, and delay of gratification. Furthermore, policies designed to reduce poverty can help. Entitlement programs can be linked to encouraging poor families to emphasize the importance of education and schooling to their children and to engage in behaviors reflecting values relegated to education. The same can be said in relation to social well-being. Children who have social support from nurturing families, nurturing relatives and neighbors, and nurturing communities are likely to experience higher levels of educational well-being than children with little social support. Social well-being matters to educational well-being. As such, public policy must be designed to foster social well-being. Health well-being is yet another nonschool factor affecting educational well-being. Children cannot effectively learn when they must battle illness. Health is a major detractor to education. Policies designed to enhance health well-being of children are a step in the right direction.

We then turned our attention to discussing the many positive outcomes of educational well-being on other well-being outcomes. We cited much evidence suggesting that educational well-being serves to increase economic well-being, political stability, social well-being, control of population growth, and happiness. Such research elevates the importance of educational well-being in societal welfare. Education should not be viewed only as a desirable societal goal but also as a means to other societal ends.

Although we discussed issues of gender disparity throughout, we devoted a major section in this chapter to equity issues dealing with both girls/women and the disabled. The basic finding is that female students have made enormous strides in achieving equity in education, and this equity seems to be highly instrumental in their educational well-being. We also reviewed much of the evidence related to the disabled, and we concluded that there has been much progress in this area too, in both the developed and the developing countries. Nevertheless, inequity is much more pronounced in the developing than in the developed countries. Hence, much more work is needed to achieve full equity among the disabled. But again, more good news to cheer.

NOTES

1 For a comprehensive list of agreements, see Education for All, 2017.

2 The issue of gender differences in both verbal and math proficiency is a complex phenomenon riddled with many competing theories and evidence. Readers interested in understanding the issues related to this complex phenomenon may consult Hyde, Fennema, and Lamon (1990) and Hyde and Linn (1988).

3 Besides compulsory education, hundreds of other educational policies play a significant role in educational well-being (e.g., policies related to class size, teacher-pupil ratio). For example, much evidence has supported the notion that students learn much better when class sizes are reduced (e.g., Blatchford, Moriarity, Edmonds, & Martin, 2002).

4 This is not to say that teachers who are highly motivated but have less experience do not do better than teachers with much experience. The system is replete with teachers with experience who do not do better than the less-experienced teachers because of burnout.

5 For a literature review of the "gender pipeline" concept, see Blickenstaff (2005).

6 Enhancing productivity means using inputs better to produce outputs (i.e., getting more output per unit of labor, capital, energy, or other resource inputs). We can also think about productivity enhancement in terms of providing more and/or better products (good and services) that are consumed by people or organizations for less money and effort.

REFERENCES

Acemoglu, D., & Angrist, J. D. (2002). How large are the social returns to education? Evidence from compulsory schooling laws. *NBER Macroeconomics Annual, 2002*.

Adelman, I. (2000). Fallacies in development theory and their implications for policy. In G. M. Meier & J. E. Stiglitz (Eds.), *Frontiers of development economics: The future in perspective*. Washington, DC: The World Bank.

Alesnia, A., & Perotti, R. (1996). Income distribution, political instability, and investment. *European Economic Review, 40*(6), 1203–1228.

Angrist, J. D., & Krueger, A. (1991). Does compulsory school attendance affect schooling and earnings? *Quarterly Journal of Economics, 106*(4), 979–1014.

Arrieta, G. A., & Cheynut, A. (2002). A world fit for us. United Nations Special Session on Children. [Opening remarks]. Retrieved June 29, 2017, from https://www.unicef.org/specialsession/documentation/childrens-statement.htm.

Becker, G. (1993). *Human capital: A theoretical and empirical analysis, with special reference to education*. Chicago: University of Chicago Press.

Behrman, J. R., & Hoddinott, J. (2005). Programme evaluation with unobserved heterogeneity and selective implementation: The Mexican PROGRESA impact on child nutrition. *Oxford Bulletin of Economic Statistics, 67*, 547–569.

Blatchford, P., Moriarity, V., Edmonds, S., & Martin, C. (2002). Relationships between class size and teaching: A multimethod and analysis of English infant schools. *American Educational Research Journal, 39*, 101–132.

Blickenstaff, J. C. (2005). Women and science careers: leaky pipeline or gender filter? *Gender and education, 17*, 369–386.

Blum, R. W., & Libbey, H. P. (2004). School connectedness—strengthening health and education outcomes for teenagers. *Journal of School Health, 74*, 231–242.

Bongaarts, J. (2010). The causes of educational differences in fertility in sub-Saharan Africa. *Vienna Yearbook of Population Research, 8*, 25–29.

Bourdieu, P. (1986). The forms of capital. In J. G. Richardson (Ed.), *Handbook of theory and research for the sociology of education*. New York: Greenwood Press.

Branham, D. (2004). The wise man builds his house upon the rock: The effects of inadequate school building infrastructure on student attendance. *Social Science Quarterly, 85*, 1112–1128.

Bryk, A. S., & Thum, Y. M. (1989). The effects of high school organization on dropping out: An exploratory investigation. *American Educational Research Journal, 26*, 353–383.

Cain, G. G., & Watts, H. W. (1970). Problems in making policy inferences from the Coleman Report. *American Sociological Review, 35*, 228–242.

Campbell, F. A., Pungello, E. P., Miller-Johnson, S., Burchinal, M., & Ramey, C. T. (2001). The development of cognitive and academic abilities growth curves from an early childhood educational experiment. *Developmental Psychology, 37*, 231–242.

Coleman, J. S. (1994). Social capital, human capital, and investment in you. In A. C. Petersen & J. T. Mortimer (Eds.), *Youth unemployment and society*. Cambridge, MA: Cambridge University Press.

Crocker, R. E. (2002). *Learning outcomes: A critical review of the state of the field in Canada*. Ottawa: Canadian Education Statistics Council.

Dee, T. (2003). Are there civic returns to education? NBER Working Paper No. 9588. Cambridge, MA: National Bureau of Economic Research.

Department of Education and Employment (1998). *The learning age: A renaissance for a new Britain, a summary*. Retrieved July 1, 2017, from http://www.leeds.ac.uk/educol/documents/summary.pdf.

Eckermann, L. (2017). History of well-being and the global progress of women. In R. J. Estes and M. J. Sirgy (Eds.), *Pursuit of human well-being: The untold history*. Dordrecht, NL: Springer.

Education for All. (2017, May 16). In Wikipedia, the Free Encyclopedia. Retrieved June 29, 2017, from https://en.wikipedia.org/w/index.php?title=Education_For_All&oldid=780633811.

EFA Global Monitoring Report Team (2006). *EFA global monitoring report 2007: Strong foundations: Early childhood care and education*. Paris: United Nations Educational, Scientific and Cultural Organization.

Entwisle, D., Alexander, K., & Olson, L. (2005). First grade and educational attainment by age 22: A new story. *American Journal of Sociology, 110*, 1458–1502.

European Court of Human Rights. (2010). *European convention on human rights*. [Amended document]. Strasbourg, France: European Court of Human Rights. Retrieved June 28, 2017, from https://ec.europa.eu/digital-single-market/sites/digital-agenda/files/Convention_ENG.pdf.

Furstenberg, F. R., & Hughes, M. E. (1995). Social capital and successful development among at-risk youth. *Journal of Marriage and the Family, 57*, 580–592.

Galor, O., & Weil, D. N. (2000). Population, technology, and growth: From Malthusian stagnation to the demographic transition and beyond. *American Economic Review, 90*, 806–828.

Glewwe, P., Hanushek, E. A., Humpage, S. D., & Ravina, R. (2011). School resources and educational outcomes in developing countries: A review of the literature from 1990 to 2010. Working Paper 17554. Cambridge, MA: National Bureau of Economic Research. Retrieved June 28, 2917, from https://core.ac.uk/download/pdf/6653965.pdf

Goldberg, A., Russell, M., & Cook, A. (2003). The effect of computers on student learning: A meta-analysis of studies from 1992to 2002. *Journal of Technology, Learning, and Assessment, 2,* 1–30.

Gutmann, A., & Ben-Porath, S. (1987). *Democratic education.* New York: Wiley.

Habibi, G. (1999). UNICEF and children with disabilities. *Education Update, 2,* 4–5.

Hattie, J. (2008). *Visible learning: A synthesis of over 800 meta-analyses relating to achievement* (1st ed.). New York: Routledge.

Hattie, J., & Yates, G. C. R. (2014). *Visible learning and the science of how we learn.* London: Routledge.

Hedges, L. V., Laine, R. D., & Greenwald, R. (1994). Does money matter: Meta-analysis of studies of differential school inputs on student outcomes. *Educational Researcher, 23,* 5–14.

Higgins, S., Hall, E., Wall, K., Woolner, P., & McCaughey, C. (2005). *The impact of school environments: A literature review.* Newcastle: The Centre for Learning and Teaching at the University of Newcastle. Retrieved June 28, 2017, from https://www.researchgate.net/publication/232607630_The_Impact_of_School_Environments_A_Literature_Review

Hyde, J. S., Fennema, E., & Lamon, S. J. (1990). Gender differences in mathematics performance: a meta-analysis. *Psychological Bulletin, 107,* 139–159.

Hyde, J. S., & Linn, M. C. (1988). Gender differences in verbal ability: A meta-analysis. *Psychological Bulletin, 104,* 53–80.

International Baccalaurate. (2017). Education for a better world. [Web site]. Retrieved June 30, 2017, from http://www.ibo.org/

Irogbe, K. (2014). *The effects of globalization in Latin America, Africa, and Asia: A global south perspective.* London: Lexington Books, a Division of Rowman and Littlefield.

Jhurree, V. (2005). Technology integration in education in developing countries: Guidelines to policy makers. *International Education Journal, 6,* 467–483.

KC, S., & Lentzner, H. (2010). The effect of education on adult mortality and disability: A global perspective. *Vienna Yearbook of Population Research,* 201–235.

Kozol, J. (1991). *Savage inequalities.* New York: Crown Publishers.

Layard, R. (2005). *Happiness: Lessons from a new science.* London: Penguin Books.

Leventhal, T., & Brooks-Gunn, J. (2000). The neighborhoods they live in: The effects of neighborhood residence on child and adolescent outcomes. *Psychological Bulletin, 126,* 309–337.

Libbey, H. P. (2004). Measuring student relationships to school: Attachment, bonding, connectedness, and engagement. *Journal of School Health, 74,* 274–282.

Lindqvist, B. (1999). Education as a fundamental right. *Educator's Update, 2,* 6–7.

Lleras-Muney, A. (2002). The relationship between education and adult mortality in the U.S. Working Paper 8986. Cambridge, MA: National Bureau of Economic Research. Retrieved June 28, 2017, from http://www.nber.org/papers/w8986.

Lochner, L., & Moretti, E. (2001). The effect of education on crime: Evidence from prison inmates, arrests, and self-reports. Working Paper No. 8605. Cambridge,

MA: National Bureau of Economic Research. Retrieved June 28, 2017, http://www.nber.org/papers/w8605.

Lonsdale, M. (2003). *Impact of school libraries on student achievement: A review of the research. A Report for the Australian School Library Association.* Camberwell, Victoria: Australian Council for Educational Research. Retrieved June 28, 2017, from http://files.eric.ed.gov/fulltext/ED482253.pdf.

Lutz, W., & Samir, K. C. (2011). Global human capital: Integrating education and population. *Science, 333*(6042), 587–592.

Marcus, R. F., & Sanders-Reio, J. (2001). The influence of attachment on school completion. *School Psychology Quarterly, 16*, 427–444.

Meier, D. W. (2000). *Will standards save public education?* (1st ed.). Boston: Beacon Press.

Michalos, A. C. (1985). Multiple discrepancies theory (MDT). *Social Indicators Research, 16*, 347–413.

Michalos, A. C. (2008). Education, happiness and wellbeing. *Social Indicators Research, 87*, 347–366.

Milligan, K., Moretti, E., & Oreopoulos (2003). Does education improve citizenship? Evidence from the U.S. and the U.K. Working Paper No. 9584. Cambridge, MA: National Bureau of Economic Research. Retrieved June 28, 2017, http://www.nber.org/papers/w9584.

Moon, B. (2007). Research analysis: Attracting, developing and retaining effective teachers: A global overview of current policies and practices. *Working Paper*, United Nations Educational, Scientific and Cultural Organization. Retrieved June 28, 2017, from http://citeseerx.ist.psu.edu/viewdoc/download?doi=10.1.1.47 2.8545&rep=rep1&type=pdf.

Murnane, R. J. (2007). Improving the education of children living in poverty. *Future Child, 17*, 161–182.

National Institute of Child Health and Human Development Early Child Care Research Network (2005). Duration and developmental timing of poverty and children's cognitive and social development from birth through third grade. *Child Development, 76*, 795–810.

Organization for Economic Cooperation and Development. (2006). *Education at a glance 2006.* Paris: Organization for Economic Cooperation and Development.

Organization for Economic Cooperation and Development. (2010). *Improving health and social cohesion through education.* Paris: OECD Publishing. Retrieved June 28, 2017 from http://dx.doi.org/10.1787/9789264086319-en.

Oreopoulos, P. (2003). Do dropouts drop out too soon? Evidence from changes in school-leaving laws. Working Paper No. 10155. Cambridge, MA: National Bureau of Economic Research. Retrieved June 28, 2017, http://www.nber.org/papers/w10155

Oreopoulos, P. (2006). The compelling effects of compulsory schooling: Evidence from Canada. *Canadian Journal of Economics, 39*(1), 22–52.

Parent-Teacher Association. (2017, February 18). In Wikipedia, the Free Encyclopedia. Retrieved June 28, 2017, from https://en.wikipedia.org/w/index.php?title=Parent-Teacher_Association&oldid=766164568.

Peters, S. J. (2007). "Education for All?": A historical analysis of international inclusive education policy and individuals with disabilities. *Journal of Disability Policy Studies, 18*(2), 98–108.

Petrakis, P. E., & Stamatakis, D. (2002). Growth and educational levels: A comparative analysis. *Economics of Education Review, 21*(5), 513–521.

Prentice, A. L., & Houston, S. E. (1975). *Family school and society in the nineteenth century Canada.* Toronto: Oxford University Press.

Programme for International Student Assessment. (2017, June 22). In *Wikipedia, The Free Encyclopedia.* Retrieved June 28, 2017, from https://en.wikipedia.org/w/index.php?title=Programme_for_International_Student_Assessment&oldid=786919694.

Psacharopoulos, G. (1985). Returns to education: A further international update and implications. *Journal of Human Resources, 20*, 583–604.

Psacharopoulos, G. (1994). Returns to investment in education: A global update. *World Development, 22*, 1325–1343.

Psacharopoulos, G., & Hinchliffe, K. (1973). *Returns to education: An international comparison.* Amsterdam: Elsevier.

Psacharopoulos, G., & Patrinos, H. A. (2004). Returns to investment in education: A further update. *Education Economics, 12*, 111–134.

Putnam, R. D. (1995). Bowling alone: America's declining social capital. *Journal of Democracy, 6*, 65–78.

Ratcliffe, R. (2013, January 29). The gender gap at universities: Where are all the men? *The Guardian.* Retrieved June 28, 2017, from http://www.theguardian.com/education/datablog/2013/jan/29/how-many-men-and-women-are-studying-at-my-university.

Rauner, M. (1998). *The worldwide globalization of civics education topics from 1955 to 1995.* (Doctoral dissertation). Stanford University, Stanford, CA. Available through https://searchworks.stanford.edu/view/3934707.

Romer, O. (1990). Endogenous technological change. *Journal of Political Economy, 98*(5), part 2, 71–102.

Sabates, R. (2008). Educational attainment and juvenile crime: Area-level analysis using three cohorts of young people. *British Journal of Criminology, 48*, 395–409.

Schultz, T. (1971). *Investment in human capital: The role of education and research.* New York: The Free Press.

Schumpeter, J. A. (1943). *Capitalism, socialism and democracy.* New York: Harper.

Sen, A. (2000). *Development as freedom.* New York: Anchor Books.

Sen, A. (2002a). *Rationality and freedom.* Boston: Harvard University Press.

Sen, A. (2002b). *Capability and well-being.* In M. Nussbaum & A. Sen (Eds.), *The quality of life.* Oxford: Oxford University Press.

Skirbekk, V. (2008). Fertility trends by social status. *Demographic Research, 18*(5), 145–180.

Smith, W. (Ed.). (1848). Diogenes Laertius. *A dictionary of Greek and Roman biography and mythology.* London: John Murray.

Solow, R. M. (1957). Technical change and the aggregate production function. *Review of Economics and Statistics, 39*, 312–320

Stiglitz, J. E., & Greenwald B. C. (2014). *Creating a learning society: A new approach to growth, development, and social progress.* New York: Columbia University Press.

Streeten, P. (1981). *First things first: Basic human needs in developing countries.* A World Bank Publication. Washington, DC: World Bank.

Suhrcke, M., & de Paz Nieves, C. (2011). *The impact of health and health behaviours on educational outcomes in high-income countries: A review of the evidence.* Copenhagen: WHO Regional Office for Europe. Retrieved June 28, 2017, from http://www.euro.who.int/__data/assets/pdf_file/0004/134671/e94805.pdf.

Taras, H., & Potts-Datema, W. (2005a). Chronic health conditions and student performance at school. *Journal of School Health, 75*, 255–266.

Taras, H., & Potts-Datema, W. (2005b). Sleep and student performance at school. *Journal of School Health, 75*, 248–254.

Taras, H., & Potts-Datema, W. (2005c). Obesity and student performance at school. *Journal of School Health, 75*, 291–295.

Taras, H., & Potts-Datema, W. (2005d). Childhood asthma and student performance at school. *Journal of School Health, 75*, 296–312.

UN Women. (2015). *Progress of the world's women 2015–2016: Transforming economies, realizing rights.* Retrieved June 29, 2017, from http://www.unwomen.org/en/ digital-library/publications/2015/4/progress-of-the-worlds-women-2015#sthash.kPQ5KvDx.dpuf.

United Nations. (1948). *Universal declaration of human rights.* Retrieved June 28, 2017, from http://www.un.org/en/universal-declaration-human-rights/.

United Nations. (1989). *Implementation of the World Programme of Action concerning disabled persons and the United Nations Decade of Disabled Persons.* [United Nations General Assembly document]. Retrieved June 30, 2017, from http://www.un.org/documents/ga/res/44/a44r070.htm.

United Nations. (2015a). *Goal 4: Ensure inclusive and quality education for all and promote lifelong learning.* Retrieved June 29, 2017 from http://www.un.org/sustainabledevelopment/education/.

United Nations. (2015b). *Goal 5: Achieve gender equality and empower all women and girls.* Retrieved June 30, 2017, from http://www.un.org/sustainabledevelopment/gender-equality/.

United Nations Children's Fund (UNICEF). *Statistics, 2015.* Retrieved July 20, 2015, from https://data.unicef.org/.

United Nations Development Programme. (1990). *Human development report, 1990: Concept and measurement of human development.* NY: Oxford University Press.

United Nations Development Programme. (1992). *Human development report, 1992: Global dimensions of human development* NY: Oxford University Press.

United Nations Development Programme. (2013). *Human development report, 2013: The rise of the south: Human progress in a diverse world.* New York: United Nations Development Programme. Retrieved June 29, 2017, from http://hdr.undp.org/sites/default/files/reports/14/hdr2013_en_complete.pdf.

United Nations Development Programme. (2014). *Human development report, 2014: Sustaining human progress—reducing vulnerabilities and building resilience.* New York: United Nations Development Programme. Retrieved June 29, 2017 from http://hdr.undp.org/sites/default/files/hdr14-report-en-1.pdf.

United Nations Educational, Scientific and Cultural Organization. (1953). *Progress of literacy in various countries: A preliminary statistical study of available census data since 1900.* Paris: United Nations Educational, Scientific and Cultural Organization.

United Nations Educational, Scientific and Cultural Organization. (1994). *The Salamanca statement and framework for action on special needs education*. Paris: United Nations Educational, Scientific and Cultural Organization.

United Nations Educational, Scientific and Cultural Organization. (2004). *Higher education in a globalized society*. UNESCO Education Position Paper. Paris: United Nations Educational, Scientific and Cultural Organization. Retrieved June 29, 2017, from https://www.washingtonpost.com/news/worldviews/wp/2016/11/22/47-percent-of-the-worlds-population-now-use-the-internet-users-study-says/?utm_term=.63ccde5c98fe.

United Nations Educational, Scientific and Cultural Organization. (2005). *The UNESCO Teacher Training Initiative in Sub-Saharan Africa*. Retrieved June 1, 2017, from http://unesdoc.unesco.org/images/0014/001436/143611e.pdf.

United Nations Educational, Scientific and Cultural Organization. (2015). *UNESCO Science Report, 2015*. Paris: United Nations Educational, Cultural, and Scientific Organization.

United Nations Enable (2003–2004). *Developmental and psychiatric disabilities*. Retrieved June 30, 2017, from http://www.un.org/esa/socdev/enable/disdevelopmental.htm#_Toc35445324.

United Nations Office of the High Commissioner (1976). *International Covenant on Economic, Social and Cultural Rights*. Retrieved June 28, 2017, from http://www.ohchr.org/EN/ProfessionalInterest/Pages/CESCR.aspx.

United States Department of Education (2004). *No Child Left Behind: Closing the achievement gap in America's public schools*. (Slide presentation). Retrieved June 29, 2017, from http://www.ed.gov/nclb/landing.jhtml.

Valk, J-H., Rashid, A. T, & Elder, L. (2010). Using mobile phones to improve educational outcomes: An analysis of evidence from Asia. *The International Review of Research in Open and Distributed Learning, 11*(1). Retrieved June 29, 2017, from http://www.irrodl.org/index.php/irrodl/article/view/794/1487.

Van Leeuwen, B., & Foldvari, P. (2008). Human capital and economic growth in Asia 1890–2000: A time-series analysis. *Asian Economic Journal, 22*(3), 225–240.

Van Zanden, J. L., Baten, J., d'Ercole, M. M., Rijpma, A., Smith, C., & Timmer, M. (Eds.). (2014). *How was life? Global well-being since 1820*. Paris: Organization for Economic Cooperation and Development Publishing.

Wigley, S., & Akkoyunlu-Wigley, A. (2006). Human capabilities versus human capital: Gauging the value of education in developing countries. *Social Indicators Research, 78*, 287–304.

Wiseman, A. W. (2015). *How the world learns: Comparative educational systems*. Chantilly, VA: The Teaching Company.

Witter, R. A., Okun, M. A., Stock, W. A., & Haring, M. J. (1984). Education and subjective well-being: A meta-analysis. *Educational Evaluation and Policy Analysis, 6*(2), 165–173.

World Bank. (2015). *World development report, 2015: Mind, society, and behavior*. Washington, DC: World Bank. Retrieved June 28, 2017, from http://www.worldbank.org/en/publication/wdr2015.

World Bank. (2017). Education statistics. [Databank]. Retrieved from http://data. worldbank.org/data-catalog/ed-stats.

World Values Survey (2010–2014). World Values Survey. Official aggregate v.20150418. World Values Survey Association. Madrid: Asep/JDS (aggregate file producer). Retrieved from http://www.worldvaluessurvey.org/WVSDocumen tationWV6.jsp.

Zajda, J., Biraimah, B., & Gaudelli, W. (Eds.). (2008a). *Education and social inequality in the global culture*. Dordrecht, NL: Springer.

Zajda, J., Davies, L., & Majhanovich, S. (Eds.) (2008b). *Comparative and global pedagogies: equity, access and democracy in education*. Dordrecht, NL: Springer.

Part III

Ak'b'al—Third day of the Maya calendar. Mixed media on paper—22″ × 30″. © 2015 Lylia Forero Carr. Used with permission.

Chapter 6

Toward a More Positive Future for All

ADVANCES IN HUMAN WELL-BEING: CONCLUDING THOUGHTS

We began this book with an emphasis on the need to "reframe" the way in which we perceive and experience the many dramatic changes that have taken place in human well-being over the past 125 years. Efforts to advance well-being certainly have been undermined by the numerous social, political, and economic calamities that have interfered with social progress in all regions of the world. The large numbers of deaths, disabilities, and dislocations of millions of people because of the two "great" world wars, the Armenian holocaust in Eurasia, and the Jewish Holocaust throughout Europe are especially noteworthy. So, too, are the stubborn social and political problems and the associated discrimination in virtually all societies based on gender, race, age, sexual orientation, and other personal traits that individuals cannot change. Both world wars and efforts to combat discrimination have consumed vast amounts of fiscal and human resources that otherwise could have been used to aid in advancing more positive outcomes in our collective well-being.

Even so, enormous accomplishments have been realized during these same time periods, especially in the health, education, and economic sectors. They, in turn, have served as the foundation for the even more dramatic accomplishments that took place in the late twentieth century and the early decade and a half of this still young twenty-first century. We detailed many of the most important of these advances in the preface, but we have not attempted to provide an encyclopedic-type presentation of the transformational changes that have taken place over such an extended period. To produce such a list was not one of our goals.

We have, however, set a framework within which governments and major nongovernmental leaders can work to realign public and private policies to make them more consistent with a positivist approach to advancing well-being. Such policies tend to be more participatory and transparent and, always, are supportive of other initiatives implemented by societies to improve the quality of life of their citizens. In presenting this framework, we have sought to identify the major drivers of human well-being documented in the chapters on health, the economy, and education. Doing so ensures that the well-being policies developed by local and national governments engage a fuller spectrum of state- and nonstate actors in the framing of policies that will add to the quality of life of *all* their citizens. This approach also offers a higher level of data-driven decision making for use by governments, business and corporate leaders, leaders in the not-for-profit sector, and leaders at all levels of social and political organization to work more cooperatively in helping to bring about the world we all seek.

The following summary of the major findings reported in the book is structured using the same framework found in the book itself. Throughout the summary, we have sought to identify positive alternatives that societies can adopt in promoting the well-being of their citizens. We focus first on the policy implications of the various philosophical traditions presented in chapter 2 vis-à-vis our personal and collective quest for well-being.

THE PHILOSOPHICAL FOUNDATIONS
OF HUMAN WELL-BEING

As discussed in chapter 2, the pursuit of *well-being* has been one of the most enduring quests of human civilization. The concept of well-being permeates our philosophies, religions and religious traditions, rituals and rites of passage, music, visual arts, and, of course, the performing arts in all their varieties. We reviewed the concept of well-being from a philosophical point of view—and shed light on how philosophers over many centuries have treated this concept from a Western perspective, an East Asian perspective, a South Asian perspective, and an Islamic perspective.

We treated a selection of major notions of well-being from the known history of the *Western world*—expressed in terms of the good life, harmony, and pleasure. The notion of the good life dates to ancient Greece. It involves people being honest, courageous, just, generous, compassionate, hospitable, and so on. In other words, the good life is a virtuous life. The concept of harmony as well-being became popular in the period 550–250 BCE. Philosophers during that time discussed harmony as it was reflected in the various attributes of the good life such as the soul's harmony with itself (i.e., striving to bring harmony to the soul to improve the individual's chances for trading up rather than down in the next life—trading up means to come back as a higher form of being); harmony among the members of one's species, nature in general, and in keeping with the principles of ideal law (i.e., living in a community and willingly following the community's customs and conventional laws in a manner consistent with divine law); harmony as blending daimones with a Supreme Being (i.e., daimones are considered entities exalted for having special status—better than souls but lesser than gods; for example, love is viewed as a cosmic force bringing together elements such as earth, air, fire, and water to produce a world in which daimones are blended with a Supreme Being); harmonious balance among an individual's internal atoms and the external atoms of his or her environment (i.e., good health is achieved by achieving harmony between the atoms in one's body and the atoms in the environment); harmonious balance among the individual's physical constitution, humors, diet, exercise, geography, seasonal climates, heavenly bodies, and government; harmonious combination of well-ordered souls in well-ordered cities (i.e., well-being is constituted when rational souls are reconciled with ideal cities); ascetic harmony with nature (i.e., the best life is that one lived by, or in harmony with, our animal nature); harmonious mixture of an active life with goods of the soul, goods of the body, and external goods (i.e., a good life requires a good mind and body—internal goods—as well as external goods such as noble birth, friends, wealth, and honor); and harmony with nature through virtue (i.e., the good life involves living in harmony with nature through virtuous action). From 550 to 250 BCE, much philosophical discourse related to human well-being focused on pleasure. Four views of well-being as pleasure were articulated: a life of personal pleasure regardless of its impact on others; a life of measured pleasures exceeding pains; a life filled with experiences of transient pleasures; and pleasure in the form of peace of mind and a healthy body.

The rise of Christianity during the time of the Roman Empire created another shift in the Western conception of well-being. In contrast to the ancient Greek view of well-being as controlled primarily by the individual through purposeful action, the Christian view of well-being was fatalistic. Human well-being was equated to spiritual well-being, and spiritual well-being is attained only in Heaven in the afterlife. As such, human well-being cannot be influenced directly by individual and purposeful action. However, if people follow the religious path toward God, they could enjoy a semblance of well-being on Earth, followed by true well-being in Heaven. Earthly happiness (or imperfect happiness) constituted a life of many satisfying experiences and a few dissatisfying ones. Imperfect happiness or earthly happiness superseded spiritual happiness during the Enlightenment period—the intellectual and scientific movement of eighteenth-century Europe was characterized by a rational approach to religious issues. This view of well-being is depicted in terms of a set of beliefs such as "Well-being is essentially earthly happiness"; "Earthly happiness is viewed as a preponderance of pleasure over pain"; "Personal happiness is more of a tranquil state, more reflective on avoiding pain than experiencing pleasure"; "Personal happiness can be achieved by being generous and moral, not greedy and immoral"; "Public happiness is essentially utilitarian in character—that is, ethical decisions can be made by selecting courses of action that can maximize pleasure and minimize pain for the greatest number of people"; and "Personal and public happiness can conflict in that decisions geared to maximize personal happiness can conflict with public happiness and vice versa." Following the Enlightenment period, the philosophical discourse shifted toward values—community, meaningful work, and God. This shift was a pushback to the greed manifested in economic life and embraced capitalism. There is more to human well-being than happiness in the hedonic sense. Well-being involves a meaningful and purposeful life (figure 6.1).

With respect to the East Asian conception of well-being, we recognize differences when viewed from the religious lens of Confucianism, Buddhism, and Daoism. As previously discussed in chapter 2, the East Asian conception of well-being can best be captured in terms of the following dimensions:

- *prosperity and wealth* (i.e., glorifying the extended family with plenty of material resources),
- *love of virtue* (i.e., upholding virtues such as family responsibilities and obedience; commitment to group norms, solidarity, and harmony; commitment to hard work and education; austerity, humility, self-control, and frugality),
- *good health and peace of mind* (i.e., good health can be achieved through acupuncture, herbal remedies, massage, and lifestyle changes designed to calm the spirit, regulate diet; proper exercise and breathing; moderate emotions; and moderation in drinking, eating, and sexual activities; in contrast, peace of mind can be achieved through the yin and yang—countervailing negative emotional states through being calm, quiet, and tranquil),
- *longevity* (i.e., living a long life through health rituals, herbs and medicine, mineral elixirs, visualization and breathing practices, ascetic dietary regimens, astrology, sexual practices, and physical exercise) (figure 6.2); fulfilling destiny and following the will of Heaven (i.e., being filial to one's ancestors, having filial children, maintaining the health and wealth of the family, and protecting the family from life's hazards), and
- *following the will of Heaven* (i.e., ensuring safety—safety for the self, the family, the community, and one's country).

Figure 6.1. Ancient Roman columns in Rome, Italy. *Source*: (Photo by GreenDragonfly Legs at https://commons.wikimedia.org/w/index.php?curid=58192831; Creative Commons Attribution-Share Alike 4.0 International license)

With respect to the South Asian view of well-being as discussed in chapter 2, the Buddhist tradition in South Asia emphasizes life without suffering. In other words, a state of well-being is a state that is devoid of suffering. This view is further translated to reflect several states: *Sukha* (i.e., satisfaction, happiness, ease, agreeability); *Hita* (i.e., sound beneficial, or healthy state mostly a result of gift-giving or religious practice); *Kusala* (i.e., suitability, competence, and cleverness); *Aucitya* (i.e., appropriateness); *Svasti* (i.e., auspiciousness); *Svasthya* (i.e., established in oneself); and *Islam* (i.e., intactness, peace, safety, and security). Well-being is pursued through a caste system. The caste system categorizes people into four hierarchical classes

至聖孔子
名丘字仲尼山東
兗州府曲阜縣人

Figure 6.2.   Confucius (551 BC—479 BC). *Source:* **(Photo of drawing, gouache on paper, ca. 1700, author unknown; Granger collection; at https://commons.wikimedia. org/w/index.php?curid=3318964; public domain)**

that reflect occupational divisions: priest, warrior, merchant, and laborer. Religiously, well-being, at least among the priests, warriors, and merchants, was construed in terms of reward and punishment in the afterlife. Those who lived a good, productive life and stuck to social customs (*dharma*) would be rewarded in the afterlife by being reincarnated in exalted states.

Turning to the Islamic view of well-being, the guidelines to human well-being are spelled out in the *Qur'an*, which is considered by Muslims to be the literal word of *Allah* (God) as revealed to the prophet Muhammad through the angel Gabriel (figure 6.3). Well-being based on the *Qur'an* is a state of permanent bliss experienced in the afterlife (i.e., Heaven). It can be achieved only through submission to the will of *Allah*. That is, to achieve this state of well-being, the individual must have absolute faith in *Allah* (as the one and only God) and follow the teachings of the *Qur'an* in conducting his or her daily affairs. To submit to *Allah* and ultimately attain well-being in this world (at least partly) and the next, people must follow Islamic law and the moral code (the *Sharia*). Specifically, people have two natures: one is angelic, and the other is demonic. As such, people are in a constant state of internal conflict between good and evil. They win the battle in favor of the good when they mobilize their will and inner strength to do good and prevent sinful conduct and evil. This battle is the essence of what Muslims call the *jihad*—the inner struggle to resist temptations of the carnal self and to act in accordance with the will of *Allah*. Thus, the *jihad* is to embrace the *Sharia* and follow its many prescriptions. Well-being is not construed as subjective states of experience (e.g., life satisfaction, positive/negative affect, hedonic well-being, or happiness) but a lifelong devotion of worshipping and serving *Allah*, which means following the *Sharia*.

Well-being as conceptualized by the philosophical approaches just presented shares many common characteristics. At the center is a commitment

Figure 6.3. Islamic designs, ceiling of Alhambra Palace, Granada. *Source:* **(Photo by Vaughn Williams; at https://upload.wikimedia.org/wikipedia/commons/b/be/Abencer-rajes.jpg; Creative Commons Attribution 2.0 Generic license)**

to the use of nonviolence in resolving conflicts, a deep concern for the well-being of others, and the sublimation of the personal ego to the needs of larger collectives of which they are part. Consistency in the engagement of virtuous behavior in interpersonal relationships also is a shared value of all the perspectives, especially as viewed through the eyes of family members, community fellowships, and religious and other organizations. Ethical and virtuous behaviors in all these arenas are enriched by the individual's participation, which, as we have already demonstrated, promotes advances in well-being in the health, economic, and education sectors as well as that of the whole society.

In as much as the various philosophical traditions discussed in the book share many values in common with one another, their overlapping and mutually supporting approach to well-being should come as no surprise to most readers. We do, though, need to explain that the underlying foundations on which these approaches are based must be applied appropriately to the policy development approaches adopted by nations to attain the fullest possible increases in the levels of collective well-being.

We need to ensure that the high level of accountability necessary for the application of these value systems is transparent to the governed and to the intended beneficiaries of the various national and global policy frameworks that are put into place, including those of businesses and other major nongovernmental organizations that underwrite activities within a country. The overlapping of social values and policies of all organized entities functioning within societies is an essential component of advances in human well-being (Estes & Sirgy, 2017).

HEALTH WELL-BEING

To assess health well-being as an outcomes state at the country level, we focused on four of the most sensitive indicators of health care worldwide: advances in the average years of life expectancy and advances in reducing infant, child, and maternal death rates. The data show significant gains in life expectancy—from a world average of just 48 years in 1950 to a world average that exceeded 69.1 years for men and 73.8 years for women in 2015. This increase represents a major achievement on the part of the world community in advancing health well-being. The country with the highest current life expectancy rates is Japan, with an average number of 86.8 years of life expectancy for both sexes; the country with the least favorable average years of life expectancy is Sierra Leone, where men currently live on average 49.3 years and women, 50.8 years. By 2050, years of average life expectancy in economically advanced countries will likely increase to about 100 and by the end of the century, to 120 years. Average years of life expectancy are expected to continue to increase in developing countries as well and, most likely, at a pace even faster than that which occurs in economically advanced societies, given the already high years of life expectancy that characterize economically well-off countries. This trend reflects a remarkable change in worldwide development and is clearly related to social progress associated with national and regional development strategies.

Average years of life expectancy increased for all regions: It rose from a high of the late fifties and early sixties to the late sixties and low to middle seventies in just forty-three years. Life expectancy growth rates are especially impressive for East Asia and the Pacific and Latin America and the Caribbean. This pattern is expected to continue well into the future. The average years of life expectancy for sub-Saharan Africa is expected to approximate those reported for other regions. The impressive regional gains are the result of significant investments made by economically advanced countries in improving the general health status of people living in less-developed countries.

Data from population pyramids point out the dramatic age and gender differences that exist between developed and developing countries—high concentrations of the populations of young people in developing countries and high concentrations of persons aged sixty years of age and older in developed countries. This marked difference has a profound impact on the nature of the health care that is needed in both sets of countries. That is, developed countries invest more of their health care dollars in providing for the complex and long-term health needs of their aging populations. The costs for doing so are extraordinarily high, especially in situations where the elderly have not set aside private resources in support of their own care as they age. Health services at a high level are needed in developing countries to care for the complex preventive curative care typically needed by children, youth, and older young people. The demands for sophisticated health care for all age groups for both sets of nations are universally high and increase as populations age.

Reducing the number of infant and child deaths has been a major challenge confronting all the world's nations. Infant and child deaths are also directly associated with maternal deaths, given the enormous demands that are made on the bodies of mothers, especially mothers living under difficult economic circumstances. Recent estimates indicate that there have been substantial gains in infant and child survival rates since 2002. Still, though, the threats to child survival remain serious and will require significantly increased international development assistance and other efforts to reduce them. As individual nations and as a world community, we have a long way to go in achieving our child survival targets. Infant and child death rates are highest among the developing nations of sub-Saharan Africa and Southern Asia—five of ten child deaths occur in the nations of sub-Saharan Africa and three in ten occur among the low-income nations of Southern Asia. Child survival also is a major problem for financially poor mothers and their children living in many developed countries. The challenges are especially severe among population groups living in rural and remote communities.

Equally significant gains have been achieved in reducing maternal mortality. Women of reproductive age (fifteen–forty-five years) are especially vulnerable to illnesses, disabilities, and death associated with pregnancy and childbirth. The threats to life are especially high in developing countries where large segments of the population reside in rural communities that have few or inadequate health resources. We provided evidence clearly showing the significant gains that have been achieved in reducing rates of maternal mortality for each major world region over the twenty-four-year period, 1989 to 2013. The most significant achievements in reducing maternal mortality rates occurred in the nations of sub-Saharan Africa, South Asia, and Southeast Asia. These gains parallel other broad-based developmental achievements made by the nations of these regions, including access to basic education, transportation and communication networks, and more secure supplies of safe drinking water and effective systems of solid waste disposal. Furthermore, early intervention in the form of regular prenatal checkups, the provision of prenatal food supplements, and access to skilled personnel prior to and during the delivery process are responsible for the significant gains, especially in those countries at great risk.

The world regions that experienced the lowest levels of net gains in reducing maternal mortality rates were Latin America and the Caribbean, East Asia and the Pacific, and the Arab states of the Middle East and West Asia. Continuing poverty for some of the countries in these regions, in combination with the absence of skilled health personnel to assist with the birthing process, may be the major impediment to reducing their rates of maternal mortality. We also discussed the rising importance of emergency medicine in reducing infant, child, and maternal mortality rates. In that regard, we were glad to report that emergency medical services have become far more accessible than during earlier decades.

An important discussion of health well-being focused on the drivers of health and health care. Some of the drivers are *environmental* (quality of physical environment, employment conditions), others are *social* (culture, gender, ethnicity), and still others involve the actual *providers and recipients* of health services. Among the major drivers of health policy are the public and private investments made by governments, nongovernmental organizations, business leaders, and consumers. Public health data show that all countries currently have spent approximately 10.1 percent of their gross domestic product (GDP) on health and health care services in 2011. This percentage has increased significantly from the 4.7 percent of GDP allocated to the sector in 1990 and from that of 5.6 percent of GDP in 1998. Thus, steady and somewhat higher levels of GDP are allocated to health and health services for each period studied and are likely to continue to increase as the world's population continues to age. The region with the highest levels of investments in health in 2011 was Latin America and the Caribbean (7.6 percent) followed by Eastern Europe and the Commonwealth of Independent States, sub-Saharan Africa, and North America, each of which invested an average of approximately 6.3 percent of their GDP in health and health care. The United States is an outlier among the region's countries in that it spends somewhat more than 17 percent of its GDP on health care each year. The geopolitical regions with the lowest levels of investment of national and regional resources in health care are East Asia and the Pacific (4.8 percent) and the Arab States of the Middle Eastern and North African region (4.3 percent). These comparatively low levels of investments in health care limit development in other sectors as well, but especially in the economic and education sectors that are discussed more fully in other sections of this book. The most recent data available concerning average annual GDP expenditures for health among the countries of Southeast Asia and the Pacific region (1.2 percent in 1998) suggest a very slow rate of progress for these nations as well.

Technological innovation in health and health care continues to increase in type and influence. These innovations do not occur in isolation but are closely linked to the large number and variety of consumer technological products that have emerged during the same period and that today they can connect to the large technological systems that store medical records. In time, these systems will be used to record, organize, analyze, and plan even further advancements in the health sector by drawing on the rich patient databases contained in electronic health records.

ECONOMIC WELL-BEING

We discussed economic well-being in chapter 4. The content of this chapter reinforces many of the lessons learned concerning advances in human well-being that were reported in the health and education chapters for the period 1990 until the present. The chapter also reinforces the discussions of human well-being and economic well-being that appear in other sections of the book. We started the chapter by discussing the economic growth of nations. Economic growth has reached historically high levels in virtually all regions and countries of the world. The current rate of global economic growth currently averages 3.4 percent per annum. The world average per capita income levels rose from $4,261 in 1990 to $5,486 in 2000 to $9,511 in 2010 and, in 2015, to $10,093—an increase of 137 percent in just twenty-five years. These contemporary global economic growth rates are unparalleled in modern history and provide substantially more of the resources needed to employ a larger workforce and reduce rates of extreme poverty. Continuing high rates of economic growth in developing countries serve to improve the quality of health, education, and economic well-being in poor nations as well and, in time, in economically advanced countries.

We noted that economic well-being is more of a subjective, than objective, phenomenon because people tend to assess their standard of living against dominant economic norms that operate within their respective societies. The degree to which the economic status of a people reflects the values that are implicit in the society's organizing economic principles, the higher is the degree of economic well-being experienced by that population. Population groups whose economic status is at considerable negative variance with dominant societal economic norms experience profoundly lower levels of economic well-being. Thus, poor people living in rich societies often feel much poorer than they would if they were not surrounded by the high levels of economic consumption experienced by many in their society.

The world's most rapidly developing countries for 2015 are emerging markets located in East and Southeast Asia and in sub-Saharan Africa. Among the twenty most rapidly developing countries economically, China tops the list followed the Philippines, Kenya, India, and Indonesia. The combined population of these countries exceeds 3.1 billion people, or approximately 42 percent of the world's total population. The fact that such a large share of the world's population, including three of the world's population super giants (China, India, and Indonesia), is benefiting from more accelerated rates of economic growth is good news. We can fully expect that this trend will continue over at least the near term and that an increasingly larger pool of developing nations will benefit from the social gains realized by these countries.

Another major indicator of economic well-being, median household income, averaged $9,733 worldwide in 2013, and median per capita income averaged $2,920. These averages are substantially higher than the median household and per capita income levels reported in 1990. Median household and individual per capita incomes are higher today than those reported for 2013 and are likely to continue to rise appreciably between 2017 and 2030. The changes are expected to occur among the poorest nations of East, South, and Southeast Asia—the regions with the largest concentrations of extreme poverty. The poorest nations of sub-Saharan Africa are expected to benefit significantly from these trends as well.

Many governments have used a variety of approaches to alleviate poverty and enhance economic well-being. The most innovative of these approaches involves the use of a combination of tax incentives and private skills training for persons with highly uneven employment histories. Public subsidies of private job training have been among the most commonly used policy approaches and have been among the most effective in promoting sustained levels of well-paying jobs for previously poor people.

Other types of public–private initiatives frequently exist between governments and business enterprises, such as in the armaments and munitions industries, in road building, in providing research funds in support of a wide range of research investigations, and backers of the last resort in student loans and the financing of research laboratories in universities, pharmaceutical firms, and other types of businesses. Similar types of relationships exist between developed and developing countries, including the provision of large amounts of critically needed financial assistance to stimulate economic development and economic well-being in developing and least developing countries.

Another approach to enhancing the incomes of impoverished families is the migration of adult members of the households to foreign countries as contract laborers. This approach has been used for several decades and has been proved highly effective in generating substantial sums of income in the form of foreign remittances to families. Indeed, both countries of origin and receiving countries make the process of obtaining work visas easier for persons wanting to engage in contract labor. Families receiving foreign remittances, in turn, benefit from the income they receive, which adds appreciably to their living situation and quality of life.

Other approaches to raising the median household and per capita income levels of families living in or near-poverty involve cash grants to subsidize the ability of poor families to purchase basic goods and services. Cash grants to the poor, however, have not been designed to lift the poor out of poverty but rather to provide only for their subsistence needs. To lift the poor out of poverty requires programs of social support, including improved health and education services designed to bring the poor into the mainstream of society.

Among the not-so-recent innovative approaches for improving the economic well-being of poor families is the Universal Basic Income (UBI) initiative, the essence of which is a utopian approach that involves the payment by governments of income to every individual regardless of wealth or other income sources. The expectation is that the scheme would solve a host of economic problems that are endemic to every society such as chronic joblessness, poverty, and other recurrent economic problems.

Furthermore, foreign aid continues to be an efficient, effective mechanism for transferring large sums of development assistance from rich to poor countries. For example, the Organization for Economic Cooperation and Development has set and, for the most part, almost has achieved the goal of having its member nations contribute a minimum of 0.7 percent of their GNI to alleviate poverty. The most generous countries are in North America and Northern Europe, though not necessarily the countries with the largest economies. In terms of dollars, though, the United States, the United Kingdom, Germany, and Japan allocated the highest number of actual dollars to international development assistance in 2013 and 2016.

FDI is another method of alleviating poverty. FDI is critical to propelling the growth of new emerging economies and those of poorer developing countries. FDI investments have proven to be highly effective in growing entire industries, creating large numbers of new jobs, and helping the economies of developing and socially least developing countries to transition from agricultural and extraction industries to urban-based manufacturing and services—the two stable segments of most modern economies. Prominent examples of countries that have benefited from high levels of FDI in the past include Germany, Japan, Singapore, South Korea, and Taiwan, among others. Major beneficiaries of FDI include China, India, Malaysia, the Philippines, and, in recent years, the newly independent countries of Central Asia (e.g., Kazakhstan, Tajikistan). This has in the past decade been bolstered by a growing movement of private wealth being channeled to poor countries through socially conscious and development-oriented fund and venture philanthropy vehicles, seeking to work in parallel with the traditional activities of large global foundations and government aid.

EDUCATIONAL WELL-BEING

In chapter 5, we focused on educational well-being and documented the progress that has occurred in this domain since 1990. We explored the trends of educational well-being, the causes of these trends, and their effects on other dimensions of well-being such as economic well-being, social well-being, and health well-being. We provided evidence of the marked gains in educational well-being worldwide. The evidence also suggests that the rate of growth of educational well-being is greater in some of the world regions than in others.

To reiterate, the *Universal Declaration of Human Rights* clearly states that everyone has the right to an education. Education shall be free, at least in the elementary and fundamental stages. Elementary education shall be compulsory. Technical and professional education shall be made generally available, and higher education shall be equally accessible to all based on merit. Much of the world to date has embraced the notion that education is indeed a human right.

Traditionally, development economists treat education as a tool of economic growth. Education contributes to economic development by enhancing workers' knowledge and skill level. Education should not be considered as an expense or a consumption element; instead, it is an investment for future income. This perspective on education has allowed development economists to argue that education is a basic need; other basic needs include health care, food, clean water supply, and sanitation. More recently, development economists have embraced the notion that education is an important element of human freedom. Specifically, human freedom is a direct function of three factors of development: educational, health, and economic arrangements. Human freedom can be achieved by the *ability* to realize one's own well-being. Educational arrangements enable the individual to improve his or her own well-being.

We delineated an important distinction between educational well-being outcomes, antecedents, and consequences. Educational well-being outcome is essentially the desired state of education around the world. These educational outcomes were treated in terms of two dimensions: quantity and quality. The quantity dimension of educational well-being refers to the average years of total schooling (age fifteen plus). The quality, as an indicator of educational well-being, reflects learning. In this context, a quality education is viewed in terms of mastering levels of proficiency in mathematics, reading, and science. As such, a country or world region that registers higher levels of learning proficiency in mathematics, reading, and science is considered to have higher levels of educational well-being outcome compared to those registering lower levels of learning proficiency. We mentioned that statistics for quality indicators of educational well-being are collected by both national and international agencies that administer educational achievement tests (mathematics, reading, and science tests). These agencies include the Programme for International Student Assessment, Trends in International Mathematics and Science Study, and the Progress in International Reading Literacy Study.

When considering educational well-being outcomes, we made the distinction between "quantity" indicators of educational well-being and "quality" indicators. A key quantity indicator of educational well-being is *average years of total schooling (age fifteen plus)*. The data collected between 1970 and 2010 reflect a positive world trend. The gains are indeed remarkable, especially in sub-Saharan Africa, Latin America, East Asia, South Asia, Southeast Asia, Europe, the Middle East/North Africa (MENA) region, Oceania, the former states of the Soviet Union, and North America. Furthermore, the data show a positive trend in educational attainment in both developing and developed countries. Gender disparity in educational attainment is also narrowing—female students are catching up with their male counterparts in both developed and developing countries, which is positive news. South Asia and the MENA regions seem to be lagging other world regions, but even so the gap in gender disparity is narrowing significantly.

In our review, the quality dimension of educational well-being is captured in terms of learning proficiency in reading, mathematics, and science (as reflected in the Programme for International Student Assessment results). The data show that proficiency in mathematics in the developed countries is high but remained flat between 2000 and 2012. In contrast, improvement in proficiency in mathematics in the developing world is both positive and remarkable. The data show little disparity between boys/men and girls/women in proficiency in mathematics in the developing countries. When we examined proficiency in mathematics by gender by world region, we noted that proficiency in mathematics was higher than the world average in East Asia, followed by Oceania, North America, and Europe. Regions below the world average were the former states of the Soviet Union, MENA, Southeast Asia, South Asia, sub-Saharan Africa, and Latin America, in that order. We also noted that proficiency in mathematics is increasing among both male and female students in East Asia (with male students doing better than female students, but female students catching up in 2009 and 2012). In Oceania, proficiency in mathematics seems to be declining for both male and female students (with the latter doing worse). In North America, progress in proficiency in mathematics is flat (for both male and female students, with the male students doing slightly better than the female students). A similar trend is evident in Europe (progress is flat with male students doing slightly better than female students). In the world regions scoring below average (i.e., South Asia, Southeast Asia, the former Soviet Union, MENA, and Latin America), the data show marked fluctuations for both genders.

The data show a similar pattern in terms of the rate of improvement in language proficiency (i.e., reading). The rate of improvement in language proficiency among students in the developing countries is positive and significant compared to the rate of change in the developed countries—the rate of change in language proficiency among students in the developed countries seems flat. Unfortunately, the discrepancy in language proficiency among students in the developing versus developed countries is high—that is, the students in the developed countries outperform the students in the developing countries by a significant margin. We noted a reverse phenomenon for gender disparity. That is, female students slightly outperform male students on reading proficiency tests in the developing countries but much more markedly in the developed countries. Examining language proficiency by gender disparity by world region, we noted that reading proficiency for the world at large was stable in 2000, 2003, 2006, and 2009 but rose markedly in 2012 for both male and female students. Reading proficiency was noted to be higher than the world average in East Asia, followed by Oceania, North America, and Europe—a profile highly like that for proficiency in mathematics. Regions that were below the world average are the former Soviet Union, MENA,

Southeast Asia, South Asia, sub-Saharan Africa, and Latin America, but not necessarily in that order.

With respect to science proficiency, again, the difference between developed and developing countries is huge, but the trend is like the trends for mathematics and reading proficiency. That is, the rate of improvement is much more pronounced among students in the developing than the developed countries. This observation reinforces the main theme of this book—that gains in human well-being are much more evident among the developing than developed countries. With respect to gender disparity, the data show no disparity in either developing or developed countries, which is, of course, good news. Female students have made significant strides in science education.

We have discussed further factors that may account for educational well-being outcomes, both quantity and quality outcomes. Specifically, we examined educational policies and their impact on educational well-being. A major educational policy that plays a significant role in educational well-being outcomes is compulsory education (number of years that children are legally obliged to attend school). Many countries mandate a school-leaving age of twelve, but most countries enforce a school-leaving age of sixteen. Accumulating evidence suggests that compulsory education is correlated with educational attainment and learning proficiency. Also, based on the evidence, government investment in education is considered a major factor impacting educational well-being. We also examined the effects of the educational technologies on educational well-being and asserted that information and communication technologies in education are changing the educational landscape by enhancing both learning proficiency and educational attainment. Although we have a digital divide, all forecasts point to the likelihood that the digital divide will shrink soon, further contributing to educational well-being, especially in the developing world. Again, good news!

With respect to workforce issues in the education sector, we provided evidence showing that teacher quality is positively related to student performance. In other words, students do better with experienced teachers. We used Finland as a case in point. Finland is a strong performer in education, which may be directly attributed to teacher quality. There are significant problems with the educational workforce in various parts of the world. Perhaps the significant disparity between the educational well-being of students in the developing and the developed countries may be explained (at least in part) by workforce problems. There are problems of recruiting and retaining young, qualified teachers, problems related to recruiting and retaining teachers with expertise in specialist subject areas such as mathematics and science, and problems of teacher absenteeism. In some countries in sub-Saharan Africa, the shortage of teachers is a national crisis. South and West Asia are also facing the problem of teacher shortage in the drive to provide every child with at least a primary education. Other world regions such as North America are not exempt from the problems of teacher recruitment and retention. Teacher shortages have been endemic in developed countries, such as the United States, for many years. We also discussed the effects of school infrastructure (or lack of infrastructure) on educational well-being outcomes. Examples of infrastructure problems include lack of availability of toilets and sanitation in schools and the frequency and extent of electric power surges in schools. Infrastructure problems are common in many developing countries, especially in the sub-Saharan region.

We discussed at length how nonschool factors influence educational well-being. To date, we have enough evidence to suggest that educational outcomes are more related to nonschool than school factors. Students' family backgrounds and the socioeconomic makeup of the community were the best predictors of student achievement. In other words, we now know that nonschool factors such as economic well-being, social well-being, and health well-being play a major role in educational well-being.

We also covered how education plays an important role in human well-being at large. We looked at much of the evidence suggesting that education serves to increase economic well-being, political stability, social well-being, control of population growth, and happiness.

In closing we argued that educational policies must be contextualized. That is, successful policies and programs applied in one country cannot and should not be applied in another country without considering the "context." We further suggested that education is an important factor in globalization. For countries to compete in the global marketplace, education must be a priority in policy making, and specific strategies to enhance education in a global economy should be considered. We also made the point that education plays an important role in the making of global citizens.

CONCLUSIONS

We, the authors, have taken you, the reader, on a rather long and heavily data-based journey that reflects the truth about the extraordinary gains in human well-being that have been achieved from the early nineteenth century to the present.

Today, for example, we have at our "electronic" fingertips the full sum of human knowledge covering the period 600 BCE to the present, in some cases even earlier. We can pursue our understanding of the lessons taught to us by history in comfortable armchairs, in a state of health and well-being that has never existed before for large masses of people. For most of us, we have on average eight decades of life within which to pursue these interests. We do so in a more disease-free state than ever previously existed and, for those of us struggling with disabilities, using an array of handheld computers, telecommunications systems, robotics, and prostheses of every describable type.

We are healthier and better educated on average than was the case for people living just a generation ago. We share electronic access to a range of publishing outlets, electronic data sources, and systems of higher education and vocational training that previously were closed to all but the privileged few. In both economically advanced and developing countries, we have, on average, more money on a per capita and household income level than ever previously was the case. Residents of economically advanced countries also have available to them robust personal and family savings plans, commercial investments, and, though declining, access to various types of retirement programs. Though mostly paid for by individuals and families themselves, governmental agencies increasingly are assuming responsibility for the administrative costs associated with the management of these large "trust" funds.

We travel the planet in large numbers and at speeds never previously attained anywhere except among members of royalty and the elite classes. This reality is in sharp contrast to most people who considered bus, possibly rail, travel as a luxurious, but affordable, means of transportation across long distances and international borders. Since 1998, we have maintained an impressive internationally funded and staffed space station that continuously orbits the earth. We also have a telescope in space, the Hubble, that brings us images of stars and galaxies that we never imagined even existed. Active planning is under way that eventually will make interplanetary travel possible, indeed to Mars and beyond.

Our vision for the future is one of reaching stars whose brief twinkles amazed boys and girls (and, yes, adults) just a generation ago. No one ever expected that we would eventually be able to travel to them. Even so, we now hold the stars in our hands and dare to dream the dream about interspatial travel, about which the myths of our ancient forbearers concerned themselves.

Dramatic advances in health, education, and economics are at the foundation of the impressive accomplishments just outlined. Without these gains, we would still be struggling with widespread illiteracy, poverty, and infectious and communicable diseases that now can be prevented entirely or successfully contained. The situation that exists today has been improved very dramatically. Our inexorable, determined drive to "improve our lot" and to work—albeit at times more gradually in some places than others—toward higher *collective* standards of life on this planet is a unique characteristic of our human race. We have made such incredible social progress and advances in personal and collective well-being that the father of economics, Adam Smith (1723–1790), would have observed them in complete amazement

(Smith, 1776/2014). These accomplishments have occurred in an historical context informed by millennia-old values, traditions, norms, and virtues that continue to inform humanity's steady advances in well-being.

The journey we have taken in writing this book has been a challenging one. It was made more challenging because we have asked you, the reader, to engage with us in the process of reframing your perspectives concerning the flood of social, political, and economic challenges and narratives with which you and we are daily confronted. They are, indeed, real challenges that require great care and collective action in solving. We have asked you, though, to focus with us on the positive changes that are occurring in your own and other societies around the world rather than on placing your emphasis on the mostly negative, life-taking, and ill-being news with which we are bombarded daily. The authors recognize that this is a demanding request, but we believe that this is the most effective approach for affirming the positive advances in well-being that have been accomplished since the nineteenth century. We conclude with a widely cited quote from the nineteenth-century Danish existentialist philosopher Søren Kierkegaard (1813–1855) (Kierkegaard, n.d.):

Life can only be understood backwards; but it must be lived forwards.

This book has been an attempt to do just as Kierkegaard has instructed. Hopefully, we have achieved this goal.

REFERENCES

Estes, R. J., & Sirgy, M. J. (Eds.). (2017). *The pursuit of human well-being: The untold global history*. Dordrecht, NL: Springer.

Kierkegaard, S. (n.d.). Brainy Quote. Retrieved July 4, 2017, from BrainyQuote.com Web site: https://www.brainyquote.com/quotes/quotes/s/sorenkierk105030.html.

Smith, A. (1776/2014). *The wealth of nations*. Amazon.com: CreateSpace Independent Publishing Platform.

Part IV

K'an—Fourth day of the Maya calendar. Mixed media on paper—22″ × 30″. © 2015 Lylia Forero Carr. Used with permission.

Appendix A

Selected Country Performances on the Human Development Index, 1990–2015

Table A.1. Human Development Index—Highest Ratings, 2015 (Base = 188)

Country	Human Development Index (HDI)	Life expectancy at birth	Expected years of schooling	Mean years of schooling	Gross national income (GNI) per capita	GNI per capita rank minus HDI rank
	Value	(years)	(years)	(years)	(2011 PPP $)	
	2015	2015	2015	2015	2015	2015
Norway	0.949	81.7	17.7	12.7	67,614	5
Australia	0.939	82.5	20.4	13.2	42,822	19
Switzerland	0.939	83.1	16.0	13.4	56,364	7
Germany	0.926	81.1	17.1	13.2	45,000	13
Denmark	0.925	80.4	19.2	12.7	44,519	13
Singapore	0.925	83.2	15.4	11.6	78,162	−3
Netherlands	0.924	81.7	18.1	11.9	46,326	8
Ireland	0.923	81.1	18.6	12.3	43,798	11
Iceland	0.921	82.7	19.0	12.2	37,065	20
Canada	0.920	82.2	16.3	13.1	42,582	12
United States	0.920	79.2	16.5	13.2	53,245	1
Hong Kong, China (SAR)	0.917	84.2	15.7	11.6	54,265	−2
New Zealand	0.915	82.0	19.2	12.5	32,870	20
Sweden	0.913	82.3	16.1	12.3	46,251	2
Liechtenstein	0.912	80.2	14.6	12.4	75,065	−11
United Kingdom	0.909	80.8	16.3	13.3	37,931	10
Japan	0.903	83.7	15.3	12.5	37,268	10
Korea (Republic of)	0.901	82.1	16.6	12.2	34,541	12
Israel	0.899	82.6	16.0	12.8	31,215	16
Luxembourg	0.898	81.9	13.9	12.0	62,471	−12

Data Source: United Nations Development Programme: Human Development Reports. (2015). Table 1: Human Development Index and its components. Retrieved July 8, 2017, from http://hdr.undp.org/en/composite/HDI

PPP: purchasing power parity; SAR: special administrative region

Table A.2.   Human Development Index—Lowest Ratings, 2015 (Base N=188)

Country	Human Development Index (HDI)	Life expectancy at birth	Expected years of schooling	Mean years of schooling	Gross national income (GNI) per capita	GNI per capita rank minus HDI rank
	Value	(years)	(years)	(years)	(2011 PPP $)	
	2015	2015	2015	2015	2015	2015
Afghanistan	0.479	60.7	10.1	3.6	1,871	1
Malawi	0.476	63.9	10.8	4.4	1,073	16
Côte d'Ivoire	0.474	51.9	8.9	5.0	3,163	−20
Djibouti	0.473	62.3	6.3	4.1	3,216	−22
Gambia	0.452	60.5	8.9	3.3	1,541	3
Ethiopia	0.448	64.6	8.4	2.6	1,523	5
Mali	0.442	58.5	8.4	2.3	2,218	−9
Congo (Dem. Rep. of the)	0.435	59.1	9.8	6.1	680	15
Liberia	0.427	61.2	9.9	4.4	683	13
Guinea-Bissau	0.424	55.5	9.2	2.9	1,369	3
Eritrea	0.420	64.2	5.0	3.9	1,490	1
Sierra Leone	0.420	51.3	9.5	3.3	1,529	−1
Mozambique	0.418	55.5	9.1	3.5	1,098	4
South Sudan	0.418	56.1	4.9	4.8	1,882	−12
Guinea	0.414	59.2	8.8	2.6	1,058	4
Burundi	0.404	57.1	10.6	3.0	691	5
Burkina Faso	0.402	59.0	7.7	1.4	1,537	−8
Chad	0.396	51.9	7.3	2.3	1,991	−19
Niger	0.353	61.9	5.4	1.7	889	1
Central African Republic	0.352	51.5	7.1	4.2	587	4

Data Source: United Nations Development Programme: Human Development Reports. (2015). Table 1: Human Development Index and its components. Retrieved July 8, 2017, from http://hdr.undp.org/en/composite/HDI

PPP: purchasing power parity; Dem. Rep.: Democratic Republic

Table A.3. Human Development Trends by Major World Regions and United Nations Classification, 1990–2015

World Regions	Human Development Index (HDI) Value		Change in HDI Score
	1990	**2015**	**1990–2015**
Arab States	0.556	0.687	0.85
East Asia and the Pacific	0.516	0.720	1.35
Europe and Central Asia	0.652	0.756	0.59
Latin America and the Caribbean	0.626	0.751	0.74
South Asia	0.438	0.621	1.40
Sub-Saharan Africa	0.399	0.523	1.09
Least developed countries	0.347	0.508	1.54
Small island developing states	0.570	0.667	0.63
Organization for Economic Cooperation and Development	0.785	0.887	0.49
World	**0.597**	**0.717**	**0.74**

Data Source: United Nations Development Programme: Human Development Reports. (2015). Table 2: Trends in the Human Development Index, 1990–2015. Retrieved July 8, 2017, from http://hdr.undp.org/en/composite/trends

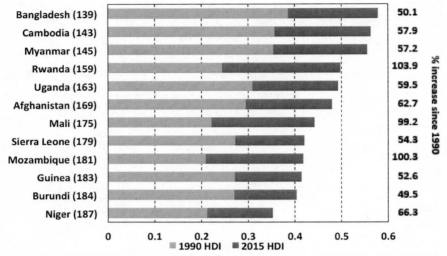

Figure A.4 Human Development Index—Greatest Improvers, 1990–2015 (Base N=169)

Data Source: United Nations Development Programme: Human Development Report. (2015). Table 2: Trends in the Human Development Index, 1990–2015 Retrieved July 8, 2017, from http://hdr.undp.org/en/composite/trends

Appendix B

Supplemental Readings on Advances in Well-Being

CHAPTER 1: ADVANCES IN HUMAN WELL-BEING

Anderson, R. E. (2014). *Human suffering and quality of life*. Dordrecht, NL: Springer.

Anderson, R. E. (2017). *Alleviating world suffering: The challenge of negative quality of life*. Dordrecht, NL: Springer.

Dorling, D. (2013). *Population 10 billion*. London: Constable.

Estes, R. J. (2014). Development trends among the world's socially least developed countries: Reasons for cautious optimism. In B. Spooner (Ed.), *Globalization in progress: Understanding and working with world urbanization*. Philadelphia: University of Pennsylvania Press.

Estes, R. J. (2015). Trends in world social development: The search for global well-being. In W. Glatzer, L. Camfield, V. Møller, & M. Rojas (Eds.), *Global handbook of quality of life: Exploration of well-being of nations and continents*. Dordrecht, NL: Springer.

Estes, R. J., & Sirgy, M. J. (2014). Radical Islamic militancy and acts of terrorism: A quality-of-life analysis. *Social Indicators Research, 117*(2), 615–652.

Estes, R., & Tiliouine, H. (2014). Development trends in Islamic societies: From collective wishes to concerted actions. *Social Indicators Research, 116*, 67–114.

Kinney, C. (2011). *Getting better: Why global development is succeeding—and how we can improve the world even more*. New York: Basic Books.

Land, K. C., Michalos, A. C., & Sirgy, M.J. (Eds.) (2012). *Handbook of social indicators and quality of life research*. Dordrecht, NL: Springer.

Layard, R. (2006). *Happiness: Lessons from a new science*. New York: Penguin Group.

Organization for Economic Cooperation and Development (2013). *How's life? 2015: Measuring well-being*. Paris: OECD Publishing. doi: http://dx.doi.org/10.1787/how_life-2015-en

Seligman, M. E. P. (2002). *Authentic happiness: Using the new positive psychology to realize your potential for lasting fulfillment*. New York: The Free Press.

Sirgy, M. J. (2011). Theoretical perspectives guiding QOL indicator projects. *Social Indicators Research, 103*, 1–22.

CHAPTER 2: THE CONCEPT OF WELL-BEING: PHILOSOPHICAL WISDOM FROM THE AGES

Almeder, R. (2000). *Human happiness and morality*. Buffalo, NY: Prometheus Press.

Annas, J. (1993). *The morality of happiness*. New York: Oxford University Press.

Annas, J. (1998). Virtue and eudemonism. In E. F. Paul, F. D. Miller Jr., & J. Paul (Eds.), *Virtue and vice* (pp. 37–55). New York: Cambridge University Press.

Aristotle (1962, 1986). *Nicomachean ethics*. (M. Ostwald, Trans.). New York: Holt, Rinehart, & Winston.

Austin, J. (1968). Pleasure and happiness. *Philosophy, 43*, 51–62.

Belliotti, R. A. (2004). *Happiness is overrated*. Oxford, UK: Rowman & Littlefield.

Benditt, T. M. (1974). Happiness. *Philosophical Studies, 25*, 1–20.

Brandt, R. B. (1967). Happiness. In O. Edwards (Ed.), *The encyclopedia of philosophy* (pp. 413–414). New York: Macmillan Publishing Co/The Free Press.

Carson, T. (1981). Happiness, contentment, and the good life. *Pacific Philosophical Quarterly, 62*, 378–392.

Collard, D. (2003). *Research on well-being: Some advice from Jeremy Bentham* (WeD Working Paper, 2). Bath, UK: ESRC Research Group on Wellbeing in Developing Countries.

Cottingham, J. (1998). *Philosophy and the good life*. New York: Cambridge University Press.

Crisp, R. (2015). Well-Being. In E. Zalta (Ed.), *The Stanford Encyclopedia of Philosophy* (Summer Edition). http://plato.stanford.edu/archives/sum2015/entries/well-being/.

Davis, W. (1981). A theory of happiness. *American Philosophical Quarterly, 18*, 111–120.

Davis, W. (1981). Pleasure and happiness. *Philosophical Studies, 39*, 305–318.

Feldman, F. (2010). *What is this thing called happiness?* New York: Oxford University Press.

Frankl, V. (1963). *Man's search for meaning: An Introduction to Logotherapy*. New York: Simon and Schuster.

Frankl, V. (1967). *Psychotherapy and existentialism*. New York: Simon & Schuster.

Gauthier, D. P. (1967). Progress and happiness: A utilitarian consideration. *Ethics, 78*, 77–82.

Goldstein, I. (1973). Happiness: The role of non-hedonic criteria in its evaluation. *International Philosophical Quarterly, 13*, 523–534.

Griffin, J. (1986). *Well-being: Its meaning, measurement, and moral importance*. Oxford, UK: Clarendon Press.

Hayborn, D. M. (2001). Happiness and pleasure. *Philosophy and Phenomenological Research, 62*, 501–528.

Hayborn, D. M. (2008). *The pursuit of unhappiness*. Oxford: Oxford University Press.

Inoguchi, T. (2015). Multiple modes of well-being in Asia. In W. Glatzer, L. Camfield, V. Møller, & M. Rojas (Eds.), *Global handbook of quality of life* (pp. 597–607). Dordrecht, NL: Springer.

James, W. (1902). *Varieties of religious experience: A study in human nature.* New York: Longmans Green.

Joshanloo, M. (2014). Eastern conceptualizations of happiness: fundamental differences with western views. *Journal of Happiness Studies, 15,* 475–493.

Joshanloo, M., Weijers, D., Jiang, D.-Y., Gyuseog Han, G., Bae, J., Pang, J. S., . . . Natalia, A. (2014). Fragility of happiness beliefs across 15 national groups. *Journal of Happiness Studies* 16, 1–26.

Kekes, J. (1982). Happiness. *Mind, 91,* 358–376.

Kekes, J. (1988). *The examined life.* Lewisburg, PA: Bucknell University Press.

Kekes, J. (1992). Happiness. In L. C. Becker & C. B. Becker (Eds.), *Encyclopedia of ethics* (pp. 430–435). New York: Russell Sage.

Kenny, A. (1966). Happiness. *Proceedings of the Aristotelian Society, 66,* 93–102.

Kesebir, P., & Diener, E. (2009). In pursuit of happiness: Empirical answers to philosophical questions. In E. Diener (Ed.), *The science of well-being: The collected works of Ed Diener* (pp. 59–74). Dordrecht, NL: Springer.

Keyes, C. L. M. (2002). The mental health continuum: From languishing to flourishing in life. *Journal of Health and Social Behavior, 43,* 207–222.

Kraut, R. (1979). Two conceptions of happiness. *Philosophical Review, 138,* 167–197.

Lane, R. E. (2001). *The loss of happiness in market democracies.* New Haven, CT: Yale University Press.

Mayerfield, J. (1999). *Suffering and moral responsibility.* New York: Oxford University Press.

McGill, V. J. (1967). *The idea of happiness.* New York: Praeger.

Mill, J. S. (1979). *Utilitarianism.* Indianapolis, IN: Hackett.

Nozick, R. (1989). *The examined life.* New York: Simon and Schuster.

Parducci, A. (1995). *Happiness, pleasure, and judgment: The contextual theory and its applications.* Mahwah, NJ: Lawrence Erlbaum Associates.

Peterson, C., Park, N., & Seligman, M. E. P. (2005). Orientations to happiness and life satisfaction: The full life versus the empty life. *Journal of Happiness Studies, 6,* 24–41.

Phillips, D. (2006). *Quality of life: Concept, policy and practice.* London: Routledge.

Plato. (1892). *The dialogues of Plato.* (B. Jowett, Trans.). New York: Random House. (Original work published 360 BC).

Rath, T., & Harter, J. (2010). *Well-being: The five essential elements.* Washington: Gallup Press.

Ricard, M. (2007). *Happiness: A guide to developing life's most important skill.* Boston: Little, Brown and Company.

Russell, B. (1975). *The conquest of happiness.* London: Unwin. (Original work published 1930).

Scruton, R. (1975). Reason and happiness. In R. S. Peters (Ed.), *Nature and conduct* (pp. 139–161). New York: Macmillan.

Simpson, R. (1975). Happiness. *American Philosophical Quarterly, 12,* 169–176.

Smith, T. W. (1979). Happiness. *Social Psychology Quarterly, 42*, 18–30.

Sumner, L. W. (1996). *Welfare, happiness, and ethics.* New York: Oxford University Press.

Tatarkiewicz, W. (1976). *Analysis of happiness* (E. Rothert & D. Zielinskin, Trans.). The Hague, NL: Martinus Nijhoff.

Telfer, E. (1980). *Happiness.* New York: St. Martin's Press.

Thomas, D. A. L. (1968). Happiness. *The Philosophical Quarterly, 18*, 97–113.

Veenhoven, R. (1984). *Conditions of happiness.* Boston: Reidel.

Veenhoven, R. (1988). The utility of happiness? *Social Indicators Research, 20*, 334–354.

Veenhoven, R. (1991). Is happiness relative? *Social Indicators Research, 24*, 1–34.

Veenhoven, R. (1996). Happy-life expectancy: A comprehensive measure of quality of life in nations. *Social Indicators Research, 38*, 1–58.

Warburton, D. (1996). The functions of pleasure. In D. Warburton & N. Sherwood (Eds.), *Pleasure and quality of life.* Chichester, UK: Wiley.

Warner, R. (1987). *Freedom, enjoyment, and happiness: An essay on moral psychology.* Ithaca, NY: Cornell University Press.

Waterman, A. S. (1993). Two conceptions of happiness: Contrasts of personal expressiveness (eudaimonia) and hedonic enjoyment. *Journal of Personality and Social Psychology, 64*, 678–691.

Weijers, D. (2011). Hedonism. *Internet Encyclopedia of Philosophy.* Retrieved September 29, 2017, from http://www.iep.utm.edu/hedonism/.

Wolf, S. (1997). Happiness and meaning: Two aspects of the good life. *Social Philosophy and Policy, 14*, 207–225.

CHAPTER 3: HEALTH: THE CORNERSTONE OF HUMAN WELL-BEING

Agner, E., Miller, M. J., Ray, M. N., Saag, K. G., & Allison, J. J. (2010). Health literacy and happiness: A community-based study. *Social Indicators Research, 95*, 325–338.

Ano, G. G., & Vasconcelles, E. B. (2005). Religious coping and psychological adjustment to stress: A meta-analysis. *Journal of Clinical Psychology, 61*, 461–480.

Baltes, B. B., Clark, M. A., & Chakrabarti, M. (2010). Work-life balance: The roles of work-family conflict and work-family facilitation. In P. A. Linley, S. Harrington, & N. Garcea (Eds.), *Oxford handbook of positive psychology and work* (pp. 201–212). Oxford: Oxford University Press.

Baltes, P. B., & Baltes, M. M. (Eds.) (1990). *Successful aging: Perspectives from the behavioral sciences.* Cambridge, MA: Cambridge University Press.

Biddle, S. H. J., & Ekkekakis, P. (2005). Physical active lifestyles and well-being. In F. A. Huppert, N. Baylis, & B. Keverne (Eds.), *The science of well-being* (pp. 141–168). Oxford: Oxford University Press.

Blanchflower, D. G., & Oswald, A. J. (2008). Is well-being U-shaped over the life cycle? *Social Science & Medicine, 66*, 1733–1749.

Bowden, R. G., Lanning, B. A., Doyle, E. I., Slonaker, B., Johnston, H. M., & Scanes, G. (2008). The effects of weight loss attempts, exercise initiation, and dietary practices on health-related quality of life. *Applied Research in Quality of Life, 3*, 149–160.

Bowling, A. (1995). *Measuring disease: A review of disease-specific quality-of-life measurement scales.* Buckingham: Open University Press.

Chambers, L. W., Ounpuu, S., Krueger, P., & Vermeulen, M. (1997). Quality of life and planning for health boards. In H. L. Meadow (Ed.), *Developments in quality-of-life studies* (vol. 1, p. 11). Blacksburg, VA: International Society for Quality-of-Life Studies.

Chen, K-H., & Yao, G. (2010). Investigating adolescent health-related quality of life: From a self-identity perspective. *Social Indicators Research, 96*, 403–415.

Cohen, S., Miller, G. E., & Rabin, B. S. (2001). Psychological stress and antibody response to immunization: A critical review of the human literature. *Psychosomatic Medicine, 63*, 7–18.

Cornelisse-Vermaat, J. R., Antonides, G., Van Ophem, J. A. C., & Van Den Brink, H. M. (2006). Body mass index, perceived health, and happiness: Their determinants and structural relationships. *Social Indicators Research, 79*, 143–158.

Diener, E., & Chan, M. Y. (2011). Happy people live longer: Subjective well-being contributes to health and longevity. *Applied Psychology: Health and Well-Being, 3* (1), 1–43.

Evans, R. G., & Stoddart, G. L. (1990). A model of the determinants of health. *Social Science and Medicine, 31*, 1347–1363.

Ferrans, C. E., & Powers, M. J. (1985). Quality of life index: Development and psychometric properties. *Advances in Nursing Science, 8*, 15–24.

Fredrickson, B. L. (2001). The role of positive emotions in positive psychology: The broaden-and-build theory of positive emotions. *American Psychologist, 56*, 219–226.

Fredrickson, B. L. (2010). *Positivity: Top-notch research reveals the 3-to-1 ratio that will change your life.* New York: Three Rivers Press.

Frisch, M. B. (2007). *Quality of life therapy: Interventions to improve the quality of life of patients with emotional or physical problems.* New York: Wiley.

Hunt, S. M., McEwen, J., & McKenna, S. P. (1986). *Measuring health status.* London: Croom Helm.

Keyes, C. L. M. (2002). The mental health continuum: From languishing to flourishing in life. *Journal of Health and Social Behavior, 43*, 207–222.

Langner, T. S., & Michael, S. T. (1963). *Life stress and mental health.* New York: Free Press.

Lee, C. (1998). *Women's health: Psychological and social perspectives.* London: Sage Publication.

Phillips, D. (2006). *Quality of life: Concept, policy and practice.* London: Routledge.

Rahtz, D. R., Sirgy, M. J., & Lee, D-J. (2004). Further validation and extension and the quality-of-life/community-healthcare model and measures. *Social Indicators Research, 69*, 167–198.

Sirgy, M. J., Hansen, D. E., & Littlefield, J. E. (1994). Does hospital satisfaction affect life satisfaction? *Journal of Macromarketing, 14*, 36–46.

Sirgy, M. J., Mentzer, J. T., Rahtz, D., & Meadow, H. L. (1991). Satisfaction with healthcare marketing services consumption and life satisfaction among the elderly. *Journal of Macromarketing, 11*, 24–39.

WHO (2001). *International classification of functioning, disability and health.* Geneva: WHO.

CHAPTER 4: ECONOMIC WELL-BEING: AN ESSENTIAL ELEMENT IN THE ADVANCEMENT OF WELL-BEING

Chen, K-H., & Yao, G. (2010). Investigating adolescent health-related quality of life: From a self-identity perspective. *Social Indicators Research, 96*, 403–415.

Clark, A. E., & Oswald, A. J. (1996). Satisfaction and comparison income. *Journal of Public Economics, 61*(3), 359–381.

Clark, A. E., Frijters, P., & Shields, M. A. (2008). Relative income, happiness, and utility: An explanation for the Easterlin paradox and other puzzles. *Journal of Economic Literature, 46*, 95–144.

Cummins, R. A. (2000). Personal income and subjective well-being: A review. *Journal of Happiness Studies, 1*(2), 133–158.

Diener, E., & Chan, M. Y. (2011). Happy people live longer: Subjective well-being contributes to health and longevity. *Applied Psychology: Health and Well-Being, 3* (1), 1–43.

Diener, E., & Seligman, M. E. P. (2004). Beyond money: Toward an economy of well-being. *Psychological Science in the Public Interest, 5*, 1–31. Republished in E. Diener (Ed.) (2009), *The science of well-being: The collected works of Ed Diener* (pp. 201–265). Dordrecht, NL: Springer.

Diener, E., Horwitz, F., & Emmons, R. A. (1985). Happiness of the very wealthy. *Social Indicators Research, 16*, 263–274.

Diener, E., Sandvik, E., Seidlitz, L., & Diener, M. (1993). The relationship between income and subjective well-being: Relative or absolute? *Social Indicators Research, 28*, 195–223.

Diener. E., Oishi, S., & Lucas, R. E. (2015). National accounts of subjective well-being. *American Psychologist 70*(3), 234–243.

Dolan, P., Peasgood, T., & White, M. P. (2008). Do we really know what makes us happy? A review of the economic literature on factors associated with subjective well-being. *Journal of Economic Psychology, 29*, 94–122.

Duncan, O. (1975). Does money buy satisfaction? *Social Indicators Research, 2*, 267–274.

Dunn, E. W., Aknin, L. B., & Norton, M. I. (2008). Spending money on others promotes happiness. *Science, 319*, 1687–1688.

Easterlin, R. A. (1974). Does economic growth improve the human lot? Some empirical evidence. In P. A. David & M. W. Reder (Eds.), *Nations and households in economic growth* (pp. 89–125). New York: Academic Press.

Easterlin, R. A. (1995). Will raising incomes of all increase the happiness of all? *Journal of Economic Behavior and Organization, 27*, 2735–2747.

Easterlin, R.A. (2001). Income and happiness: Towards a unified theory. *Economic Journal, 111*, 465–484.

Estes, R. J. (2012). Development challenges and opportunities confronting economies in transition. In K. Land, A. Michalos, & M. J. Sirgy (Eds.), *Handbook of social indicators and quality of life research* (pp. 433–457). Dordrecht, NL: Springer.

European Commission (2001). *Employment and social policies: A framework for investing in quality*. Brussels: Commission of the European Communities.

Evans, R. G., & Stoddart, G. L. (1990). A model of the determinants of health. *Social Science and Medicine, 31*, 1347–1363.

Ferrans, C. E., & Powers, M. J. (1985). Quality of life index: Development and psychometric properties. *Advances in Nursing Science, 8*, 15–24.

Ferrer-i-Carbonell, A. (2005). Income and well-being: An empirical analysis of the comparison income effect. *Journal of Public Economics, 89*, 997–1019.

Fredrickson, B. L. (2001). The role of positive emotions in positive psychology: The broaden-and-build theory of positive emotions. *American Psychologist, 56*, 219–226.

Fredrickson, B. L. (2010). *Positivity: Top-notch research reveals the 3-to-1 ratio that will change your life*. New York: Three Rivers Press.

Frey, B. S., & Stutzer, A. (2002). *Happiness and economics*. Princeton, NJ: Princeton University Press.

Frisch, M. B. (2007). *Quality of life therapy: Interventions to improve the quality of life of patients with emotional or physical problems*. New York: Wiley.

George, L. K. (1992). Economic status and subjective well-being: A review of the literature and an agenda for future research. In N. E. Cutler, D. W. Gregg, & M. P. Lawton (Eds.), *Aging, money, and life satisfaction: Aspects of financial gerontology*. New York: Springer.

Gill, D. L., Chang, Y-K., Murphy, K. M., Speed, K. M., Hammond, C. C., Rodriguez, E. A., . . . Shang, Y-S. (2011). Quality of life assessment for physical activity and health promotion. *Applied Research in Quality of Life, 6*, 181–200.

Graham, C. (2009). *Happiness around the world: The paradox of happy peasants and miserable millionaires*. New York: Oxford University Press.

Graham, C. (2012). *The pursuit of happiness: An economy of well-being*. Washington, DC: Brookings Institution Press.

Headey, B., Muffels, R., & Wooden, M. (2008). Money does not buy happiness: Or does it? A reassessment based on the combined effects of wealth, income and consumption. *Social Indicators Research, 87*, 65–82.

Hirata, J. (2011). *Happiness, ethics and economics*. London: Routledge.

Kasser, T. (2002). *The high price of materialism*. Cambridge: MIT Press.

Keyes, C. L. M. (2002). The mental health continuum: From languishing to flourishing in life. *Journal of Health and Social Behavior, 43*, 207–222.

Lane, R. E. (2000). *The loss of happiness in market democracies*. New Haven, CT: Yale University Press.

Langner, T. S., & Michael, S. T. (1963). *Life stress and mental health*. New York: Free Press.

Lee, C. (1998). *Women's health: Psychological and social perspectives*. London: Sage Publication.

Phillips, D. (2006). *Quality of life: Concept, policy and practice*. London: Routledge.

Porter, C. (2014, March 11). A relentless widening of disparity in wealth. *New York Times*. Retrieved October 22, 2015, from http://www.nytimes.com/2014/03/12/business/economy/a-relentless-rise-in-unequal-wealth.html?_r=0.

Rahtz, D. R., Sirgy, M. J., & Lee, D-J. (2004). Further validation and extension and the quality-of-life/community-healthcare model and measures. *Social Indicators Research, 69*, 167–198.

Simsek, O. F. (2009). Happiness revisited: Ontological well-being as a theory-based construct of subjective well-being. *Journal of Happiness Studies, 10*, 505–522.

Sirgy, M. J. (1998). Materialism and quality of life. *Social Indicators Research, 43*, 227–260.

Sirgy, M. J., Hansen, D. E., & Littlefield, J. E. (1994). Does hospital satisfaction affect life satisfaction? *Journal of Macromarketing, 14*, 36–46.

Sirgy, M. J., Mentzer, J. T., Rahtz, D., & Meadow, H. L. (1991). Satisfaction with healthcare marketing services consumption and life satisfaction among the elderly. *Journal of Macromarketing, 11*, 24–39.

Stutzer, A. (2004). The role of income aspirations in individual happiness. *Journal of Economic Behavior and Organization, 54*, 89–109.

Sumner, L. W. (1996). *Welfare, happiness, and ethics*. New York: Oxford University Press.

Ware, J. E., Snow, K. K., Kosinski, M., & Gandek, B. (1993). *SF-36 Health Survey: Manual and interpretation guide*. Boston: The Health Institute: New England Medical Center.

Warr, P. (1987). *Work, unemployment, and mental health*. Oxford: Oxford University Press.

WHO (2001). *International classification of functioning, disability and health*. Geneva: WHO.

CHAPTER 5: EDUCATION: DRAMATIC GAINS IN EDUCATIONAL WELL-BEING

Chevalier, A., & Feinstein, L. (2006). Sheepskin or Prozac: The causal effect of education on mental health. London: Centre for the Economics of Education, London School of Economics.

Hallinger, P. (2003). Leading educational change: Reflections on the practice of instructional and transformational leadership. *Cambridge Journal of Education, 33*, 329–351

Holmes, E. (2005). *Teacher well-being: Looking after yourself and your career in the classroom*. New York: Routledge Falmer.

Hoy, W. K., & Miskel, C. G. (1996). *Educational administration: Theory, research, & practice*. New York: McGraw-Hill.

Michalos, A. C. (1993). *Global report on student well-being. Volume IV: Religion, education, recreation, and health*. New York: Springer Verlag.

Michalos, A. C. (2008). Education, happiness and wellbeing. *Social Indicators Research, 87*, 347–366.

Salinas-Jimenez, M. M., Artes, J., & Salinas-Jimenez, J. (2011). Education as a positional good: A life satisfaction approach. *Social Indicators Research, 103*, 409–426.

CHAPTER 6: TOWARD A MORE POSITIVE FUTURE FOR ALL

Estes, R. J. (1993). Toward sustainable development: From theory to praxis. *Social Development Issues, 15*(3), 1–29.

Estes, R. J. (2010). The world social situation: Development challenges at the outset of a new century. *Social Indicators Research, 98*, 363–402.

Inglehart, R. (1997). *Modernization and post-modernization: Cultural, economic, and political change in 43 societies*. Princeton, NJ: Princeton University Press.

Seligman, M. E. P. (2011). *Flourish: A visionary new understanding of happiness and well-being*. New York: The Free Press.

Sirgy, M. J. (1986). A quality of life theory derived from Maslow's developmental perspective: "Quality" is related to progressive satisfaction of a hierarchy of needs, lower order and higher. *American Journal of Economics and Sociology, 45*(July), 329–342.

Sirgy, M. J. (2001). *Handbook of quality-of-life research: An ethical marketing perspective*. Dordrecht, NL: Kluwer Academic Publishers.

Sirgy, M. J. (2002). *The psychology of quality of life*. Dordrecht, NL: Kluwer Academic Publishers.

Sirgy, M. J., & Wu, J. (2009). The pleasant life, the engaged life, and the meaningful life: What about the balanced life? *Journal of Happiness Studies, 10*, 183–196.

United Nations Development Programme (2016). *Human development report, 2015: Human Development for Everyone*. New York: Oxford University Press.

Veenhoven, R. (2008). Healthy happiness: Effects of happiness on physical health and the consequences for preventative health care. *Journal of Happiness Studies, 9*, 449–469.

Veenhoven, R. (2009). Well-being *in* nations and well-being *of* nations: Is there a conflict between individual and society? *Social Indicators Research, 91*, 5–21.

Veenhoven, R. and coworkers (1994*). World database of happiness: Correlates of happiness*. Rotterdam: Erasmus University.

Part V

Chikchan—Fifth day of the Maya calendar. Mixed media on paper—22″ × 30″. © Lylia Forero Carr. Used with permission.

Index

health, 69–72, *70*, 75; investment in well-being, 45–46, 222; investment to alleviate poverty, 90, 131, 227; for-profit, economic well-being and, 92–93. *See also* organization(s), not-for-profit
Bustreo, Dr. Flavia, 61

capability, defined, 147
Caribbean. *See* Latin America and the Caribbean
caste system, 35–36, 40, 219–20
catalyst(s), learning and, 195
Central Asia, 166, 228
charities, private: investment in educational well-being, 163–64; investment to alleviate poverty, 125; religious, investment in health well-being by, 50, 80, 91
chi (qi), 48
children, mortality rates of. *See* mortality rates, child
children, survival rates of. *See* mortality rates, child
China, 116, 129, 226; civic education, 198–99; classical medical traditions of, 29–32; declining poverty rates, 13; population and gender distribution, *6, 7*; population growth issues, 55; regional poverty in, 119; traditional view of happiness, 32; well-being conception of, 28–32, *31*
Christianity, well-being concepts in, 25, 217–18
Clark-Decés, Isabelle, 32
Coleman Report (*Equality of Educational Opportunity*), 174–75
Commonwealth of Independent States, 71, 92, 140n2, 166, 225
communities, rich and poor: economic well-being and, 93–94; wealth gap and, 114–16, *115*
communities, rural, xiii, 5, 11, 13, 60; child mortality rates, 61; emergency health services for, 68; maternal survival rates and, 63–66, *64*

comparative advantage, 194, 194–95
competency-based education, 197–98
Confucianism, 29, 32, 218
Confucius, *220*; happiness view of, 29, 40, 218
context, public policy formulation and, 192–93, 232
contract labor, 112–13, 130, 140n7, 227
Convention against Discrimination in Education, 190
Convention of the Rights of the Child (UNICEF), 191
corruption, 103–4, 120, 172
Côte d'Ivoire (Ivory Coast), rapid economic growth in, 101
Creating a Learning Society (Stiglitz, J. E. and Greenwald, B. C.), 193–94; creative mind-set, 196; learning strategies of, 195–96; learning types, 194–95
credit, 104, 107
crime, *161*; education and, 183, 184; Universal Basic Income and, 114

daimones, 24, 217
Daoism, 29, 218
data processing systems, technological advances in health and health services and, 72–75, *73–75*
Declaration on the Rights of Disabled Persons (United Nations), 190–91
deprivation, economic well-being and, 93–94, 117. *See also* poverty
destiny, East Asian dimension of well-being, 29, 32
developed countries: average life expectancy and, 53, 54; educational attainment, 153–55; gross domestic product and years of schooling in, 181; knowledge gap, 193–94; population pyramids of, 223; unemployment, *182*; Weighted Index of Social Progress in, 105–6
developing countries, 2015, 226; average life expectancy, gender-based, 5–7, *6*; compulsory

About the Authors

Richard J. Estes is professor emeritus of social work and social policy of the School of Social Policy & Practice of the University of Pennsylvania. He specializes in international and comparative social welfare, social policy, and social development. He has been the recipient of many national and international awards for his contributions to research on comparative quality of life, well-being, and social development. In addition to the present volume, his books include *The Social Progress of Nations*, 1984; *Trends in World Social Development*, 1988; *Health Care and the Social Services*, 1984; *Towards a Social Development Strategy for the Asia and Pacific Region* (with Edward Van Roy), 1992; *Social Development in Hong Kong: The Unfinished Agenda*, 2005; *Medical, Legal and Social Science Aspects of Child Sexual Exploitation*, 2007; *Advancing Quality of Life in a Turbulent World*, 2007; *The State of Social Progress of Islamic Societies: Social, Economic, Political, and Ideological Challenges* (with Habib Tiliouine, 2016). He is also the co-editor of *The Pursuit of Human Well-Being: The Untold Global History* (with M. Joseph Sirgy, 2017).

M. Joseph Sirgy is a management psychologist (PhD, University of Massachusetts, 1979), Virginia Tech Real Estate Professor of Marketing with Virginia Polytechnic Institute and State University (Virginia Tech). He has published extensively in the areas of marketing, business ethics, and quality of life (QOL). He is the author/editor of many books related to QOL and well-being research. In 1998, he received the Distinguished Research Fellow Award from the International Society for Quality-of-Life Studies, which in 2003 honored him as the Distinguished QOL Researcher for research excellence and a record of lifetime achievement in QOL research. In 2012, he was awarded the EuroMed Management Research Award for outstanding achievements and groundbreaking contributions to well-being and QOL research. He is also the co-editor of *The Pursuit of Human Well-Being: The Untold Global History* (with Richard J. Estes, 2017).